ENTERPRISING CARE?

Unpaid voluntary action in the 21st century

Irene Hardill and Susan Baines

This edition published in Great Britain in 2011 by

The Policy Press
University of Bristol
Fourth Floor
Beacon House
Queen's Road
Bristol BS8 1QU
UK

t: +44 (0)117 331 4054
f: +44 (0)117 331 4093
tpp-info@bristol.ac.uk
www.policypress.org.uk

North American office:
The Policy Press
c/o International Specialized Books Services
920 NE 58th Avenue, Suite 300
Portland, OR 97213-3786, USA
t: +1 503 287 3093
f: +1 503 280 8832
info@isbs.com

British Library Cataloguing in Publication Data
A catalogue record for this book is available from the British Library.

Library of Congress Cataloging-in-Publication Data
A catalog record for this book has been requested.

ISBN 978 1 84742 721 2 hardcover

Cover design by The Policy Press
Front cover: image kindly supplied by www.istock.com
Printed and bound in Great Britain by TJ International
Ltd, Padstow

To Ian and Dave

Contents

List of tables, figures and boxes

List of abbreviations

ACEVO	Association of Chief Executives of Voluntary Organisations
AVM	Association of Volunteer Managers
BIG	Big Lottery Fund
BME	black and minority ethnic
BGOP	Better Government for Older People
CDP	Community Development Project
CIPFA	Chartered Institute of Public Finance and Accountancy
CRAC	Career Development Organisation
CSH	Central Surrey Health
CSR	corporate social responsibility
CURS	Changing Urban and Regional System
CV	curriculum vitae
DRC	Disability Rights Commission
DWP	Department for Work and Pensions
emda	East Midlands Development Agency
ESRC	Economic and Social Research Council
EU	European Union
EVM	Excellence in Volunteer Managers
FSA	Financial Services Authority
FTE	full-time equivalent
GSCE	General Certificate in Secondary Education
HESVA	Higher Education Student Volunteering Awards
ICA	International Co-operative Alliance
ICT	information and communication technology
IiV	Investing in Volunteering
IT	information technology
IVR	Institute for Volunteering Research
KE	knowledge exchange
KT	knowledge transfer
LAA	Local Area Agreement
LFS	Labour Force Survey
LSP	Local Strategic Partnership
MBA	Master of Business Administration
NAVSM	National Association of Voluntary Service Managers
NAVHO	National Association of Voluntary Help Organisers
NCV	National Centre for Volunteering
NCVO	National Council for Voluntary Organisations
nef	New Economics Foundation

NGO	non-governmental organisation
NHS	National Health Service
NOPWC	National Old People's Welfare Committee
NOS	National Occupational Standards
NPM	New Public Management
NVMF	National Volunteer Managers Forum
OPAG	Older People's Advisory Group
OTS	Office of the Third Sector
PCT	primary care trust
PSA	Public Service Agreement
REF	Research Excellence Framework
SAVM	Scottish Association of Volunteer Management
SOC	Standard Occupational Classification
SOLACE	Society of Local Authority Chief Executives and Senior Managers
SRB	Single Regeneration Budget
TSOL	total social organisation of labour
TSRC	Third Sector Research Centre
UK	United Kingdom
UN	United Nations
US	United States
VCS	voluntary and community sector
VCSO	voluntary and community sector organisation
VHO	voluntary help organiser
VM	voluntary manager

Notes on the authors

Irene Hardill is Professor of Public Policy, Department of Social Sciences, Northumbria University, UK. Prior to this she held a chair at Nottingham Trent University in the Graduate School, Business, Law and Social Sciences. She has extensive research experience in theorising work (paid and unpaid), volunteering and the voluntary and community sector, and has published recently in the *Journal of Social Policy*, *Ageing and Society*, *Social Policy and Society*, *Policy & Politics* and *21st Century Society*. Professor Hardill has produced over 100 publications, including five books. Her work has featured in a number of ESRC publications for its academic and wider impact. She has co-edited a special issue of *Social Policy and Society* on remixing the economy of welfare with Dr Baines. Professor Hardill is membership secretary of the Academy of the Social Sciences, and is former vice chair of the Regional Studies Association.

Susan Baines is Reader in Social Policy at the Research Institute for Health and Social Change, Manchester Metropolitan University, UK, a post she has held since summer 2007. Before that she was in Newcastle University Business School. Her research is about the challenges facing the public and voluntary sectors, including innovation, partnership, and notions of enterprise in the context of public services. She has a particular interest in care and unpaid work in the household and community. These have been themes of recent articles published in *New Technology, Work and Employment*, *Social Policy and Administration*, *Social Policy and Society* and the *Social Enterprise Journal*. As a result of working closely with external funders and users of research for many years, she has become increasingly interested in the process and theory of knowledge exchange, and has also, with Irene Hardill, published on this subject.

Acknowledgements

This book draws on research funded by Age Concern England, the Economic and Social Research Council (RES R000 22 0592, 809318004, 172250051, 185-31-0110) and the Big Lottery. Some of the research was undertaken in partnership with Professor Peter Dwyer, Eddy Hogg, John Ramsey, Dr Mabel Lie, Professor Jane Wheelock, Rob Wilson, Mike Bull and Jenny Fisher.

We are indebted to the volunteers and voluntary organisations of Brightville and Irontown, the organisations affiliated to AgeUK in the East and West Midlands, in the East and in North City and to John Ramsey, Professor James Goodwin, Gill Sergeant, Angela Barnes, Oliver Moss, Amanda Williams, Perri 6, Ian Viles, Liz Blackman, Lorraine Clarke, Phil Poulter, Brenda Davies, Cressida Laywood, Mary Rayner, Sue Pearson, Rebecca Taylor, Keith Shaw, Suzanne Martin, Elaine Scogings, Jane Wilson and Diane Webb. We are grateful to Dan Wheatley for help with Chapter Four and Eddy Hogg for help with Chapter Seven and a special thank you to Adele Irving for her research assistance.

Acknowledgements

ONE

Fixing Britain's 'broken' society: from the Third Way to Big Society

> The making of a good society depends not on the State but on citizens, acting individually or in free association with one another, acting on motives of various kinds. (Beveridge, 1948, p 320)

Introduction

On 20 January 1961, when President John F. Kennedy was sworn in as the 35th President of the United States (US), he uttered the famous words, 'my fellow Americans: ask not what your country can do for you – ask what you can do for your country'. Almost five decades later in another liberal democracy, the new British Prime Minister David Cameron launched his Big Society drive to empower communities in Liverpool on 20th July 2010, describing social action as his 'great passion'.

> The Big Society is about a huge culture change ... here people, in their everyday lives, in their homes, in their neighbourhoods, in their workplace ... feel both free and powerful enough to help themselves and their own communities. The success of the Big Society will depend on the daily decisions of millions of people – on them giving their time, effort, even money, to causes around them. So government cannot remain neutral on that – it must foster and support a new culture of voluntarism, philanthropy, social action. (Cameron, 2010a)

The words uttered by Prime Minister Cameron about the Big Society are not dissimilar to those of former British Prime Minister Tony Blair (1999) who, in a speech at the annual conference of the National Council for Voluntary Organisations (NCVO) on 14 February 1999, said: 'each day, in communities across the country, people act out their vision of Britain – rejecting selfishness and embracing community'. He went on to express a vision that 'we mark the Millennium with an explosion in giving, "acts of community", that touch people's lives'.

Today, high-profile 'acts of community' regularly appear in the press. In 2000, for example, Prince William of Wales spent part of his gap year (breaking his studies between school and university) working as a volunteer for the charity Raleigh International, in Chile. During 2009, the then UK New Labour Prime Minister Gordon Brown spent part of his summer holiday giving time helping out at a voluntary project in his Kirkcaldy and Cowdenbeath seat in Fife, Scotland.

In recent years, in a number of countries, including the UK and the US, volunteering and the work of the voluntary and community sector (VCS) have been climbing up the policy agenda and much is now expected of volunteering and the VCS. Esping-Andersen (1990, 1999) identifies the UK and US as liberal democracies in his well-known conception of welfare regimes, which classifies economies along a continuum between the state and the market. In the case of liberal democracies, market solutions are promoted and there is political commitment to minimising the role of the state. While Esping-Andersen (1990, 1999) does not include the voluntary sector in his model, in liberal democracies it is the voluntary sector that has played a crucial role in reducing the state as it is the VCS that is increasingly delivering public services.

In the case of the UK, the VCS is playing an increasingly important role in public service delivery. We saw the role of the VCS intensified under New Labour (1997–2010) with policies to broaden the supplier base in health and care and investments in upskilling voluntary and community sector organisations (VCSOs) to bid for and deliver contracts. There is a commitment to volunteering from across the mainstream British political spectrum (Di Domenico et al, 2009; Alcock, 2010) and the 'Big Society' agenda of the coalition government promises a continuation of this direction of travel; albeit in a new regime of budget cuts, service cuts and demands for more for less, including from unpaid volunteers.

Through volunteering, individuals are said to be 'transformed' into better citizens (Russell, 2005); and communities and wider society, it is claimed, benefit through building social capital (Putnam, 2000; Devine and Roberts, 2003). As has already been noted, the new UK coalition government (as did the previous Labour administration) has strategies to expand and diversify volunteering across all three sectors of the economy. *Building the Big Society* (Cabinet Office, 2010a) promises a range of measures to encourage volunteering, with a specific proposal for a flagship 'National Citizen Service' to give 16-year-olds a chance to get involved in their communities, learn to be active citizens and mix with people from different backgrounds.

In an article in 2003, we pointed to the paradox that while much was expected of volunteering across policy domains (social capital, economic development, public service modernisation), all this was oddly 'unjoined up' with the overarching welfare-to-work agenda (Hardill and Baines, 2003). There is evidence that volunteering is changing in ways that are uncomfortable for some – and are not well understood. Quantitative data on volunteering is relatively plentiful and much empirical research on volunteering has used survey methods to determine volunteer motivation against socioeconomic variables and other factors such as time devoted to volunteering. Such quantitative research provides a valuable body of evidence for patterns of individual attitudes to volunteer activity across a very wide range of organisational, national and cultural contexts.

Moreover, until recently, theoretical insight into the *work* of volunteering has been relatively underdeveloped (Taylor, 2004). In 2004, we embarked on research that we report on in this book, which aimed to test the utility of theories and frameworks around work and care through fine-grained, micro-sociological research; we have used more holistic methods to encompass the social, economic and cultural complexity of volunteering.

In this book, we specifically seek to offer a theoretically nuanced understanding of voluntary work in the 21st century in liberal democracies by linking three key social science concepts: the 'sociology of work', the 'ethic of care' and 'enterprise/entrepreneurial behaviour' (for a fuller account, see Chapter Two). We seek to contribute to knowledge by offering a feminist-inflected understanding of individual action in that part of the economy that is beyond the state and the market (see the section 'The voluntary and community sector' later in this chapter). We offer a conceptualisation of volunteering at three spatial scales: the individual (and their household), the organisation and the community.

From the *individual* perspective, questions include: Do people volunteer as an expression of care for non-household members? Is it as part of a strategy for personal success, to 'get on' in terms of the labour market? We see the individual as embedded within household, kinship and wider networks (see pp 24-5). From the *organisational* perspective, we consider increased VCS partnership working with the public sector (Wilding et al, 2006) and the associated trend towards the professionalisation of volunteering with selection, training and appraisal, as in paid jobs. The professionalisation of volunteering has been accompanied by a growth in the number of paid jobs in the sector, including increasing numbers of volunteer managers, which some argue is an embryonic profession. Many voluntary organisations, volunteers and their activities are embedded in a *community* context (Omoto and Snyder, 2002). Community is seen as a space of 'opportunity, responsibility, employability and inclusion' (Levitas, 2000, p 191) and includes communities of identity and interest, as well as place (Willmott, 1986). It is an important theme in this book because community both influences the causal processes shaping volunteering and can be the target of volunteer efforts (Levitas, 2000; Williams, 2003). Subjectively, neighbourhood and community mean different things to different people at different times; each individual's activities, networks and travel patterns shape their concept of neighbourhood and community (Massey, 1994). The community context, therefore, is complex and contested.

Our arguments about volunteering at each of these levels will be illustrated by empirical evidence largely, but not exclusively, from the UK – from research funded by the Economic and Social Research Council (ESRC) and charities (such as Age Concern England) that we have undertaken since 2004 (see the section 'Researching volunteering and the voluntary and community sector' later in this chapter).

Unpaid voluntary work

There continues to be much debate among both academics and policy makers as to what exactly volunteering is (Kendall, 2003; Ellis Paine et al, 2010; Rochester el al, 2010). In advanced capitalist economies, voluntary work takes place through formal organisations (in the public, private and voluntary and community sectors) and more informally, through community groups, for example (Gibson-Graham, 2006). For the purposes of this book, volunteering is regarded as an activity that is freely chosen, does not involve remuneration and helps or benefits strangers (Zappala, 2000, p 1). Some authors add a fourth dimension – that of 'organisation' – but Ellis Paine et al (2010, p 8) suggest that the degree to which volunteering activities are organised should be seen as a dimension of volunteering; a way of understanding it rather than a defining principle.

In official datasets and much commentary, volunteering is divided between 'formal' (undertaken through an organisation or group) and 'informal' (neighbouring and time giving on a one-to-one basis, sometimes referred to as the 'fourth sector') (Williams, 2003, 2008). When formal and informal volunteering are conflated together, just under three out of four adults (73%) in England are volunteers at least once in 12 months, according to national data from the Department for Communities and Local Government (DCLG, 2008). But this binary divide has been criticised in a number of ways. For example, Saxton and Baker (2009) question the definitions and therefore the measurement of volunteering in official statistics in England. Ellis Paine et al (2010) suggest thinking of volunteering as either organised, collective action or individual action. In this framework, collective volunteering takes place in groups that are more grassroots, with no formal structure (Billis, 1993). Individual action embraces informal volunteering and some forms of civic engagement (Billis, 1993, p 19). However, we suggest drawing on feminist theorisations of 'work'; in particular, the conceptual framework developed by Glucksmann (1995, 2000) and others (Taylor, 2004; Williams, 2011): the 'total social organisation of labour' (TSOL), that cuts across binaries, and highlights the 'fuzzy edges' of different forms of 'work'. The TSOL we argue helps understand voluntary action (see pp 12–14).

In this book, our main concern is organised or formal volunteering for social welfare, which has been the target of interventions sponsored by government. As others have argued, such volunteering in practice can be hard to distinguish from more informal activities often associated with care for others (Schervish and Havens, 2002). For example, some people give time via social welfare organisations and visit the same clients informally too. Informal neighbouring and care within kin groups have traditionally been key to the wellbeing of communities (Young and Wilmott, 1957, chapter six) and the categories of formal and informal volunteering are perceived differently by different groups. For example, the contribution of some minority ethnic groups may be undervalued because its lack of formality does not conform to narrow definitions of volunteering (Lukka and Ellis, 2001). All this is significant because some writers (notably Williams, 2003; Williams and Windebank, 2006) argue that a culture of engagement in groups is relatively alien to most people in deprived communities, unlike one-to-one aid. New Labour's preference for promoting formal volunteering in such communities, according to this reasoning, was felt to be inappropriate (Williams, 2003).

Historical accounts of volunteering in England identify two main impulses – philanthropy and mutual aid (Davis Smith, 1995). During the Industrial Revolution, there was a visible shift from informal and individual charitable acts to organised formal volunteering by philanthropic institutions and voluntary associations dominated by middle-class elites (see Box 1.1;Taylor, 2005). Philanthropy is associated with altruism towards people who are perceived as outsiders (Davis Smith, 1995). The 19th century saw working-class membership of a range of self-help organisations (such as temperance societies, cooperatives and friendly societies) grow and was driven by a different set of material circumstances and cultural values from those that encouraged philanthropic work among the middle classes. Working-class societies were concerned with protecting members and mutual aid rather than helping the less fortunate and were guided by the need to survive insecurity and poverty (Taylor, 2005). Mutual aid is characterised by individuals with a shared experience or situation working together to bring about change (Davis Smith, 1995; see Box 1.2).

Box 1.1: Nineteenth-century acts of philanthropy

North and South (Gaskell, 2003)

One of the central characters in this novel is Margaret Hale, daughter of a former Church of England clergyman, who moves to a northern industrial town. Margaret does not undertake paid work but does undertake philanthropic acts. She befriends Mr Nicholas Higgins, a factory worker and his sick daughter Bessy, who is about Margaret's age, and visits the family as often as she can – taking small food parcels and so on, 'she would go and see Bessy Higgins. It would not be so refreshing as a quiet country walk, but still it would perhaps be doing the kinder thing' (p 180).

Bleak House (Dickens, 1976)

The 'telescopic philanthropist' Mrs Jellyby is 'a lady of very remarkable strength of character who devotes herself entirely to the public' (p. 64). She pursues projects in distant places – Africa is one of her obsessions – at the expense of her 'duty' to her own family. This is a sharp satiric picture of a Victorian woman who devotes all her energies to public causes while neglecting her home and children.

In the Beveridge Report (Beveridge, 1948), a sharp distinction was made between philanthropy and mutual aid (Deakin, 1995). According to Davis Smith (1995), philanthropic good works have received an undue share of attention from previous writers and he sets out to rescue mutual aid and self-help[1] from comparative neglect. Mutual aid and self-help are characterised by a common concern and a shared decision to do something about it (Wann, 1995). As such, they represent

Box 1.2: Nineteenth-century acts of 'mutual aid'

The Rochdale Pioneers

In 1844, a group of 28 Lancashire cotton weavers faced harsh working conditions and low wages and could not afford the high price of food and household goods. They decided that by pooling their scare resources, they could open their own store selling food items that they could not otherwise afford. Within three months, they expanded their selection to include tea and tobacco, and they were soon known for providing high-quality, unadulterated goods.

Source: ICA (2005)

a distinct alternative to those forms of voluntary action that are based on philanthropy and altruism and enshrined in charitable law (Hyatt and England, 1995).

Notwithstanding dramatic changes over half a century in people's attachment to places, community relationships are still particularly significant in the lives of some groups. Older women, for example, act as 'neighbourhood keepers' according to a study that revisited the communities researched by Young and Willmott in the 1950s (Phillipson et al, 1999; see also Lupton, 2003; Mumford and Power, 2003, p 31).

The identity of women with the local and the community has a long history. The 19th-century philanthropist Josephine Butler argued that state-controlled welfare systems were 'masculine' while parochial service, which recreated domestic life, was essentially 'feminine' (Prochaska, 1988). Some feminists suspect that present-day calls for more reliance on unpaid work through voluntary organisations and groups within communities mean a return to traditional gender roles and relations (Frazer, 1999). Little (1997) has uncovered ways in which voluntary activity supports a gendered form and image of one kind of community, the rural English village. Her analysis of rural women's participation in voluntary work can be seen as a reflection of their powerlessness and of the hegemonic power of paid work over unpaid.

Work – meaning paid employment – is of central importance to social policy in the UK, as it is elsewhere. Policies to move people without jobs into employment have concentrated on 'making work pay'. It has been argued that all these welfare-to-work policies send a signal that only paid work is important and devalue non-marketised activity (Lister, 2002). Moreover, McDowell (2004) contends that the dominance of an individualistic ethos that pervades both the labour market and the welfare state is undermining notions of collective welfare and an ethic of care.

The voluntary and community sector

Volunteering is often conflated with the VCS, although the boundaries between sectors of the economy are becoming increasingly indistinct (Lewis, 2005). Indeed, volunteering takes place in all three sectors of the economy and around two thirds of individuals who volunteer in England, volunteer for organisations within the VCS (Low et al, 2007). Other settings for volunteering include the National Health Service (NHS), private companies and higher education institutions. In 2008, the NHS consulted on a national strategy to raise the profile of volunteering and encourage a more diverse range of volunteers in health and social care services, where 'volunteering has a potentially critical role to play in supporting improved health and wellbeing' (DH, 2008, p 4). Volunteering in the private sector via secondments and employee schemes is also promoted (Murphy et al, 2005).

But what is the VCS? Within the academy, as in the world of policy, no single term is used to capture that part of the economy beyond the public and private sectors. It is variously known as the voluntary and community sector/social economy/third sector. For the sake of brevity, we adopt in this book the inclusive 'voluntary and community sector (including social enterprises)', commonly abbreviated to VCS. The confusion over nomenclature, however, is significant. It reflects the diversity of claims to expertise that are not well established or widely accepted.

Under New Labour, the term 'third sector' became widely used. In 2006, for England, the Office of the Third Sector within the Cabinet Office was created, with a Minister of the Third Sector, initially Ed Miliband MP. The notion of a 'third sector' that is neither the bureaucratic state nor profit-driven business was not invented by New Labour, but it gained official acceptance during its second and third terms; perhaps on account of its verbal echo of Third Way politics (Haugh and Kitson, 2007). After the 2010 General Election, the coalition government quickly renamed the 'Office of the Third Sector' the 'Office for Civil Society'. The coalition government's rejection of the label 'third sector' is indicative of the extent to which definitions in this area are invested with political dimensions and sectional interests (Ridley-Duff and Bull, 2011).

In mainland Europe, the term '*économie sociale*' has a long history. It was first used in 1830 by French economist Charles Dunoyer (Mouleart and Ailenei, 2005). The French sociologist Frédéric Le Play contributed significantly to the rise and acceptance of this concept in socioeconomic analysis (Archambault, 2001). '*Économie sociale*' has been an official term in the European Union (EU) since 1989 and it remains currently in vogue within the EU.

The VCS includes a host of organisations (VCSOs) that deliver social and environmental benefits and are neither profit-making nor statutory-value driven; it is composed of charities, community groups, social enterprises (profits reinvested for social goals) and 'umbrella' organisations that represent and support parts of the wider VCS. As a result, it has been described as being a 'loose and baggy monster' (Kendall and Knapp, 1995). Moreover, within what seems to be one organisation, there can be a number of trading entities; part of an organisation's activities can be undertaken as a registered charity, while other activities can be undertaken as a social enterprise/trading arm/ community interest company. So, what seems to be one organisation can in fact be a complex web of trading entities.

In addition to achieving goals related to their underlying values and mission (often related to relieving hardship), some VCSOs have taken on new roles, which are both welcomed and contested. These include:

• *labour market intermediaries*, facilitating the re-entry of the socially excluded into employment (Wardell et al, 2000; McDonald and Warburton, 2003; Baines, 2004; Cabinet Office, 2007);
• *agents for public service delivery* – services traditionally offered by the welfare state are contracted out to VCSOs, thereby reducing the cost to the state of welfare provision (Blackmore, 2005; Lewis, 2005; Paxton et al, 2005);
• *social partners* working to achieve civil renewal and community regeneration and/or participation in governance (Tonkiss and Passey, 1999).

But not all VCSOs have taken on such roles.

Milligan and Fyfe (2004, 2005), in their study of social welfare VCSOs in Glasgow, describe the VCS as having a 'bifurcated/binary structure', composed of traditional grassroots activities and organisations, as well as corporatist voluntary organisations engaged in the delivery of public services. They also comment that the nature of the volunteering experience and organisational structure, including reliance on paid labour and community focus of some VCSOs, has been radically altered by an increasing commitment to public service delivery. Some VCSOs, they observed, gravitated to areas of deprivation because of state funding programmes but were also located in parts of the city in response to the needs of specific user groups (Milligan and Fife, 2005).

Theoretical work on the way VCSOs manage their volunteers by Rochester et al (2010; Zimmeck, 2001) identifies two models. In the workplace model, volunteering in such organisations resembles paid work as the organisation adopts more formal styles of volunteering. Organisations with a service delivery role may find that eligibility for funding requires some demonstrable way of indicating how volunteers will contribute to the work of the organisation. A further driver is the trend for organisations to demonstrate their effectiveness and efficiency as potential providers of public services (Rochester, 2006). It is in the more bureaucratic organisations that the management of volunteers is undertaken by paid staff. It is in such organisations that, it is argued, the nature of the volunteer experience is changing with the professionalisation agenda. In contrast to this bureaucratic organisational form is the collectivist-democratic organisation (Rochester et al, 2010, p 153), which is more egalitarian and which only minimal applies rules and procedures with regard to volunteering (see also Zimmeck, 2001, p 19).

The book

As we briefly mentioned earlier, our research on volunteering and the VCS has been inspired by feminist-inflected approaches of individual and collective action in that part of the economy beyond the state and the market. Such approaches have challenged and shifted the boundary between what is considered economic and non-economic. Gibson-Graham (2006) have re-imagined the economy, making visible non-capitalist forms. Their 'diverse economy' offers a more nuanced view of the economy by including practices excluded by capitalist theory. Rather, they see 'economic value as liberally distributed', in an alternative economy (2006, pp 59-60). In their rethinking of the economy and its representation in their action research, they have used the image of an iceberg to form a pedagogical version of their diverse economy. Such activities as wage labour, market exchange of commodities and capitalist enterprise, what is usually regarded as 'the economy', comprises but a small subset of the activities by which we produce, exchange and distribute values. In the submerged part of the iceberg, they identify a myriad of activities, sites and people, which include volunteering, the voluntary sector and the community-building effect of giving. This section contains individuals, households, organisations and communities, and formal and informal voluntary work.

In Chapter Two, we present the theoretical underpinnings of the book. When we focus on individual volunteers, we link the traditions from the sociology of work with the emerging notion of the ethic of care as a theoretical framework. In the light of heightened expectations that voluntary organisations – and volunteers – create new solutions to deprivation and social exclusion, we enrich these guiding concepts with selected insights from evolving thought about enterprise and entrepreneurial behaviour. We use a third set of conceptual resources to confront the ever-more competitive environment for voluntary action and expectations that it will innovate and expand frontiers. We, therefore, invoke the growing, diverse and increasingly critical literature on 'entrepreneurship', a term that some writers consider should be broadened to represent the creation of social as well as economic value (Chell, 2007). A strand of sociological theory identifies the 'entrepreneurs of the self'; individual projects of personal success as opposed to bureaucracy and notions of service and 'public value' (such as Giddens, 1991; Beck, 1992; du Gay, 2007). People utilise these narrative resources selectively and creatively to construct their social worlds (Down, 2006). We use these concepts to understand individual action.

In so doing, we link the three social science concepts of 'work', 'care' and 'entrepreneurship' in a novel way in Chapter Two and draw on them throughout the book. In our research and in this book, we have adapted a conceptual model developed by Omoto and Snyder (2002) as a framework for understanding volunteering. They characterise volunteering as a process situated at, and building bridges between, three levels (individual, organisational and community). We have added a fourth level, the household/family, as volunteering can impact on, be facilitated by or be undertaken with other household and family members. The decision of one individual within a household to volunteer may well impact on other household members, as creating space and time to volunteer may have implications for other household members – one may be required to undertake more tasks of social reproduction to enable their partner to volunteer, for example.

For Omoto and Snyder (2002, p 38), community is both a context and a process for voluntary efforts; highlighting how concerns about and connections to communities can motivate and sustain the action of individuals. Community extends beyond the simple context of the spatially bounded physical definition of community. Rather, community is a psychological entity or conceptualisation that is likely to have significant consequences for understanding voluntary efforts and broader civic participation. VCSOs are for the most part based in communities and some grew out of attempts to change aspects of the community in which they are embedded in some way. Volunteers, volunteer efforts and many voluntary organisations are therefore embedded in a community context. This community context can influence the volunteer process and can be the target of volunteer efforts.

Volunteering in Omoto and Snyder's (2002) model has three stages that unfold over time (antecedents, experiences and consequences). The antecedents of volunteerism centre on what motivates some people to volunteer; while experiences centre on what may promote or deter continuing involvement, including the interpersonal relationship between volunteer and recipient of services. The third stage is consequences of volunteering, which include changes in attitudes, knowledge and behaviour.

In Chapter Three, we combine the heuristic developed by Omoto and Snyder (2002) as a framework for understanding why individuals volunteer with cultural theory, known as Grid and Group. As we are concerned with explanations, dynamics and processes, rather than counting phenomena, we draw on Grid and Group as a heuristic devise for explaining and categorising the multiple positions people take up with regard to voluntary work (for a fuller account, see Hardill et al, 2007). Cultural theory aims to understand the ways in which different people and social groups respond to threats and opportunities. It arose out of the work of Douglas (1992), who proposed that social structures generate attitudes towards the world.

Grid and Group has been widely adapted in analysis of responses to public policy, for example public sector management reform (Hood, 1998; 6 et al, 2002) and local economic development (Jayne, 2003). It is an approach sensitive to the local specificities and preoccupations that are likely to explain stances towards volunteering in organisations providing caring services in a community. In this way, we can offer a more nuanced and useful account of variations than the lists of motivations that characterise much literature in this field. Using these heuristic devices, we aim to offer a more holistic perspective, a more textured and complex picture of people's 'work' and caring practices, choices and constraints (for a fuller discussion, see Hardill et al, 2007).

In Chapter Four, we link the feminist–inspired heuristic of TSOL to explore the work of volunteer managers (VMs) (those staff members who manage volunteers); examining the work they undertake, their careers and their search for a professional identity. VMs often work above contracted hours and undertake unpaid volunteer roles. Glucksmann's (2000) conceptual framework, TSOL, encompasses activities that cut across boundaries between paid and unpaid work, market and non-market, formal and informal sectors (see Figure 1.1). TSOL proposes a sophisticated model of work that highlights its fuzzy edges, with the existence of activities that can be work or non-work according to context. Taylor (2004, Figure 1.2) and Williams (2011, Figure 2) build on TSOL to situate paid and unpaid work within a continuum of work that can take place in public, institutional or familial settings and can be either paid or unpaid in any of them. In recognising the neglected dimension of unpaid activity in the public sphere, TSOL can encompass the work identities and the practical realities of people whose lives include volunteering and who may or may not also perform work within market-like exchange relations. Such a framework facilitates an examination of the interconnections between paid and unpaid work. Following Taylor (2004) and Williams (2011), Figure 1.2 shows possible types of work along the dimensions of paid and unpaid, formal and informal, with the types considered in this book in the shaded segments.

In Chapter Five, we focus on VCSOs, which it is claimed are tending to become more like state agencies as a result of taking on the delivery of services under government contracts. They are also said to resemble private sector enterprises in response to an increasingly competitive

Figure 1.1: Framework of the total social organisation of labour

PAID		
Formal paid employment in public, private or voluntary sector	**Informal economic activity**	**Household/ family work**
e.g. paid care assistant	e.g. paid babysitting for friends or neighbours	e.g. paid babysitting within the family
PUBLIC/ FORMAL	**PUBLIC/ INFORMAL**	**PRIVATE/ INFORMAL**
e.g. unpaid care assistant	e.g. unpaid care for sick or elderly neighbour	e.g. unpaid care for sick or elderly relative
Formal unpaid work in public, private and voluntary sector	**Informal unpaid work**	**Private domestic labour**
UNPAID		

Source: Taylor (2004, Figure 2)

Figure 1.2: Typology of kinds of community self-help in the total social organisation of labour

PAID

(1) Formal paid job in private or public sector	(2) Formal paid job in voluntary sector	(3) Informal employment	(4) Reimbursed favours	(5) Paid family/ household work
eg waged job; self-employed	eg formal job in voluntary organisation	eg wholly undeclared waged work; informal self-employment	eg favour for friends and neighbours recompensed with gift or in-kind labour	eg paid exchanges within the family

FORMAL ⸻ **INFORMAL**

eg unpaid internship	eg unpaid work in formal community-based group	eg unpaid children's soccer coach without formal police check	eg unpaid kinship exchange, neighbourly favour	eg self-provisioning of care within household
(6) Formal unpaid work in private and public sector	(7) Formal unpaid work in VCS	(8) 'Below the radar' unpaid labour in groups	(9) One-to-one unpaid labour	(10) Self-provisioning

UNPAID

Source: Adapted from Williams (2011)

environment for resources. The notion of social enterprise 'draws on the exceptional effort of individuals and organisations working in the most testing circumstances to meet social needs and empower communities' (Amin, 2009a, p 47). 'Social enterprise' is a term that can be applied to charities and voluntary groups that adopt income-generating strategies, including public sector contracts, although such organisations often do not recognise themselves as being enterprises or entrepreneurial. While traditionally the literature on entrepreneurship has focused on the start-up of new firms, contemporary definitions of entrepreneurship tend to centre on the pursuit of opportunity. Stevenson and Gumpert, 1985; Stephenson and Jarillo, 1990, for example, have argued that entrepreneurial value-creating processes can take place in any type of organisation; a point echoed by Chell (2007), who goes on to contend that definitions of entrepreneurship might usefully be modified to incorporate the creation of social as well as economic value.

Understanding communities has long enthralled both social scientists and policy makers, but what we understand as community has changed from being place-based with studies of spatially bound communities to recognising that communities can also be framed around identity and interest (Willmott, 1986, 1989); these imagined communities can be transnational (O'Reilly, 2000).

In Chapter Six, we focus on volunteering and the VCS within communities of place and in Chapter Seven on communities of identity/attachment/interest. It is interesting to note that one dimension of the Big Society is the neighbourhood/community with the theme of 'Your Square Mile', or community.

Researching volunteering and the voluntary and community sector

In this book we draw on qualitative empirical evidence of individuals (paid workers and volunteers), organisations and communities, largely but not exclusively from the UK. We draw on work we have undertaken collectively and work we have undertaken with others. The stream of research we have undertaken together began in 2004 when we obtained funding from the ESRC under the research grants scheme for a micro-sociological study of the work of volunteers in a case study community (RES 000220592).

Our case study community of place was Brightville, in the East Midlands, which developed in the 19th century and had a diverse industrial base spanning coal mining and textiles. It coalesced with a nearby industrial town, Irontown, but to this day, Brightville's residents retain a strong sense of a separate identity from Irontown. Brightville is composed of two types of 'poor' area: one of largely working-class, 19th-century terraced housing and the other of peripheral post-war social housing – both have been a poverty cluster since their inception (Lupton, 2003). According to the Index of Multiple Deprivation, Brightville is economically deprived (CRESR, 2002) – the kind of place that typically tends to have relatively low levels of volunteering. Yet, from a series of visits prior to the start of the study, we were aware of vibrant, active volunteer initiatives there. This led us to think of it as a place rich in the elusive quality of 'community spirit'

In order to understand the complex structuring of volunteering at the level of the individual and the organisation, we talked to former volunteers, current volunteers (in management roles as well as delivering the services of the organisation) and paid workers who also volunteer. These 27 interviews followed a 'life history' design, which we adopted because of its capacity to capture the overlap between the individual and social and institutional structures (Dex, 1991). The interviews were recorded and transcribed in full and analysed by theme, paying careful attention to language used and emphasis given.

During the fieldwork, we worked more interactively than we anticipated. We used a range of qualitative data-gathering tools, including:

- repeated, systematic observation at a number of voluntary organisations working in the community;
- the collection of documentary evidence from these organisations;
- face-to-face interviews with key informants (officers in local economic development and social inclusion, managers and workers in organisations using volunteers);
- a series of focus groups with groups of volunteers;
- 'life history' interviews with a selection of volunteers.

The VCSOs where we undertook the fieldwork, and individual volunteers, showed more interest in our research than we expected and we signalled this in our end of award report. Some of the one-to-one interviews we undertook were very interactive. We ended up being interviewed/questioned by some research participants about why we were interested in volunteering and what voluntary work we did – we interpreted this as linked to the interviewees' confidence in us, trust and curiosity in why we were working in the community and what was going to happen to the findings. As we mentioned above, we chose the community carefully following advice. It is economically distressed, with an address that is perceived to be a 'bad one', but it is a community with an amazing spirit. A community where people feel undervalued and where people are not often consulted; indeed, there is a perception that the people who live there are 'problematic'. During our fieldwork we asked their views and as a result they felt that they were real research participants.

We were asked to undertake some community activities during the data-gathering stage of the research, such as speaking engagements to the organisers and volunteers of two of the voluntary organisations. We were also asked to help craft the community's bid for funding to a community regeneration initiative, the East Midlands Local Alchemy scheme, which was run jointly by the East Midlands Development Agency (emda) and the New Economics Foundation (nef). Local Alchemy was a bottom-up initiative designed to foster social capital in deprived communities, to maximise the energy (social capital) that people already have for community regeneration. The bid was successful and a local facilitator (not dissimilar to the community organisers of the Big Society: see Chapter 8) worked within the community to stimulate community groups and bring about change.

The community had expectations of what it wanted from us, however we had not budgeted for these events in our application form (in terms of our time and travel expenses). Towards the end of the project, we held a dissemination seminar for the community, which over 50 people attended, including some regional policy makers. The seminar was funded by a local social enterprise.

We built on the community engagement element of the first project by submitting an Impact Grant bid in 2006 to the ESRC (RES 809318004). This scheme was open to current and recent (within the last 12 months) ESRC grant holders to undertake new and additional knowledge transfer (KT) activities that were likely to have an impact on policy or practice. In 2006, we bid for funds to undertake a number of KT activities, including within our case study community.

In 2007, we undertook an ESRC Impact Grant project entitled *Delivering public services in the mixed economy of welfare: Putting research into practice* (RES 172250051), which also involved Robert Wilson of Newcastle University and John Ramsey of AgeUK. Part of this project, which was intended to promote practical learning from research, involved the identification of 10 case studies of VCSOs, five in each of two English regions: the North East and the East Midlands. They were selected through local networks and on the recommendation of the 24-strong project reference group of experts from the VCS and the public sector that advised the research team (Baines et al, 2008). The cases were not intended to be typical, but rather instances of service delivery that were thought to be successful and likely to offer useful learning material for others.

In this book we also draw on research undertaken in 2007-08 by Irene Hardill and Professor Peter Dwyer (Salford University), which was commissioned by Age Concern England (now called AgeUK), the national federation of charities active across England delivering help to older adults. It sought to identify and evaluate existing effective practice in delivering services to excluded older people in remote rural communities, across three English regions – the East and West Midlands and the East of England (Dwyer and Hardill, 2008; Hardill and Dwyer, 2011). Local branches of the national federation that funded the research were invited to put forward low-level services for inclusion in the study. Subsequently, six services (two in each of the three regions) were chosen. The services each promote the wellbeing of service users in different ways, through offering information and advice or overcoming social isolation. A total of 69 participants were interviewed in the course of the fieldwork for this project. Of these, 25 were key informants (including VSO chief executives and public sector commissioners) and 44 were older people who made use of one of the six village services under consideration. We also used AgeUK as a case study of a community of interest that is supported by the volunteer efforts of over 50,000 largely older people.

Two research projects carried out by Susan Baines and others are also referred to in this book. One of these was a Big Lottery-funded study of older volunteers entitled *Volunteering, self-help and citizenship in later life*, led by Professor Jane Wheelock and also involving Dr Mabel Lie (both of Newcastle University). This research was undertaken from 2004 to 2006 in partnership with a charity working with and for older people in the North East of England. The study was designed to assess the conditions under which older people become volunteers, their capacity to remain volunteers and constraints that impact on volunteering for them. The project began with focus groups to help plan the fieldwork and ensure that it was informed by as wide a range of volunteers as possible. There followed a questionnaire survey of the charity's current and former volunteers. The most substantial part of the research consisted of 76 in-depth interviews with people aged 55 and over involved with the charity. Most (four fifths) had responded to the volunteering questionnaire and the rest were users of the charity's leisure and learning services. It is the interview data with volunteers that we draw on in this book.

From 2009 to 2010, Susan Baines led a project funded by the ESRC under its Business Engagement Opportunities scheme in partnership with NHS Manchester, with colleagues Mike Bull and Jenny Fisher (both of Manchester Metropolitan University). The project was about the contribution of VCSOs to health and their capacity to become service providers to the NHS. One element of the project was a short-term placement by Jenny Fisher with Co-operatives UK to investigate opportunities for cooperative business models to respond to the 'personalisation' agenda in which service users entitled to public funding can receive cash in lieu of services. (Cash payments to adults who qualify for social care have been available in various forms since 1996 in England and pilots in the NHS commenced in 2009.) Working in close collaboration with Co-operatives UK, Jenny followed up the experiences of two cooperative social care providers that had been formed with support from Co-operatives UK to help people retain individual control over their care but share organisational burdens. The data we draw on in this book consist of site visits to the cooperatives and to key meetings (the Co-operative UK annual conference and a 'roundtable' on personalisation organised by the Association of Chief Executives of Voluntary Organisations; ACEVO), interviews with the cooperative founders and analysis of documentary material (reports, working documents, meeting minutes, organisations' websites and media publicity).

Conclusion

After this introductory chapter, the book is divided into seven additional chapters, which explore in greater detail the themes described in this chapter. In Chapter Two, we begin by looking at the theoretical underpinnings of the book. Three bodies of knowledge – the sociology of work, the ethic of care and enterprise – are used to offer insights into understanding why people give their time for no monetary reward by undertaking voluntary work. These three bodies of knowledge are analysed using Omoto and Snyder's (2002) framework in subsequent chapters. Chapter Three offers an understanding of individual pathways into volunteering by combining two heuristics: the heuristic of Omoto and Snyder (2002) and cultural theory, also known as Grid and Group. We begin by mapping individual pathways to volunteering, linking these pathways to the ethic of work, care and enterprise. Through these frameworks, we are able to explore, more holistically, volunteer motivation using TSOL and invoking the ethic of care and work, as well as to map the ways in which, for example, unpaid voluntary work precedes paid work in the VCS or is undertaken alongside paid work.

In Chapter Four, the focus moves to paid VMs; examining the work they undertake, their careers and their search for a professional identity drawing on TSOL. VMs often work above contracted hours and undertake unpaid volunteer roles. In Chapter Five, the focus switches to VCSOs. We begin by looking at the diversity of organisations in the sector, embracing cooperatives and social enterprises. Indeed, within one organisation there may be more than one trading entity. We review the contract culture agenda and move to social enterprise, using empirical description to examine the impact of the professionalisation agenda, the formalisation of volunteering and the need to be more enterprising. In Chapter Six, volunteering within communities is highlighted. The chapter begins with a brief review of community studies, and communities and public policy, and this is followed by studies of community engagement in a community of place. In Chapter Seven, we turn to communities of identity/interest, using a case study of an organisation actively supporting older people in urban and rural areas. The final chapter consists of a synthesis of the evidence presented and a critical assessment of the three theoretical concepts as an explanation for voluntary action in the 21st century. The final part of the chapter is forward-looking: examining emerging future trends and the implications for unpaid voluntary action in a period of economic and social uncertainty for liberal democracies with an ageing demographic profile.

Note

[1] Davis Smith makes no distinction between mutual aid and self-help.

TWO

Theoretical underpinnings of voluntary work and voluntary organisations: work, care or enterprise?

The voluntary sector ... should not simply be celebrated. Yet, what is also obvious from the experiences of experts and practitioners ... is that however different the situations, state support and big bureaucracies of any kind only work because the voluntary sector, and especially women, stitch people into the bigger structures of society. This is often done in chaotic ways, as responses to pressures which can destroy what is valuable in a society, which appear messy and are full of contradictions. Much, however, is creative and it is this creativity which progressive politicians and policy-makers should facilitate and political and social philosophers contemplate. (Showstack Sassoon, 1996, p 184)

Introduction

Volunteering is far from new, but over the past decade and a half, it has moved from the 'shadows into the policy spotlight' (Kendall, 2010, p 1). The weight of expectation about the contribution that volunteering, of all kinds, can make to the wellbeing of individuals and communities has never been greater (Rochester et al, 2010). The involvement of governments in volunteering has expanded since the mid-1990s, as we noted in Chapter One. Under the coalition government, in the UK, this seems set to continue, with the flagship Big Society agenda intended to encourage more volunteering and local action, to empower communities and to encourage social enterprises to deliver welfare services tailored to individual needs at low cost. Volunteering is multifaceted and by no means is all volunteering concerned with caring for others, as the refreshing reassessment by Rochester et al (2010) reminds us. Most care is unpaid and usually performed in domestic settings, but increasingly also through VCSOs, where it may be paid, unpaid or a hybrid of both (Daly, 2002). Care has become more fragmented between different institutional settings (public, private, voluntary and household) since Showstack Sassoon (1996, p 185) wrote so evocatively of the 'patched together needs, resources and institutions' that enabled the economy to function. The decline of the state as a direct provider of welfare services is associated with the rise of social enterprise and the push for the VCS to become more enterprising (Amin, 2005; Bull, 2008). That is why volunteering, care and enterprise are at the heart of this book.

Following the heuristic framework of Omoto and Snyder (2002) (see Chapter One, Table 1.1), in this chapter we explore volunteering at the levels of the individual, organisation and community. We propose three sets of social science concepts around care, work and enterprise that reflect the practices and contexts of volunteering at each of these levels. With regard to care and work, the concepts we adopt are situated firmly within strands of feminist thought. This is novel because, in contrast to their extensive pioneering insights into paid employment and unpaid care, feminist theorists and activists have had very little to say about volunteering. When second-wave feminism did touch on the topic of volunteering, it was treated with suspicion as likely to keep wages low and to divert women's energies away from the struggle for change (Onyx and Leonard, 2000). The first theoretical tool we invoke is the emerging concept of the 'ethic of care', which we link tentatively to the widely cited and much criticised body of commentary that frames volunteering within the influential notion of social capital and benefits to communities. With regard to the individual and organisation, we then draw on insights from the sociology of work and highlight, in particular, a recent strand of theory that has begun to link volunteering with longstanding feminist traditions of taking unpaid work seriously. Finally, we turn to a well-established genre of research on enterprise and the entrepreneurial behaviour of individuals, most typically associated with small business research and advocacy. The creation of new social enterprises – and sometimes turning traditional VCSOs into social enterprises – has become prominent in approaches to providing services that are lacking in communities beset by deprivation and exclusion (Southern, 2011). Entrepreneurship has been controversially invoked to explain the creation of social, as well as economic value, and identified with actual or inspirational activity at the organisational level in the public sector and in the VCS. We draw selectively and critically on these ideas. We now turn to three sections which consider, in sequence, the theoretical tools by which we will craft this book: care, care ethics and communities; work beyond paid employment; and enterprise. After that, we briefly draw conclusions and set the scene for the substantive research-based chapters that will follow.

Caring for others, the ethics of care and communities

Feminist writing, in general, has not been much interested in volunteering. Care, in contrast, has become a widely used concept; firmly established in feminist writings as an activity and set of relations lying at the intersection of the state, market and family (and voluntary sector) relations (Williams, 2001; Lewis, 2005). In this section, we reflect on care, in particular on the increasingly influential concept of an 'ethic of care' as a way of helping us to think about the forms of volunteering with which this book is concerned; that is, volunteering within communities, through organisations (large and small) providing services to help people in need – including older people and young families.

'Care' is a controversial concept that arouses both advocacy and resistance. Feminism does not speak with one voice about care. It is 'a value that is marginalised in society and should be celebrated', and also one that 'imprisons women' (McLaughlin, 2006). Within the disability movement, care has been 'an infamous concept' (Kröger, 2009, p 403). For disability activists and academics, 'care' is seen as belonging in charitable discourse and notions of pity that are inappropriate and demeaning (Shakespeare, 2000). Nevertheless, antagonism between care research and disability studies has become diluted recently, with recognition of mutual interests in emancipation, citizenship rights and social justice (Kröger, 2009).

The idea of an ethic of care (which stands in contrast to an ethic of work) responds to the writing of feminist thinkers who emphasised care for others as meaningful and fulfilling to many women and took this as a premise to propose care, as a model, to be extended to the larger social arena (Gilligan, 1982; Ruddick, 1990). The ethic of care is not adopted in all care-related research, but has become one of the most popular theoretical perspectives (Kröger, 2009). A feminist ethic of care begins with a social ontology of connection: foregrounding social relationships of mutuality and trust (rather than dependence). In Sevenhuijsen's (2003, p 183) words: 'Care has to become part of the practices of active citizenship, which should be based on notions of relationality and interdependence.... New practices of caring citizenship need a relocation of care from the margins to the centre of political judgement and collective action' (Sevenhuijsen, 2003, p 183).

Although individuals care and are cared for, 'care' is a relational concept. In our framework it is most likely to operate at the levels of community and household. Care ethics understands all social relations as contextual, partial, attentive, responsive and responsible and involves values of empathy, responsiveness, attentiveness and responsibility – values most readily mobilised in our homes and communities (Lawson, 2007). Lawson (2007) has argued that we need to think through the spatial extensiveness of care ethics, although she does not explicitly make the link to volunteering. Care, as an ethic or moral orientation, places emphasis on the welfare of the collectivity as much as that of individuals (Sampson et al, 2005; Williams, F., 2005). If caring – doing things/looking out for others beyond the family – is part of citizenship, volunteering by individuals within communities can be readily linked to the ethic of care (Williams, F., 2001, 2005).

Social capital, referring to networks, norms and trust that enable individuals and groups to engage in cooperative activity, is a notion more usually invoked in the context of volunteering. Putnam (2000) argues that participation in collective activity has a significant impact on individual health and wellbeing. More controversially, he claims that shared values and collective endeavour can help to mitigate the effects of socioeconomic disadvantage. In the UK, volunteering is seen by policy makers as an important indicator of social capital in local communities (Haezewindt, 2003; Ruston, 2003). 'Social capital' is an influential concept that has been used to support policy claims about the advantages of volunteering (Kendall, 2010). Critics have, nevertheless, called social capital fuzzy, confused and uncritical of social inequalities (Portes, 2000) and noted that it is far from evident that collective capacity building for communities is compatible with developing the capacities of excluded individuals (Shucksmith, 2000). Moreover, active involvement in any form of unpaid activity for communities demands time, commitment and skills. At the level of the individual, it can have high costs (Hibbitt et al, 2001; Hardill and Baines, 2003). There is evidence, for example, that people who participate as community representatives in local regeneration projects are put under pressure, often with insufficient support (Anastacio et al, 2000), while in rural areas, the small pool of people available to help can lead to overcommitment, overwork and burnout (Osborne et al, 2002). Edwards et al (2003) point to a paradox that policy has turned its attention to the social (communities and families) through a theoretical lens (social capital) that prioritises and takes for granted the economic system. While recognising the power of all these critiques, we discern a number of parallels between the narrative on social capital and the feminist-informed political ethic of care (Daly, 2002; Williams, 2005). Civic virtues of responsibilities, of tolerance of others, of trust, are learned through care of the self and caring, loving and supporting others, as much as through paid work. Care extends into society itself, involving the networks and sets of relations of care in which people are embedded (Daly and Lewis, 2000; Lawson, 2007). Care is, therefore, a public as well as a private matter.

Debates about care signal some of the concerns that attach to volunteering – despite the almost universal consensus that it is a good thing that should be supported and promoted to the benefit of communities, organisations and individuals. Some feminists suspect that present-day calls for more reliance on unpaid work through voluntary organisations and groups within communities means a return to traditional gender roles and relations, with associated sacrifices for individual women (Frazer, 1999). For this reason, volunteering may have a dark side (Onyx and Leonard, 2000). Little (1997), for example, uncovered ways in which voluntary activity assumes and perpetuates traditional versions of women's status and caring responsibilities in one kind of community: villages in rural England. 'Care' is a central concept throughout this book. Chapter Three forefronts individuals who become volunteers, taking as a case study volunteering within a community beset by economic decline and many social problems. It considers how volunteering is embedded in community and households in ways that both facilitate and constrain individual choices to give time and energy through community-based organisations that provide care. Chapter Six returns to the same community, drawing on a long tradition of community studies to consider what it means for residents to work through local organisations to solve problems for themselves and others.

Work: thinking beyond paid employment

'Work', in its broadest sense, has been accepted as including paid and unpaid activities since second-wave feminism pioneered an understanding of women's caring in the home as 'work'. Social reproduction and reciprocal exchange have become the subjects of sophisticated theorising and debate, which rarely touch on volunteering. The omission is surprising when we reflect on the extent to which volunteering represents a strategy for renewed social cohesion and improved economic performance. Work – meaning paid employment – is of central importance to social policy in the UK, as elsewhere. Lister (2002) has argued that there is a 'fetishism' around paid work that devalues activities not mediated through the market . In many organisational contexts, the boundaries between volunteering and employment are blurred as 'volunteering opportunities' have been harnessed towards an increasing employability (Wardell et al, 2000; Parsons and Broadbridge, 2004). An example of this is the promotion of volunteering for young people to encourage them to develop skills for the labour market (see Box 2.1).

Box 2.1: Young people, volunteering and work

For young people, the Russell Commission set up by the Labour Home Secretary and the Chancellor of the Exchequer recommended that volunteering should be encouraged in order to develop their skills and increase their employability and that their volunteering should be recognised through accreditation and links to vocational qualifications (Russell, 2005). The outcome of the report was the 'V' initiative, launched in 2006 as a five year programme to promote the skills, experience and confidence that can be gained through volunteering to all young people in England – especially those who are under-represented (Hill et al, 2009). 'V' was expected to deliver 'a step change in the diversity, quality and quantity of young people's volunteering' (Hill et al, 2009, p 1). Examples of projects funded under 'V' included 'Volunteer Voices', which provided volunteer opportunities to disabled young people aged 16 to 25, whatever their background. Participating in Volunteer Voices offered accreditation to all young people involved in order to let them try out a potential career area for free (Skill: National Bureau for Students with Disabilities, 2010). The 'V' initiative attempted to reach out to young people most likely to face barriers to volunteering and in so doing, to 'solidify and galvanise the relationship between volunteering and employment' (Hill et al, 2009, p 2).

We turn now to position volunteering within a broader understanding of what constitutes 'work' in ways that draw on the insights of feminist thinking on unpaid labour and care (Parry et al, 2005). How people sustain themselves goes beyond the individual wage and profit-making business to include unpaid social reproduction, reciprocal exchange and voluntary work (Jarvis, 1999; Williams, 2003, 2008; Gibson–Graham, 2006). Gibson–Graham (2006) has developed this position to argue that a diverse economy encompasses not only production for profit, but also a wealth of alternative economic practices, including mutual aid, self-provisioning by households, community activism and caregiving. Their language conveys some of the radical diversity of these economic relations, conceptualised in terms of three practices: different types of transactions and ways of negotiating commensurability; different types of labour and compensating it; and different forms of enterprise and ways of producing, appropriating and distributing surplus. They envision 'widening the identity of the economy to include all those practices excluded by a strong theory of capitalism' (Gibson-Graham, 2006, pp 59-60).

For most of the 20th century, the concept of 'work' was synonymous with only one kind of economic activity – paid employment undertaken in the 'public world' (Beechey, 1987; Pahl, 1988). Second-wave feminist thought promoted the idea that waged work is not the only kind of purposeful activity with social significance. The novel and controversial idea that domestic activity and caring are 'work' was argued with passion in sociology (Oakley, 1974) and economics (Waring, 1988). The issue came to symbolise society's undervaluation of women and their contribution to social wellbeing (Beneria, 1999). Expanding 'work' to encompass care, however, has remained fiercely contested. In the first volume of *Feminist Economics*, Himmelweit (1995) argued that the personal, relational qualities of caring are denied by forcing it inappropriately into the category of work. Her argument rests on a definition of work as purposeful activity that takes time and energy, has opportunity costs and is separable from the person who performs it. That last quality, according to Himmelweit, differentiates work from care because care involves relationships and caring activity that is inseparable from the person who performs it. Attempts to redefine care as work, she argues, result in the unwanted effect of devaluing 'those caring and self-fulfilling activities that remain undivided into production and consumption ... precisely the activities and pursuits that people have, at various times, seen as most worthwhile and still frequently describe as desirable' (Himmelweit, 1995, p 11).

The separation of work and worker is denied by theorists who have highlighted how much paid work – especially interpersonal services usually performed by women – involves 'emotional labour' (Hochschild, 1983). 'Emotional labour' is present when workers are required to feel and express emotions in order to produce an emotional response in the 'customer' – often a feeling of being cared for (Hochschild, 1983). Hochschild's original thesis of emotional labour condemns the harm to workers that results from this commodification of their emotions. Others have developed her influential idea to propose that encounters involving emotions of care and compassion in the workplace can involve aspects of satisfaction as well as distress (Tolich, 1993). Some accounts of volunteering emphasise that it is pleasurable (Roberts and Devine, 2004). This stance is readily compatible with the idea that volunteering is best understood as a form of 'serious leisure'

(Stebbins, 1996). Rochester et al (2010) build on Stebbins (1996) to talk about volunteering outside the domains of care and welfare, in for example sport, leisure and culture. There are accounts of work, too, that emphasise its pleasurable aspects in ways that sometimes even resemble leisure activities. A privileged minority of people do work that is both intrinsically satisfying and economically rewarding, usually work with creativity at its core, as illustrated by the so-called 'symbolic analysts', such as designers and architects. Some creative activities can be work or leisure according to context. Pleasure in work also exists in more traditional occupations, engineering for example (Cockburn, 1981). Even work that itself is unpleasant and meaningless may be bearable because of the pleasurable social interaction with which it is performed (Pollert, 1981). In short, neither pleasure nor emotional involvement per se can be used to differentiate work from non-work. Both may – or may not – be experienced by individuals in work, volunteering and care. As we noted in Chapter One, Glucksmann's overarching framework, TSOL, identifies four sets of processes – production, distribution, exchange and consumption – each of which is situated within permutations of paid and unpaid activities that are labelled work or non-work, according to context. TSOL cuts across boundaries between market and non-market, formal and informal, with a model of work that can take place in public, institutional or familial settings and can be either paid or unpaid in any of them (Glucksmann, 2000). Glucksmann applies this framework in a wide range of contexts, for example to explain how care for older adults in need becomes articulated in various countries in different configurations of the public sector, market, VCS and family (Glucksmann and Lyon, 2006).

Taylor (2004) builds on TSOL to recognise volunteering as the neglected dimension of unpaid activity in the public sphere. She develops and applies to volunteering the idea from TSOL that there is no simple correspondence between pay and work, but that all work, paid or unpaid, is embedded within and defined by social relations in the contexts in which it is located. Volunteering and volunteers, she argues, are marginalised in most accounts of work and career. 'TSOL' is an important concept in this book because it can encompass the work identities and the practical realities of people whose lives include volunteering and who may or may not also perform work within market-like exchange relations. We draw on this concept in Chapter Three, when we look at the complex jigsaws of 'work' and 'care' that are pieced together by individuals through the market, household and volunteering. In Chapter Four, we turn to workers within VCSOs who support and manage volunteers (usually as paid workers, but sometimes unpaid and sometimes a combination of both). TSOL proves to be a powerful tool with which to think about the working lives and livelihoods of this group and about what makes it possible for them to perform their increasingly vital role in sustaining the mixed economy of care.

The lure of enterprise

For the last quarter of a century, measures have been in place in the UK, as elsewhere, to produce an enterprise culture in which individuals will embrace 'flexibility, individualism and entrepreneurialism, in place of collectivism and rigidity' (Bradley et al, 2000, p 58). Popular management writers have declared that reliance on large organisations as employers has been replaced with reliance on the self (Handy, 1995; Kanter, 1995). The 'modern' career, based on long-term commitment between an individual and an organisation, has come to be associated with the past (Collin and Watts, 1996; McKinlay, 2002). The contemporary 'boundaryless' career, in contrast, is said to be characterised by uncertainty, continuous learning, networks and enterprise (Arthur and Rousseau, 1996; Arthur, 2008).

There is an extensive literature on entrepreneurship that focuses on the start-up of new firms. The behaviour of individual entrepreneurs has been said to be characterised by energy, imagination, desire for achievement, tolerance of uncertainty and love of change (Chell et al, 1991). A defining characteristic of entrepreneurs is that they pursue opportunities regardless of the resources they currently control (Stevenson and Jarillo, 1990). To do this, they actively mobilise knowledge and contacts (Dubini and Aldrich, 1991). Emphasis on individuals and their traits within the entrepreneurship literature has tended to be superseded by cultural, discursive and ideological aspects of entrepreneurship and how people utilise narrative resources selectively and creatively to construct their social worlds (Down and Reveley, 2004; Down, 2006; Gartner, 2010). Definitions of entrepreneurship centre on processes that 'result in innovative, risk-taking and pro-active behaviour' (Kearney et al, 2009, p 28). Such processes, it is increasingly claimed, can and should take place in any type of organisation, including the public sector and the VCS (Zerbinati and Souitaris, 2005; Sundin and Tillmar, 2008; Petchey et al, 2009). Kearney et al (2009, p 39) argue that, 'in the private sector ... entrepreneurship brings significant benefit through increased sales, market share, profitability and growth potential.... It is these results that indicate that entrepreneurship needs engendering in the public sector as well'. Although the positive connotations of enterprise and entrepreneurship are widely assumed, there are some dissenting voices. The academic study of entrepreneurship, it has been argued, has 'suffered from an often unquestioned positive ideological stance towards entrepreneurship and small business' (Blackburn and Kovalain, 2009, p 129).

VCSOs, it is sometimes claimed, are tending to become more like private sector enterprises, with the need to anticipate change and spot opportunities in response to an increasingly competitive environment for resources (Eikenberry and Kluver, 2004; Haugh and Kitson, 2007). For small businesses in the private sector, it has been noted that 'situations of adversity can provide opportunities to respond in an entrepreneurial fashion' (Blackburn and Ram, 2006, p 77). Against this background, people in VCSOs are exhorted, or constrained, to adopt entrepreneurial practices, language, behaviour and mindsets associated with the private sector (Peattie and Morley, 2008; Zahra et al, 2009). 'Social enterprise' is a term that has become much contested, but there is some consensus that social enterprises differ from other businesses because they engage in commercial activity, primarily, as a means to achieve social goals (Pearce, 2003; Peredo and McLean, 2006). They are said to share with for-profit business the characteristics of opportunity-seeking, proactivity and networking (Shaw and Carter, 2007). But according to Parkinson and Howorth (2008), people labelled 'social entrepreneurs' by others, are more likely to use words conventionally associated with community development or regeneration than entrepreneurship and to talk of opportunity recognition in terms of social need rather than business. Whittam and Birch (2011) argue that the focus on the individual in social enterprise comes at the expense of the community.

In Chapter Five, we discuss the recent history of social enterprise and public sector contracts. We offer examples from empirical research about how VCSOs of various kinds have responded to competitive environments, mainly but not exclusively to secure resources through winning contracts to deliver services to the specifications of state agencies. Notions of entrepreneurship were not readily adopted by participants in the research. Nevertheless, there were examples of new ways of doing things that grew directly out of users and providers of care (paid and unpaid) thinking through together how to improve their experiences. The 'creation of something of value' to a given community or a cause through social enterprise is the link between VCSOs and theories about entrepreneurs as agents of change (Chell, 2007) – a theme we pick up in Chapter Five.

Entrepreneurship is used as a metaphor associated with individualisation and customer orientation, particularly in the public sector where it has replaced – or is advocated to replace – rule-bound bureaucracy, according to du Gay (1996). Du Gay (1996) describes how consumers and employees are represented as autonomous, responsible and calculating in the all-pervasive discourse of enterprise, whereby persons are required to be 'entrepreneurs of the self' in all aspects of their lives. The 'entrepreneur of the self' has become opposed to bureaucracy and notions of service and public value (du Gay, 2000). This way of framing the entrepreneur is consistent with representations of the self as a reflexive project for individual success (Giddens, 1991; Beck, 1992, 2000). The project of the self demands the sustaining of 'coherent, yet continuously revised, biographical narratives' (Giddens, 1991, p 6). In Beck's (1992, p 135) words, 'there is a shift from a socially prescribed biography, constrained by factors such as gender and class, to a biography that is continually self-produced'. Sennett (1998, p 36) has taken up this theme to reflect that the entrepreneur, once an exceptional figure like a hero of fiction, is now 'served up as an ideal Everyman'. In the context of care, the entrepreneur metaphor appears when citizens, as service users, are encouraged to make active choices about their care (Scourfield, 2007). Disabled and older people in receipt of services are re-imagined, not as beneficiaries, but as 'managers of the enterprise of their own lives' (Pavey, 2006, p 227). In Chapter Five, we contest this individualised way of thinking about people who receive and provide care, to consider the alternative of cooperative enterprise models, based on mutual aid and shared responsibility.

Conclusion

In this chapter, we have attempted to confront the complex, overlapping and sometimes contradictory relationships between waged work, unpaid care and volunteering, at the levels of the individual, organisation and community. We have noted the longstanding association of volunteering with women's unpaid roles in social reproduction and reciprocal exchange. The idea of an ethic of care was explored as a way to think about the kind of volunteering on which we will focus with examples and case studies in Chapters Six and Seven. We suggested that the 'ethic of care' is compatible with the much more widely invoked social capital, while better adapted to encompass the gendered dimensions of connection, dependence, mutuality and trust in communities. Then, we considered recent attempts to stretch definitions of 'work' to account for volunteering. We tentatively suggested an analogy between such endeavours to make conceptual inroads into the analysis of volunteering and the achievement of second wave-feminism in redefining women's caring in the home as 'work'. We recognised that emphasis on the work-like aspects of volunteering may tend to mask volunteering undertaken as an expression of care and support for others. This is discussed in Chapter Three. Finally, we highlighted the growing interest in social enterprise and demands that all VCSOs think and act entrepreneurially, to which we return in Chapter Five.

The concepts we have discussed in this chapter are considered at the levels of the individual (Chapter Three), organisations (Chapters Four and Five) and the community (Chapters Six and Seven). These levels are treated separately for the purpose of analysis, but we recognise that they intersect and overlap. Organisations, for example, can originate and operate in communities of place (neighbourhoods for example) or communities of identity (such as migrant groups). Individuals acting as volunteers for an organisation, or as paid workers supporting its volunteers, are embedded within communities. We turn now to look at the experiences of volunteers active in one community.

THREE

Understanding the journeys of individual volunteers: demanding community concern, or demonstrating job readiness?

We make a living by what we do, but we make a life by what we give. (Winston S. Churchill)

Introduction

In this chapter, we offer insights into understanding individual pathways to volunteering. As we noted in Chapter One, volunteering can be undertaken through a formal organisation or it can be a more informal activity. It is, therefore, extremely diverse. That said, it is an activity that people freely choose to do, without remuneration, to help or benefit non-household members. Every day, millions of people around the world make an important formal commitment to others by giving time to undertake unpaid voluntary work via a voluntary organisation. The types of voluntary activities undertaken are extremely varied (administration/office duties; service delivery; managerial roles and as trustees; and representing VCSOs on partnerships as diverse as crime reduction, health improvement and urban regeneration) as are the volunteers themselves, and the value of their efforts to communities and society are immense.

In England, volunteers account for 1.1 million full-time equivalent (FTE) paid employees in the VCS and 72% of VCSOs depend on a volunteer labour force with no paid staff (Wilding et al, 2006). In a study in the US, Brown (1999) found that volunteers play a key role in the US VCS, accounting for more than 10% of total working hours in these organisations. In 2006, Anheier and Salamon studied the VCS across 24 countries and concluded that over 40% of FTE VCS jobs were held by volunteers; the equivalent of 16.8 million workers.

Since the onset of the world economic crisis in 2008, there has been a reported increase in interest in volunteering from people laid off because of the recession. In a recent survey in England by the Institute forVolunteering Research (IVR) of volunteer centres (IVR, 2009), 90% reported an increase in the number of volunteers, with 75% of those looking at volunteering to improve their chances of getting another job; most people enquiring were in their thirties or forties. In this chapter, we focus on understanding individual pathways to volunteering, what motivates and moves people to action, to search out and apply to help others through supporting the work of a voluntary organisation.

In recent years, research on volunteering in the UK has been framed in terms of individual needs and has been shaped by policy interest in increasing the numbers of volunteers (Kendall, 2003; Taylor, 2005). Voluntary action is increasingly linked to improving individual positions in the labour market and to solving social problems associated with worklessness (Dean, 2003). Policy statements highlight the rewards that can be enjoyed by volunteers themselves as much as or more than the contribution that they can make to the wellbeing of others. This instrumental view does not apply to individuals 'beyond' the labour market because of age, disability or care commitments. While studying individual psychological propensity to volunteer is not invalid, it tends to assume an individualistic set of explanations that fail to engage with the contexts of locality and social networks (Dean, 2003; Baines et al, 2006).

In this chapter, we examine individual pathways to volunteering by drawing on our empirical study of volunteer-using organisations and groups present in an English East Midlands community, which we call Brightville (Hardill et al, 2007; Baines and Hardill, 2008; Hardill and Baines, 2009). Much of the empirical research on volunteering has focused on motivation and debates about altruism and self-interest. Framing volunteering in such terms, in our view, tends to assume an individualistic set of explanations and offers a weak concept that fails to fully capture the social, economic and cultural complexity of volunteering. In order to understand more about how people negotiate the constraints and opportunities in their daily lives and manage to create (emotional, temporal and physical) space for volunteering (for formal voluntary organisations for example), we use a heuristic developed by Omoto and Snyder (2002) as a framework for understanding volunteering, combining this with cultural theory, known as Grid and Group, and TSOL. The remainder of the chapter is divided into four sections. The next section highlights public policy towards volunteering and is followed by a section on academic research on volunteering. Some results from an empirical study of sites of volunteering in the community Brightville are presented in the subsequent section. The final section offers a brief conclusion.

Public policy and volunteering

In recent years, UK public policy has placed an emphasis on encouraging individuals to undertake formal volunteering (through an organisation) as opposed to informal voluntary work (Williams, 2008). Under New Labour, there was a raft of initiatives dedicated to promote it, especially among the young and disadvantaged groups (DWP, 2006; Commission on the Future of Volunteering, 2008; Morgan Inquiry, 2008). Moreover, the weight of expectation about the contribution that volunteering can make to social good has never been greater as witnessed by the coalition government's Big Society; and it has broad political consensus (Rochester et al, 2010). In this section, we focus on public policy towards individuals and volunteering.

As we noted in Chapter Two, a great deal of emphasis has been placed by policy makers on exhorting more people to volunteer. During the New Labour administrations (1997-2010), volunteering was seen as a vehicle for solving social problems associated with worklessness via such schemes as the New Deal (Box 3.1) projects for young people, older adults or single mothers, or Sure Start projects (Box 3.2) that offer training for volunteering and encourage parents to use this as a route into employment (NESS, 2004). These schemes help to connect (or reconnect) individuals to the labour market through opportunities to develop skills, contacts and credentials (Doyle and Smith, 1999; Bruegel, 2000; Wardell et al, 2000; Russell, 2005). In this way, volunteering has become aligned with welfare-to-work policies. Yet one of the criticisms of the welfare-to-work agenda has been that it has tended to devalue non-marketised activity (Lister, 2002).

The 'V' initiative (2006-2011) promoted the skills, experience and confidence that can be gained through volunteering to all young people in England, especially those who were under-represented (Hill et al, 2009). A programme introduced by New Labour via the former Office of the Third Sector (OTS), now renamed the Office for Civil Society, comprised an investment of £6.6 million for volunteering programmes

---

Box 3.1: New Deal

The New Deal was introduced by New Labour in 1998. It is a programme of active labour market policies to reduce unemployment by providing training, subsidised employment and voluntary work to unemployed people. It originally focused on helping young adults (18- to 24-year-olds), but then expanded to include lone parents, disabled people and people aged over 50.

Source: DirectGov (2010)

Box 3.2: Sure Start

Sure Start developed under New Labour for families in England with the aim of delivering the best start in life for every child by bringing together early education, childcare, health and family support. Sure Start covers a wide range of programmes; both universal and those targeted at particular local areas or disadvantaged groups within England.

Over the years, Sure Start has changed. It began with local programmes, neighbourhood nurseries and early excellence centres, and bringing integrated early years services to the most disadvantaged communities. The geographical spread of Sure Start became more diverse and over 3,500 children's centres were established.

Source: DCSF (2010)

(2009-11). The Department for Work and Pensions (DWP) funded a Volunteer Brokerage Scheme until March 2011 with a target of getting 34,000 people into volunteering via referrals from jobcentres. New Labour identified a National Indicator 6 – 'participation in regular volunteering' – in Local Area Agreements (LAAs)[1] in an attempt to raise the profile of volunteering at the local level.

Under New Labour, volunteering also became strongly linked with education. In addition to promoting a work ethic among the socially excluded, the benefits of volunteering were expounded to young people through the national curriculum, with volunteering seen as part of being a good citizen. It is possible to gain an educational qualification – a General Certificate in Secondary Education (GCSE) – in citizenship, combining coursework, examinations as well as evidence of the candidate's lived experience of volunteering.

Undergraduate students are given a similar message. For them, the personal benefits of volunteering include gaining experience that can enhance their curriculum vitae (CV). There is a national awards system for higher education student volunteering, the Higher Education Student Volunteering Awards (HESVA), which has been developed and is managed by the Career Development Organisation (CRAC). Job application forms increasingly feature sections where voluntary work can be profiled. At some universities, such as the University of Brighton, volunteering can contribute towards the degree outcome (www.brighton.ac.uk/careers/jobs-volunteering/active-student-CPDM.html). Students in five Schools at the university can follow the Community Participation and Development Module. On a 10-credit module, they need to undertake 30 hours of practical work. Students on a 20-credit module need to undertake 50 hours of practical work.

As a result of the policy changes outlined above, two 'new' types of volunteer have appeared in empirical studies of volunteer sites. They participate because either:

• they have been excluded from paid work and need support to prepare for it (Parsons and Broadbridge, 2004); or
• they see volunteering as a route into a desired career (McDonald and Warburton, 2003).

Both reinforce the role of volunteering in training and retraining for the workplace; the first in terms of rehabilitation and increasing job readiness and the second with regard to career development. The first group may be directed towards volunteering by employability and welfare-to-work programmes. The second group are likely to aspire to professional status as volunteering is increasingly a requirement of professional training (Baines, 2004); they are typically young women and men whose commitment to volunteering is instrumental and short term (McDonald and Warburton, 2003).

What Kendall (2010, p 1) has called a 'relatively upbeat context for the British domestic pro-volunteering policy community' seems unlikely to be reversed under the Conservative-led coalition. Within its first month in office, the Prime Minister and Deputy Prime Minister launched the Big Society programme to create a climate that empowers local people and communities, with a National Citizen Service about understanding the importance of voluntary work and social contribution.

Volunteer motivation

While volunteering is intimately associated with the policies of New Labour, it is not new. The roots of voluntary action in the UK can be traced to two central impulses: philanthropy and mutual aid (Davis Smith, 1995). In the Beveridge Report, 1948, a sharp distinction was made between philanthropy and mutual aid (Deakin, 1995). According to Davis Smith (1995), philanthropic good works have received an undue share of attention from previous writers and he sets out to rescue mutual aid and self-help[2] from comparative neglect. Mutual aid and self-help are characterised by a common concern and a shared decision to do something about it (Wann, 1995; Richardson and Mumford, 2002). As such, they represent a distinct alternative to those forms of voluntary action that are based on philanthropy and altruism and enshrined in charitable law (Hyatt and England, 1995). In this chapter, we argue that mutual aid and philanthropy resonate strongly in volunteers' own accounts of their activity in the community.

There is a substantial literature on motives for volunteering (Knapp et al, 1995; Wardell et al, 2000; Yeung, 2004; Narushima, 2005; Dolnica and Randle, 2007). Studies in this vein categorise motivation in various ways, usually around the themes of altruism and self-interest. Volunteers are both givers and takers (Merrell, 2000); there is a 'duality of volunteering' incorporating altruism and egoism (Wardell et al, 2000). Volunteers, whatever their age, want to feel that they are useful members of society, to help others, to put something back into the community, to meet new people and to pursue learning and personal growth (see Figure 3.1; Barlow and Hainsworth, 2001; Rochester et al, 2002; Narushima, 2005).

Some studies have identified specific age-related sets of motivations. There is evidence, for example, that organisations whose mission or purpose is to promote the wellbeing of older people have a considerable advantage in involving older people as volunteers (Rochester et al, 2002). An American review claimed that older volunteers were much less likely than younger ones to be motivated by material rewards or status (Fischer and Schaffer, 1993). The most usually reported age-related motive for volunteering is to fill the vocational void left by retirement and to manage increased free time (Barlow and Hainsworth, 2001; Barnes and Parry, 2004; Davis Smith and Gay, 2005). For those older adults who still need to be connected or aspire to be reconnected to the labour market, it can be a pathway into it – opening up new paid work opportunities (Brooks, 2000).

Since Putnam's (2000) influential interpretation of social capital, however, volunteering has most typically been theorised in terms of participation in public life (Locke et al, 2001; Devine and Roberts, 2003; Evers, 2003). Devine applied Putnam's (2000) theory to ask the empirical question, do voluntary activities generate social capital? She concluded that there is a significant research gap in the area of voluntary careers and how they might lead to formal employment opportunities (Devine, 2003). Thinking about work and volunteering in this way is in harmony with the current emphasis on volunteering as an aspect of labour market policy.

Much of the research on volunteering has been largely concerned with counting and classifying instances of volunteering within different populations (Erlinghagen and Hank, 2006) and enumerating the characteristics of volunteers and their motivations to volunteer (Zappala and Burrell, 2002; Taniguchi, 2006). Leete (2006, p 172) has developed a taxonomy of volunteer motivations and Rochester et al (2010,

Figure 3.1: A guide to volunteering for Home-Start

A quick guide to becoming a home visiting volunteer

- You must be a parent or have parenting experience.
- As a Home-Start volunteer you will support a family by visiting them at home for around two hours, once a week.
- You should be able to commit at least six months of your time to Home-Start.
- You should have a non-judgemental attitude and understand about the pressures of bringing up a family.
- You will have to attend our free Volunteer Preparation Course with other new volunteers before meeting your first family.
- Expenses are paid during training and while you support a family, and help with childcare costs may also be available.
- If you want to, you may be able to take up the option of your training being formally recognised through accreditation with the Open College Network.
- You must understand that your support for families is completely confidential.
- You will have to undergo a criminal record check at enhanced level.
- You will be supported by your local Home-Start during the time you are visiting families.

How can I find out more about becoming a Home-Start volunteer?

Contact your local Home-Start for an informal chat:

Visit our website to find out more and locate your local Home-Start: www.home-start.org.uk

Call our free information line: 0800 068 63 68

Across the UK thousands of Home-Start volunteers visit families at home each week, supporting parents in situations as diverse as isolation, bereavement, multiple births, illness, disability or who are just finding parenting a struggle. They provide non-judgemental practical and emotional support and help build the family's confidence and ability to cope. Home-Start runs more services and has more volunteers supporting more families than any other family support charity in the UK.

All Home-Start schemes are supported by Home-Start UK, which provides training for staff, volunteers and trustees, information and guidance on governance, legal and human resources issues and help with fundraising and communications.

Registered office,
Home-Start UK
2 Salisbury Road, Leicester, LE1 7QR
T 0116 233 9955 F 0116 233 0232
E info@home-start.org.uk

Home-Start UK, a company limited by guarantee, company no. 5382 1UE. A charity registered in England and Wales, registered no. 1108837.

Printing Responsibly™ by Polar Print Group Limited on 50.mm post recycled paper using vegetable-oil based inks and low-alcohol print technology.

...a guide to **volunteering** for Home-Start

www.home-start.org.uk
Freephone: 0800 068 63 68

Volunteer for Home-Start and make a difference to a family in your community

...your questions answered

What is Home-Start?
Home-Start is a national charity with schemes in hundreds of local communities. We recruit and train volunteers to help families with young children. Our volunteers, who know about being a parent, support other parents by visiting them in their own homes for a couple of hours each week. We also run special family groups and hold social events for families.

What kind of families would I be helping?
All kinds of families can find it hard to cope for all sorts of reasons, maybe because of the illness or disability of a child or because of post-natal illness, bereavement or loneliness. At Home-Start we support any parent with young children who asks for our help and our supported families, like our volunteers, come from all walks of life.

Can my support and friendship really make a difference?
All parents know that those early years are vital in a child's life and at Home-Start we believe parents have the key role in creating a secure childhood for their children. It's just that sometimes they need a bit of help... **your** help.

As a volunteer what would I actually do?
Usually you visit a family in their own home once a week for a couple of hours. How you help is really down to the family itself. Some might need someone to talk to... others may need more practical support with meal planning and cooking, reading to the children, going to the local park, or finding out about local services.

Do I need any qualifications to be a volunteer?
The only real 'qualification' is experience of bringing up children. Friendliness and a caring attitude are essential as well as an understanding of the pressures of parenting. We value people who don't judge others; people who will respect the fact that they have been invited into a family's home; people who will treat a mother or father as an equal.

Do volunteers get any training?
Yes, we give high priority to the recruitment, induction, training and support of all our volunteers. You will be supported during your training and throughout your contact with families. Home-Start's highly rated Preparation Course is also accredited by the Open College Network. If your scheme offers this accreditation you will be able to gain credits through formal recognition of your Home-Start training.

What would I get out of volunteering for Home-Start?
Knowing that you have helped; a boost to your self-esteem and confidence; even a foot on the ladder towards a job. See what Philippa says in her story.....

Can I help without visiting families?
Yes. Schemes also need volunteers to help run family groups and social activities and to help raise funds. They also need volunteer trustees to help manage their work.

Philippa, a mother of three and a Home-Start volunteer...

Home-Start appealed to me because it was a charity devoted to the family. I felt I had a great deal of experience in this and therefore something to offer.

When I met my first family I immediately warmed to them. Although I was asked to give practical help, it soon became apparent that the mother needed emotional support as well. It took some months for her to talk about this, and it really felt like a breakthrough.

The most obvious reward is the sense of helping people. Being a volunteer can occasionally be emotionally draining, but there are also poignant moments; for example when a child in your Home-Start family tells you he loves you, or the mother says she doesn't know how she would manage without you, it feels wonderful.

As a Home-Start volunteer I never feel isolated. I am part of a team and know that if I encounter any difficulties I can contact my Home-Start organiser at any time for support. I have found being a volunteer for Home-Start an extremely positive experience.

> *when a child tells you he loves you it feels wonderful*

Source: Home-Start UK

p 15) have developed a three-perspective model for understanding volunteering: as unpaid work or service, as serious leisure or as activism.

Of relevance to this chapter is a thread in volunteering research (linked to but distinct from motivation) that coheres around critical responses to expectations – explicit or implicit – in policy that volunteering can be understood as a way to accrue individual benefits through formal structures (Arai and Pedlar, 2003; Devine and Roberts, 2003). From this perspective, studies have critically examined the extent to which volunteering has become like employment and highlighted some of the costs as well as advantages associated with its formalisation (Russell and Scott, 1997; Davis Smith and Gay, 2005; Milligan and Fyfe, 2005). All this has been seen as countering 'stakeholder ambiguity', a characteristic of the VCS that refers to a lack of a clear-cut differentiation between the various roles of employer, employee, provider, recipient, volunteer and others (Billis and Glennerster, 1998).

In this chapter, we use a framework for organising our volunteering life histories developed by Omoto and Snyder (2002). They proposed three stages of volunteering: *antecedents*, *experience* and *consequences* – each of which operates at individual, organisation and community levels (for a fuller account, see Chapter One). As we are concerned with explanations, dynamics and processes rather than counting phenomena, we also draw on cultural theory – often called Grid and Group – as a heuristic device for explaining and categorising the multiple positions that people take up with regard to voluntary work (for a fuller account, see Hardill et al, 2007; Figure 3.2). Cultural theory aims to understand the ways in which different people and social groups respond to threats and opportunities. It arose out of the work of Douglas (1992), who proposed that social structures generate attitudes towards the world. Social structures, Douglas argued, differ along two principal axes: Grid and Group. Grid refers to the degree to which individuals' choices are circumscribed by their position in society. Group refers to the degree of solidarity among members of the society.

Grid and Group has been widely adapted in analyses of responses to public policy, such as public sector management reform (Hood, 1998; 6 et al, 2002) and local economic development (Jayne, 2003). It is an approach sensitive to the local specificities and preoccupations that are likely to explain stances towards volunteering in organisations providing caring services in a community. Such an approach illuminates the ways in which volunteering can be regarded as a situated practice. In this way, we can offer a more nuanced and useful account of variations than the lists of motivations that characterise much literature in this field.

We also draw on TSOL (Glucksmann, 1995, 2000), which was described in Chapter One. TSOL cuts across binaries, highlighting 'fuzzy edges', situating paid and unpaid work along a continuum of work that can take place in public, institutional or familial settings and can be either paid or unpaid in any of them. In recognising the neglected dimension of unpaid activity in the public sphere, TSOL can encompass the work identities and the practical realities of people whose lives include volunteering and who may or may not also perform work within market-like exchange relations. Such a framework facilitates an examination of the interconnections between paid and unpaid work. Using these heuristic devices, we aim to offer a more holistic perspective, a more textured and complex picture of people's 'work' and caring practices, choices and constraints (for a fuller discussion, see Hardill et al, 2007).

Pathways to volunteering: a case study of Brightville

The community of Brightville, which we introduced in Chapter One, is located in the East Midlands region of England. It developed in the 19th century and had a diverse industrial base, spanning coal mining and textiles (for a fuller account, see Chapter Six). It coalesced with a nearby industrial town, Irontown, but to this day, Brightville's residents retain a strong sense of identity, separate to Irontown. Brightville is composed of two types of 'poor' area: one consists of largely working-class, 19th-century terraced housing and the other is a peripheral post-war social housing estate. Both have been a poverty cluster since their inception (Lupton, 2003). Brightville is economically deprived and is the kind of place that typically tends to have relatively low levels of volunteering (Williams, C.C., 2005).

We undertook research with four volunteer-using organisations with a presence in Brightville. They were chosen to capture some of the diversity of volunteer activity. All four, however, are engaged in welfare activities to support young families and older adults in the community. All employ paid workers and are heavily reliant on volunteers for service delivery. They are: a local community centre (Community Centre), a national government project (Government Project), a family support charity (Family Charity) and a community project (Community Project). All four attract volunteers from within the boundaries of Brightville, as well as from neighbouring Irontown. (The Government Project has a remit to work within defined geographical boundaries and directs enquiries from beyond them to other organisations.) Table 3.1 summarises key characteristics of each organisation.

Table 3.1: Summary of the study organisations

Name	Client group	Number of volunteers	Goals
Local community centre (Community Centre) *Established by former Brightville resident*	All residents	A pool of 3–4	Raise skills and employability in the community
National government project (Government Project) *Established by government*	Families with a child under 5	27	Parenting support and education, and training for employability
Family support charity (Family Charity) *Established by health professionals*	Families with a child under 5	63	Support families under stress
Community project (Community Project) *Established by Brightville residents*	All residents	103	Provide services to support the community

We used a combination of techniques as data-gathering tools: repeated, systematic observation; collection of documentary evidence; interviews with key informants (officers in local economic development and social inclusion, managers and workers in organisations using volunteers); focus groups; and 'life history' interviews with a selection of volunteers. This combination of data gathering was intended to provide a careful and authentic description of ordinary conscious experience and to explore the meanings and explanations that individuals attribute to their experiences. In this chapter, we draw mainly, but not exclusively, on the interviews with volunteers. We refer briefly to one of the focus groups and to key informant interviews. We use simple counting to help the reader to get a sense of the material as a whole but there is no claim that numbers are generalisable in a statistical sense to a wider population. The study was concerned with explanations, dynamics and processes rather than counting phenomena.

The interviewees from the four organisations consisted of 19 volunteers (15 women, four men) and eight paid workers (five women, three men). Five of the paid workers were also volunteers at the time of the interview, making a total of 24 volunteer interviewees. Three paid workers who we interviewed were no longer volunteers but had originally come to the site in that role. The volunteers participated in management and trustee roles as well as delivering services to the public. Three quarters of the interviewees were women. The interviews followed a 'life history' design, which we adopted because of its capacity to capture the overlap between the individual and social and institutional structures (Dex, 1991). In the interviews, we explored their personal histories of volunteering and any other unpaid work they undertake (caring for household members and relatives, informal volunteering and so on). Interviews were recorded and transcribed in full and analysed by theme, paying careful attention to language used and emphasis given.

The selection of volunteers and former volunteers for interviews was guided by key informants (who were in some cases the gatekeepers who facilitated access). Our intention was to include a range of characteristics present in the sites (age, gender, employment status, volunteer role, caring responsibility, disability and time commitment to volunteering). The length of the volunteering experience varied from one who was just completing the volunteer training course to others who had been volunteering for over a decade. Individuals' average weekly time commitment to volunteering ranged from two hours to around 15. Some individuals volunteered for other organisations. Just seven of the 19 volunteers were in waged work. Of the other 12, only two expected to engage in the labour market in the future (one of whom was in training and the other was in receipt of Jobseeker's Allowance). Others were retired (four), in receipt of Incapacity Benefit (three), partnered mothers who expressed no interest in paid work (two) and a full-time carer for a severely disabled son (one). Pseudonyms are used to protect the identity of individuals, voluntary organisations and the community.

In the following sections of this chapter, we draw on the interview data to discuss volunteers' reflections and reasoning about volunteering, care and employment in their lives. We consider the meanings that people attached to volunteering, explore how they create and maintain space (emotional, social and temporal) for voluntary work and comment on tensions between the paid/unpaid work binary. As we mentioned earlier, we have adapted a framework developed by Omoto and Snyder (2002) for organising the interview material; they proposed three stages of volunteering: *antecedents*, *experience* and *consequences* – each of which operates at individual, organisation and community levels. At the level of the individual, we also draw on cultural theory and TSOL.

The four fieldwork sites employ paid workers but are heavily reliant on volunteers giving time, on a weekly basis, to deliver services to the community. Prior to volunteering, the volunteers are required to complete an application form, undertake a training course, meet regularly with other volunteers and occasionally attend further training (see Figure 3.1). The four organisations also engage with the community through organising events, such as Fun Days in the summer, Christmas parties and fundraising coffee mornings.

Meanings of volunteering: personal histories

Interviewees talked to us about their experiences of volunteering, how they came to participate in it and how it fitted into their daily working and personal lives.

As noted above, historical accounts of volunteering in the UK identify two main impulses – mutual aid and philanthropy. Mutual aid is characterised by individuals with a shared experience or situation working together to bring about change. Philanthropy is associated with altruism, usually discussed from the perspective of 'rational utilitarianism', and can be explained in terms of either 'pure selflessness' or pragmatic self-interest; an alternative is 'identification with the needs of others' (Schervish and Havens, 2002, p 49). These historical stances towards volunteering resonate strongly with the Brightville volunteers' accounts of their attitudes and personal histories. We therefore use the terms 'mutual aid'/'giving to each other' and 'philanthropy'/'giving alms' as shorthand labels to denote the main emphasis of some of the volunteers' narratives.

Prima facie, volunteering for the Family Charity could help individualistic career aspirations because it involves training, an element of selection, regular commitment and a 'professional' approach. Yet, interviewees in this study only rarely explained their volunteering in terms of personal skills development, reflecting the language of current government websites and reports. We refer to the minority who did so with the label 'getting on'. Another factor in people's accounts of their volunteering was reacting to milestone life events (retirement or change in family circumstance, for example). This is referred to elsewhere in discussions of volunteer motivation as 'social adjustment' (Knapp et al, 1995). We describe it here as 'getting by' to distinguish it from the more instrumental stance towards personal skills development (for a fuller account, see Hardill et al, 2007).

We now draw on cultural theory – often called Grid and Group – as a framework for presenting empirical case material from the narratives of the Brightville volunteers (Figure 3.2). Table 3.2 summarises, according to the typology presented in Figure 3.2, the antecedents to volunteering for the 24 (of the 27) interviewees who currently volunteer. Eleven interviewees aged 20+ (nine women and two men), 10 of whom live in Brightville, talked about their volunteering as a response to a problem

Figure 3.2: Typology of explanations for volunteering

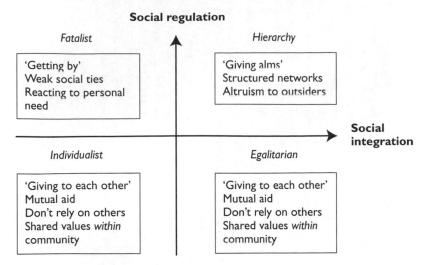

Social regulation

Fatalist

'Getting by'
Weak social ties
Reacting to personal
need

Hierarchy

'Giving alms'
Structured networks
Altruism to outsiders

**Social
integration**

Individualist

'Giving to each other'
Mutual aid
Don't rely on others
Shared values *within*
community

Egalitarian

'Giving to each other'
Mutual aid
Don't rely on others
Shared values *within*
community

Source: Hardill and Baines (2009)

or experience shared with their 'clients'. They are the group referred to as 'mutual aid'/'giving to each other'.

Martin (Table 3.2) cannot take up paid work because of mental health problems. He values volunteering because it takes him out of the house. He has a history of voluntary work, helping older Brightville residents who are housebound, with whom he has great empathy. Every week, he shops for them and helps them informally too. He also does occasional extra work for the Community Project, such as distributing leaflets. Through volunteering, he has more self-esteem and is now improving his basic literacy and numeracy skills: "So I may be on Incapacity Benefit doing nothing and not working but I am doing things for the community and helping myself in the process."

Family Charity volunteer Claire explained that she became a Family Charity volunteer to 'put something back' because she had been supported by a Family Charity volunteer herself when she had suffered from severe post-natal depression. In trying to generalise her own experience to the contribution made by the Family Charity, she commented "I think it's really to help the community help themselves."

The 'philanthropy'/'giving alms' group of volunteers comprised six women (aged 40+), living outside Brightville, who were drawn to help in the community via the structured volunteering opportunities offered by the Community Project and the Family Charity. They had identified an unmet need and they wanted to make a difference. Some explained that they feel 'fortunate' and as a result responded to advertisements

Table 3.2: Case studies of volunteering

Type/pseudonym	Brightville organisation/s	Household structure/ residence	Age	Employment status	Other unpaid activity	Explanation for volunteering
Giving alms Stella	Community project	Lives alone Irontown	60+	Retired after 32 years with Health Service	Active grandparent; church worker	"I feel that I'm fortunate and perhaps I should be doing something to help other people who are less fortunate."
Giving to each other Martin	Community project	Lives with mother Brightville	Late 20s	Incapacity Benefit	History of voluntary work, doing some skills updating	"I may be on Incapacity Benefit doing nothing ... but I am doing things for the community and helping myself in the process."
Getting on Grant	Family charity	Partner and young children Irontown	50-60	Part-time employment in a DIY shop	Shares homecare; informal volunteer to neighbours	Volunteers to improve his position in labour market. "I thought it could be a foot in the door for social work."
Getting by Lily	Community project	Lives alone Brightville	60+	Retired after 45 years with one retailer	Informal volunteer to neighbours; close to extended family	"I retired in 2003. I've always been used to being active. I was talking to [paid worker] and saying I sometimes get a bit fed up. She said, 'oh come and help us' – which I did."

or appeals for volunteers. One of the Family Charity volunteers, for example, said "I've got loads of friends – how isolated you must be to not be part of the community." They have strong social networks and some are involved in formal church activities. Most have had a history of paid work, especially in hierarchical organisations (such as the National Health Service).

Miranda has worked with several families in Brightville and claims that she is well known and liked in the area. "They call me the posh tart", she says, "but they still like me." The individuals in this group externalise the needs of the recipient, tend to stress their own relative good fortune and typically entered volunteering in response to an appeal or advertisement. Family Charity volunteers Donna and Sue both explained how they reacted to Family Charity publicity, which made them reflect on their experiences as mothers supported by strong family and friendship networks. In Sue's words, "I hate to think what it would be like to not have that, not to have somebody to ask [for help]."

Stella (Table 3.2) has helped at the Community Project for the past year. After her retirement, she thought she "really ought to do something" but was unsure what. She sees herself as – through the Community Project – helping people less fortunate than herself by working in Brightville: "I see it as they [Community Project] are trying to help people in this community, which I suppose could be described as a bit of a deprived community and I try to help them through [the Community Project]."

For four volunteers aged 40+ (two men and two women), volunteering is to help them 'get by' and is more ad hoc than for the three other groups of volunteers. They explained that they entered volunteering as a response to a milestone life event and that it fills something missing or an emotional gap in life. This is referred to elsewhere in discussions of volunteer motivation as 'social adjustment' (Knapp et al, 1995). Irontown resident Sarah explained what volunteering for the Family Charity means to her after her recent divorce and her daughter's growing independence: "The fact that there's another family that needs you is perhaps filling an emotional gap for me. I think sometimes I am actually just filling an emotional gap [with the volunteering]. Cynical me!"

While some like Sarah responded to a press campaign, Lily (Table 3.2) was prompted to volunteer when asked. Lily undertakes strongly gendered voluntary work, helping at a luncheon club run by the Community Project; which she is old enough to attend herself as a service user. Retirement and preparation for retirement may prompt the development of new sets of social contacts, drawing on attachments based in religious, voluntary, community and leisure associations, as is vividly illustrated by Lily's personal story. Lily is a neighbour of Jean, who runs the luncheon club and who recruited her. She is a retired single woman who has lived all her life in Brightville and worked for 45 years for one employer in Irontown. She had mixed feelings about leaving work and talked about retirement in terms of loss of personal identity (Barnes and Parry, 2004). She explained that she has found a new sense of importance and value by helping at the Community Project.

A fourth group, composed of three volunteers aged 30+ (two women and one man), volunteer for the Family Charity and the Community Project to 'get on' as a way of developing skills and experience of value in the labour market. Heather lives in Brightville and has gained confidence through preparing to volunteer and being a volunteer for the Community Project (training courses). She feels she has come to respect older people too. After volunteering for one year, she had sufficient confidence to begin an access course for nursing; thereby fulfilling an ambition she has held since childhood. Grant (Table 3.2) lives in Irontown and holds a part-time job, which he undertakes at the weekend, and was completing his volunteers course for the Family Charity at the time of the interview. He searched out volunteering opportunities in Brightville in the hope that volunteering would enable him to improve his chances of becoming a social worker. Grant was introduced to the Family Charity through a friend of his wife. "It was a way of getting inside the community to help people without having to spend years at college." But his hope for a new career in social care has been frustrated by the need for training: "I can't put that on to my family." At the same time, he expressed strong feelings that he has something to offer families that need help: "You are able to give something to those that maybe haven't got the support that I've got, or I've had. I mean when I went through my divorce I had nobody ... I've been there and it's horrible."

The work of the volunteers

In this subsection, we talk about the experience of volunteering and how it relates to what the interviewees understand as 'work'. Volunteering for participants in the Brightville organisations is *work-like* in a number of contrasting and overlapping ways. Volunteering is described as 'work' and compared to other forms of work; it is possible to move between volunteering and paid work (in both directions); volunteering can take the place of a job in terms of meaning and identity; organisations need 'reliable' unpaid inputs and in order to be reliable, volunteers need to 'juggle' the time they give alongside other demands on their time.

Volunteers have been recruited as paid workers. The Community Project has participated in the New Deal (Box 3.1), and used volunteers in community work. Two paid workers (Darren and Clive) are former New Dealers. They were reliable and hard working as volunteers and were 'promised' paid jobs, "If we get funding, we can get you on full time" (Darren). Clive said, "Chas said to me, 'if you volunteer it might turn into a full-time job.'" So, he finished his New Deal placement, "signed on again … volunteered for nothing … doing it five days a week". Pippa is a former Government Project volunteer who is now employed full time as an administrator. "I wouldn't have applied for the Government Project job if I hadn't done the volunteering first, I wouldn't have thought I was worth it." The transition from volunteer to paid worker has not been easy for her, as some parents resent her having the job and some Government Project staff have found it difficult to accept her as a staff member. This suggests that the boundary between employment and volunteering can be difficult and contested.

The boundary between paid work and volunteering is blurred for some paid workers at the voluntary organisations. Three Community Project employees – Emily, Chas and Jean, all of whom live in Brightville – volunteer, formally and informally, to help those they have met through work. Chas and Jean are formal befrienders and are informally helping a client who is ill by exercising her dog. Chas also undertakes informal befriending, which he sees as being a good neighbour: "I used to go and visit elderly people … not officially. I just go and see if they are all right and if they need anything." There was movement between – and a blurring of – paid and unpaid work by one of the volunteers (Sandra) and the paid worker Jean. Jean is a team support worker at the Community Project and one of her main duties is running the luncheon club twice a week, which she loves doing. Some evenings she prepares food, especially desserts, at home. At some points in the year, such as Christmas, organising and executing the meal become a volunteer task. She explained that this Christmas voluntary task began at 8am on Christmas Day. Her paid job and volunteering, therefore, blur. Jean's unpaid volunteer efforts are 'rewarded' – like the other volunteers – by a volunteer certificate at the annual Community Project awards ceremony. When Jean is on holiday or off sick, Sandra takes over her roles of cooking and organising, for which she receives remuneration.

It was typical of volunteers to refer to their voluntary activity casually as 'work'. Some made the point strongly that it is like work in terms of the commitment they give to it and of its value to others. Family Charity volunteers in the focus group, for example, claimed that they were doing some of the same tasks as social care professionals (although they also made the point that the families they support trust them because they are not paid).

When Sally explained that her initial hopes of gaining advantage in the labour market were not fulfilled, she went on to speak of volunteering as an alternative to having a job. It supports her sense of self-worth while she is not in employment, "because otherwise I'd just be a single mum, living off the Social". Claire, a partnered mother of four, is not looking for a job because "my kids are still little and I need to be there at 3pm to look after them". Yet, she similarly articulates a negative image of a wholly domestic role from which she escapes through her volunteering: "It helps me not to sit on my bum and not do anything all day and I feel as though I'm needed – and not just by the kids!" This theme of volunteering as a source of personal identity was reiterated by Brightville volunteers for whom paid work was impossible (or perceived as such) due to age, disability, ill-health or caring responsibilities.

Jean spoke about being let down by luncheon club volunteers who failed to turn up when expected. Volunteers themselves identified 'being reliable' as a key volunteer skill. Family Charity volunteer Sarah said that one has to:

> 'Be prepared to give up your time and be committed to that. I think the commitment and the time and effort that the Family Charity give to training you, the least you can do is stay with them a reasonable time for them to reap their investment. So I think you've got to be prepared to give that commitment for an appropriate length of time.'

Some respondents described juggling caring and voluntary work on a day-to-day basis in ways that recall themes from work–life balance debates. If they have young children or other dependants, they have to organise childcare to create 'space' to volunteer. Sue works for wages part time and volunteers mid-week. Her mother looks after her toddler daughter while she visits her Family Charity family. Sue acknowledges that "it's worked quite well actually – I work part time, two days per week, so I try and have a couple of days free – my mum doesn't work Wednesday so I try and arrange it [volunteering] for then." Claire does

Family Charity volunteering when her children are at school. In the holidays or if the children are ill, her mother looks after them to enable her to continue her commitments to Family Charity. Although she tries always to keep her Family Charity commitments, her children come first: "I suppose, in a way, Family Charity revolves around my family."

Demands on the part of family can put severe pressure on time available to volunteer. Sandra explained that her daughter, her daughter's partner and their baby are about to come to live with her because he has lost his job and they can no longer afford to be an independent household. Her daughter is looking for a job and expects Sandra to care for the baby while she works:

> 'We've looked at it and it's the only option – it's not something I really want and it's not what they want but it's the only way round ... you can't turn your back, can you, on your own children ... if it comes to it I would have to do it [give up volunteering] to help my family but I don't want to.'

The capacity to volunteer – like the capacity to engage in the labour market – needs to be managed alongside work and caring within the household and across the generations.

Change and consequences

Relationships between waged work, care within the family and voluntary action in the case study volunteer sites were multifaceted. Volunteering was only occasionally described by volunteers as a potential route out of unemployment or into a new career. Two of the three who did hope for new opportunities in the labour market had already been disappointed at the time of the interview, although they persisted in volunteering. On the other hand, people described personal rewards that they had not sought or anticipated. Accreditation for training and experience can be a significant benefit from volunteer activity. Donna, for example, did not identify her career as a reason for becoming a Family Charity volunteer but she did report that she had gained both skills and credentials that were valued in her workplace (she is a youth worker). She expressed delight in having a 'portfolio' of certificates (see also Dean, 2003) – including those for volunteer activity:

> 'I often look through and see my Family Charity Certificate. When I'm applying for a job it reminds me [of] what I've

done. I think it's very valuable. [The interview panel for her present job was very interested in her Family Charity certificate.] I'd imagine whichever job you go for that it looks very good on your CV.'

Increased confidence was an important gain about which many interviewees (paid workers, key informants and volunteers themselves) were extremely vocal. This is how Sandra, for example, emphasised her growth in confidence: "I was sort of 'I hope they don't ask me questions' – you know? But now it doesn't bother me and I feel I can sit there and if we have any discussion I will say something. Whereas before I wouldn't say anything but now I'll say, 'I've had this experience' and 'I've done this.'"

Some key informants talked of the confidence people gain from volunteering as an important asset to enable transitions into the workplace or enhanced workplace skills. This was not the typical perception of Brightville volunteers. Sandra's livelihood consists of three part-time cleaning jobs. She expressed no interest in building upon her increased confidence to change her work situation. At one point in the interview, she suggested that others have criticised her for not being more work oriented and that she rejects such criticism: "Somebody once said, 'why don't you get a full-time job?', but me daughter's needed me support and everything so I haven't had a full-time job. But I'm quite happy the way I am. I don't bother anybody. I live my life."

Paid worker Jean talked proudly of how Lily had gained confidence when she started volunteering after she retired. She explained that Lily would not have called the bingo numbers out but now she loves to do this. Lily is very committed to the luncheon club; Jean perceives her as a reliable volunteer. Lily gives nine hours a week to the Community Project: "It's only two mornings a week." While Lily has gained confidence and a feeling of value, she talks about the voluntary work in very personal terms. She refers to members of the club, as "a second family".

Conclusion

Volunteering is often presented in political and academic discourses as a panacea for a wide range of social and political problems, including worklessness and lack of civic participation (Milligan and Fyfe, 2004, 2005). In terms of building personal confidence that enables people to feel at ease in public arenas, the Brightville study concurs with some of the most positive expectations invested in volunteering. Volunteers recounted how they gained a role, a sense of purpose and personal wellbeing through their volunteering.

In Brightville, the most visible voluntary organisations were those offering care and family support. The women volunteers juggled volunteering around family needs and demands and volunteering was an activity that was actually an alternative form of work, which contributed to both community cohesion and their extended families. Women outside paid work described their participation in volunteering as a form of engagement in public space that contrasted with an alternative they dismissed as "just sitting at home" and this work was often a visible expression of care for non-household members. Volunteer work is work of a nature that is one ingredient of a wider scenario of the integration of work and 'home', but with community cohesion as well. It is possible that new confidence gained from volunteering could support more active engagement in forms of civic participation although our data cannot demonstrate this directly. We can show, however, that in the study sites, volunteering constitutes an important aspect of individual and community life, especially for women.

Individual narratives of volunteer engagement revealed that the capacity to give time to volunteering often depends on active support from within the household and wider family. Conversely, demands of family could be prioritised in ways that constrained (or were likely to constrain) volunteer activity. Volunteering – in common with labour market participation – is negotiated within the household and family and mediated through beliefs about family responsibilities and appropriate behaviours for men and women and for young and old (Daly, 2002; Williams, 2002). We found numerous examples of the continued strength and importance of family networks within the community, similar to the findings in other relatively deprived place-based communities (Mumford and Power, 2003).

There was little evidence in the volunteer sites discussed above of raised aspirations towards the labour market or of enskilling for employment, despite the fact that working-age volunteers 'beyond' the labour market indicated that they had been enskilled, such as through confidence raising and the acquisition of certificates (Dean, 2003). Perhaps in different communities, with different social and spatial horizons and social networks, the aspiration to paid work would be fostered through volunteering and so, in other communities, a stronger link could well exist between volunteering and the ethic of work. Mutual aid and philanthropy are terms used in analyses of the history of volunteering and they helped us to make sense of volunteers' own accounts – although volunteers themselves did not use these words. For some people in Brightville, who were excluded from the labour market, volunteering afforded an identity that was often articulated in terms of work. They typically described their volunteering as 'work' and compared it to the tasks performed for wages by others. These findings are consistent with the idea that sites of volunteering can be construed as 'spaces of hope' that embrace logics of work outside market-orientated exchange (Williams, 2002). On a more pessimistic reading of these data, it is possible to argue that volunteering can be seen as an individualised adaptation to labour market failure in a community beset by economic decline.

Notes

[1] Local Area Agreements (LAAs) were established by New Labour as three-year action plans for achieving better outcomes. They were developed by councils with their partners in Local Strategic Partnerships (LSPs). LAAs were the main way for central government and local services to work together. They also underpinned the National Performance Framework and its priorities, through which central government measured progress. They were abolished by the coalition government.

[2] Davis Smith makes no distinction between self-help and mutual aid.

FOUR

A professional paradox? 'Managing' volunteers in voluntary and community sector organisations

People with volunteer management responsibilities, who are often volunteers themselves, have a challenging job. They need to inspire people to give their time freely, maintain their motivation, ensure that they match skilled people with relevant roles, and ensure that paid staff and volunteers are able to work together. (Nick Hurd, Minister for Civil Society, Brewis et al, 2010, p 4)

Introduction

In this chapter, we focus on those people in the VCS who work for wages managing volunteers. This has become an increasingly important management issue, tied in with the professionalisation of the volunteering experience and of the sector in general (Gay, 2000a; Howlett, 2010). The sector has expanded in size and scope and while it is doing more, the number of volunteers has been static, but the number of paid staff has increased.

Growing numbers of paid staff are dealing with the management of volunteers (see Figure 4.1). In one study, Gay (2000b) explored where there was a distinct body of knowledge that marked VMs from other personnel and she identified a diverse range of skills (such as coordinating volunteers, acting in a leadership role, representing the organisation, delivering services, developing volunteers, representing the organisation and campaigning). Rochester et al (2010, p 151; see also Zimmeck, 2001) identify two models of the way VCSOs manage their volunteers. In the workplace model, volunteering in such organisations resembles paid work, as the organisation adopts more formal styles of volunteering. Organisations with a public service delivery role may find that eligibility for funding requires some demonstrable way of indicating how volunteers will contribute to

Figure 4.1: Job advertisements

Source: The Guardian, 16 January 2008

the work of the organisation or that services are delivered effectively and efficiently (Rochester and Thomas, 2006; see Chapter Five). In contrast to this bureaucratic organisational form is the collectivist-democratic organisation (Rochester et al, 2010, p 153), which is more egalitarian and there is minimal application of rules and procedures with regard to volunteering (see also Zimmeck, 2001, p 19). It is in the more bureaucratic organisations that the management of volunteers is undertaken by paid staff. In an empirical study of VMs in Australia, Onyx and Maclean (1996) found that few organisations, except very large ones, employed clearly designated managers, with volunteering very structured. In most small- and medium-sizedVCSOs, the functions of service provision and management tended to overlap, with one person designated as coordinator.

Until recently, people who worked for wages for VCSOs were seen as having no career aspirations. It was assumed either that they were there by default, unable to attain well-paid career positions elsewhere or that they were motivated by the ideal of selfless service rather than personal achievement (Harrow and Mole, 2005). The VCS is one sector of the economy often overlooked in the literature on careers (see Harrow and Mole, 2005), which has tended to focus on building careers in the public or private sector (Savage, 1988).

In the remaining part of this chapter, we focus on VMs and highlight their 'careers' in the VCS. As VMs work at the interface between volunteers and VCS organisations, we draw on theoretical work at two spatial scales: the individual and the organisation – using the TSOL framework (see Chapter One), developed by Glucksmann, for exploring the relational and interconnected nature of different forms of work (Glucksmann, 1995, 2000, 2009). This theoretical lens has been applied to voluntary work by Taylor (2004) and Williams (2011).

Managing volunteers: the issues

Until recently, the policy thrust in the UK has been to increase the number of volunteers, with little emphasis on improving the capacity of organisations to better involve and manage both existing and new volunteers. Under New Labour (1997-2010), national indicators for the VCS targeted increasing the number of volunteers rather than the nature of the volunteer experience. But volunteers themselves have consistently registered dissatisfaction with the volunteer experience. In 1997, at the beginning of the New Labour era, for example, the UK National Survey of Volunteering recorded that 71% of volunteers said that 'things could be much better organised' (Davis Smith, 1998). Such views were not confined to the UK, as a national survey in the US in 2004 revealed significant gaps and challenges in organisational volunteer management capacity, as well as a need to increase 'the ability of nonprofits and congregations to mobilize, manage and maximise their volunteer resources on behalf of America's communities' (Campbell, 2004).

Returning to the UK, a survey of 547 English VCSOs conducted in 1998 (cited in Gay, 2000a) recorded that volunteer management was becoming increasingly formalised, with four out of five of the surveyed volunteer-involving organisations having a designated volunteer coordinator/manager or equivalent post. Eighty-five per cent had a written volunteer policy and most organisations had systems to support (94%), supervise (90%) and discipline (74%) volunteers. Yet, despite a more professional approach being taken towards managing volunteers, many organisations had a narrow volunteer base. A further study undertaken in 2007 (Clark, 2007) reported that across the VCS, more than two fifths (43%) of employers had paid staff undertaking a volunteer management function.

In 2008, one of the key messages from the cross-government review by Baroness Neuberger (the Labour Government's volunteering champion) on volunteering in England was that effective volunteering requires well-managed volunteers (Commission on the Future of Volunteering, 2008): '[a]s in paid employment, this extends to everything from recruitment and retention to succession planning, team working, individual development, resources and so on' (2008, p 22). Recommendation 5.4 focused on the training and support needs of VMs (2008, p 31).

Volunteer management is not a new function. Indeed, activities such as matching volunteers with opportunities and volunteer support and training, have been recorded in the VCS since before World War One (Davis Smith, 1996; Gay, 2000a; Rochester et al, 2010).[1] Today, however, VMs are growing in significance and visibility as organisations attempt to formalise volunteering and follow good practice (Machin and Ellis Paine, 2008). Their role is to 'enable' volunteering and increase the diversity and quality of volunteering opportunities. They are individuals variously known as volunteer managers, volunteers coordinator and volunteers organisers. (For the sake of brevity we adopt the term 'volunteer manager' (VM), which is now in common usage.)

The requisite skills and knowledge have been defined by National Occupational Standards (NOS) and a Volunteer Management programme has been established under the management of Capacitybuilders (Howlett, 2010). This involves enhanced support from volunteering infrastructure organisations, training people who manage volunteers. In their recent survey, Brewis et al (2010, p 28) noted that 40% of their respondents were aware of the NOS, but the proportion of respondents was 30% in small organisations (with incomes below £10,000). Howlett (2010) also noted that the Investing in Volunteering (IiV) programme is a quality mark that recognises that organisations have the systems and procedures in place to manage volunteers effectively. IiV is aimed at the organisation rather than the individual.

VMs work at the interface between volunteers, VCSOs and policies that promote the expansion and formalisation of unpaid work. The field of volunteer management is therefore broad. A VM may directly manage or coordinate volunteers themselves. They may be paid to manage volunteers or do this in a voluntary capacity. They may lead or administer a volunteering programme. Equally, they may be involved in volunteer management in the private, public or voluntary and community sector. The characteristics of VMs are indicative of an occupation that sits awkwardly between notions of profession, career, work and volunteering. Little is known about their careers, occupational challenges and claims to professional status.

Growth in the paid workforce

Unlike in the public and private sectors, in recent years the number of paid workers in the VCS has increased to 668,000 (an increase of 105,000 since 2000), while the number of volunteers has remained largely static (Clark et al, 2010). The growth in the number of paid jobs is largely the result of new business opportunities associated with state partnering with the VCS. Therefore, in addition to achieving goals related to their underlying values and mission (often related to relieving hardship), VCSOs have taken on new roles, which are both welcomed and contested, including acting as *labour market intermediaries*, as *agents for public service delivery* and as *social partners* working to achieve civil renewal and community regeneration (see Chapters One and Five). As organisations have taken on these new roles, they have been accompanied by organisational changes, including the need to exercise more managerial control over paid staff and volunteers involved in public service delivery. Organisational change has been accompanied by the VCS becoming a sector of the economy where the concept of career for some paid staff, such as those in posts that tend to place particular demands on the individual and emphasise commitment (Erikson and Goldthorpe, 1992, p 42), may be sustained (Harrow and Mole, 2005). In this section, we begin by using published survey data of VMs and published statistics to examine the broader paid workforce.

Official statistics on VMs are not available, as it is not an occupation recognised in the Standard Occupation Classification (SOC). Onyx and Maclean (1996), in their study in Australia, found that the nature of the work of most VMs was varied and multidimensional and so did not easily fit within standard occupational descriptions. The UK Labour Force Survey (LFS) (see Box 4.1) does provide statistics for individuals

Box 4.1: The Labour Force Survey

The Labour Force Survey (LFS) is a quarterly sample survey of households living at private addresses in Great Britain. Its purpose is to provide information on the UK labour market that can then be used to develop, manage, evaluate and report on labour market policies. The questionnaire design, sample selection, and interviewing are carried out by the Social and Vital Statistics Division of the Office for National Statistics (ONS) on behalf of the Statistical Outputs Group of the ONS.

Source: ONS (2010a)

reported as working for a charity, voluntary organisation or trust, but it is difficult to identify 'volunteer managers' per se.

Using data from quarter 4, 2008 LFS (Table 4.1), we examined the records of those in the sample who indicated that they worked for a charity, voluntary organisation or trust and held managerial or professional posts – so not all will be VMs (see Box 4.2). Of those

Table 4.1: The VCS workforce

Major occupation groups (2000 SOC)	n
1 Managers and senior officials	245
2 Professional occupations	173
3 Associate professional and technical	286
4 Administrative and secretarial	187
5 Skilled trades occupations	21
6 Personal service occupations	247
7 Sales and customer service occupations	26
8 Process plant and machine operatives	18
9 Elementary occupations	68
Total	1,271

Source: Quarter 4, 2008 LFS

Box 4.2: Standard Occupation Classification 1-3

The SOC is a common classification of occupational information for the UK. Jobs are classified in terms of their skill level and skill content. The SOC is used for career information for labour market entrants, job matching by employment agencies and the development of government labour market policies. SOC 2010 is the latest update.

Major group 1: managers, directors and senior officials

A significant amount of knowledge and experience of the production processes and service requirements associated with the efficient functioning of organisations and businesses.

Major group 2: professional occupations

A degree or equivalent qualification, with some occupations requiring postgraduate qualifications and/or a formal period of experience-related training.

Major group 3: associate professional and technical occupations

An associated high-level vocational qualification, often involving a substantial period of full-time training or further study. Some additional task-related training is usually provided through a formal period of induction.

Source: ONS (2010b)

employed in managerial and professional occupations in the VCS, 66.1% were female in 2008, compared with 71.0% overall in the VCS. In the 2008 LFS sample, 6.9% of VCS managers, 5.2% of professionals and 8.4% of those employed in associate professional and technical occupations held two jobs. Of those working for a VCSO, 75.7% of men reported being married/cohabiting, compared with 64.1% of women the UK average is 79.0% among all men in managerial and professional occupations and 71.7% among women. Of those employed in managerial or professional occupations (SOC groups 1–3), the average age of VCS workers was 44.6 years, compared with an average age of all workers of 42.7 years.

Basic usual hours among managerial and professional workers in the VCS were 32.4 per week (total UK 36.8 hours per week), with unpaid overtime of 6.4 hours per week (total UK 7.4 hours per week). Among managerial and professional employees in the VCS, 70.7% reported having degree-level qualifications or equivalent. In addition to university degree qualifications, some managers in the VCS hold professional qualifications and their careers may have been pursued in other sectors of the economy, both private and public. These findings are broadly in line with the VCS in the US and Australia (Mirvis, 1992; Onyx and Maclean, 1996). Women comprised between 70% and 80% of the VCS workforce in Australia and 60% of all workers were employed on a casual or part-time basis (Industry Commission, 1994).

With regard to salaries, we use data available for chief executives. While the most recent data indicate a very slight rise in the median salary for a chief executive, from £57,264 to £57,974, nearly 70% are experiencing a pay cut or a pay freeze (36% and 34% respectively) (ACEVO, 2010). The recession and subsequent spending cuts have brought increased workload and stress levels. According to ACEVO (see Box 4.3), one third are recruited from the private sector, but the majority come from the public sector (ACEVO, 2010).

Box 4.3: ACEVO

The Association of Chief Executives of Voluntary Organisations (ACEVO) is a membership organisation for chief executives, chairs, trustees or senior managers in the VCS.

It has over 2,000 members nationwide and offers a variety of services to its members, including information and advice, professional publications, a helpline and discounted access to events.

Source: www.acevo.org.uk/about+ACEVO

Two substantial surveys of VMs have been undertaken by the IVR in England – one in 2008 and one in 2010 (Machin and Ellis Paine, 2008; Brewis et al, 2010). The most recent study was commissioned by Skills Third Sector to update the evidence base from Machin and Ellis Paine (2008) and involved a quantitative survey of over 1,000 people who manage volunteers. The survey data from these two studies reveal that within organisations in the VCS, volunteer management and coordination tasks are often only part of an individual's job remit. Brewis et al's (2010) study found that VMs had mixed levels of experience and training (one third had been managing volunteers for over 10 years) and only half had any relevant formal training. The main source of support and advice for VMs was through managers and other colleagues. Many also relied on local and national volunteering infrastructure organisations for advice and support, including local Volunteer Centres and national networks. In the following section, we explore the concept of 'career' and examine to what extent the VCS has become a sector of the economy where a career may be sustained drawing on the work of Harrow and Mole (2005).

Careers in the voluntary and community sector

Introduction

Managers in the VCS have distinctive responsibilities when compared with managers in the public and private sectors (see Box 4.4). A further defining characteristic of being a (paid) manager in the VCS when compared to organisations in other sectors of the economy is that VCSOs are characterised by stakeholder ambiguity – where the roles of employer, manager, employee, volunteer and user overlap (Billis and Glennerster, 1998). A particular complexity of these overlapping roles has been identified with VCS governance structures, with an overlap in the roles of VCS governing bodies and paid staff (Brophy, 1994; Billis and Glennerster, 1998). VCSOs tend to have a board of management and trustees who are volunteers, with charitable objectives (Ridley Duff and Bull, 2011). Community organisations usually formed by a charitable objective, normally operate at a local level and are staffed predominately or completely by volunteers (McCabe et al, 2010).

Whereas in public and private sector bureaucracies there is a clear-cut differentiation between employer and employee, employee and non-employee, provider and recipient, chairperson and director, the VCS board or management committee and staff can overlap in many combinations. In Chapter Three, we used TSOL to highlight the

Box 4.4: Management roles in the VCS

Those in management roles in the VCS:

- manage a paid and unpaid workforce;
- the unpaid volunteer workforce is more 'managed' through selection, training, appraisal procedures;
- participate in management/governance structures that involve paid and unpaid managers and trustees;
- work in lean organisations;
- deliver a wider range of 'services' because of mainstreaming;
- have a more target-driven approach to service delivery because of statutory sector contracts demands;
- have new legal implications because of public service delivery, as they become a public authority;
- play roles on partnerships (such as health, regeneration and so on);
- have funding dilemmas, which demand increasingly entrepreneurial behaviours;
- often do unpaid work for their organisation (unpaid overtime or volunteer work) and may work unpaid for a second organisation (as a trustee/volunteer).

blurring of employee/volunteer roles, as we presented case studies of paid workers who also volunteered for their employing organisation (Baines and Hardill, 2008). Stakeholder ambiguity is often accompanied by deeper tensions between the demands of a bureaucratic paid staff command structure and requirements of the democratic membership association based on voluntary effort.

While over recent decades it has become more difficult to sustain a career in both the private and public sectors in the UK, it is still assumed that the majority of employees are motivated by the prospect of increased responsibility, status and financial rewards (Giddens, 1991; Beck, 1992; Sennett, 1998). Much of the theoretical and empirical focus by social scientists in the UK and elsewhere has been on the careers of managers and professionals in the public and private sector, highlighting bureaucratic and professional practice, with very little theoretical and empirical work on careers in the VCS. In the following subsection, we look at conceptual and empirical studies of careers in general and then we look at the VCS and careers.

What is a career?

Organisationally, careers depict structures, routes and processes through which employees gain promotion and move through an organisation

(Harrow and Mole, 2005). Individual work histories – the sequences of job experiences and career – are the most observable aspects of career and they are known as the objective or external career (Bailyn, 1989). The impact of individual work histories on the way people behave and experience their careers is seen as the subjective or internal career (Bailyn, 1989). Work histories have been used as the sense-making story an individual feels about their work history (Nicholson and West, 1989). A number of themes in research on careers can be identified, including commitment and careers, gender and careers, as well as the interplay of social and spatial mobility and careers. But first, we define career.

Traditionally, the term 'career' implied some long-term progression; a ladder or linear promotion within an occupation or through a series of occupations involving increasing levels of responsibility at each stage (Evetts, 2000). Career progression is closely linked with ideas of social mobility. Linear promotion (thereby gaining social mobility) can be achieved through some combination of factors such as length of service, experience, ability and aptitude and the acquisition of further vocational qualifications (Bailyn, 1993). Promotion ladders can be nationally standardised (as in teaching or nursing) or they can be firm or company specific. Qualifications and promotions are linked in that occupational qualifications bestow competence on practitioners, which is of great significance to the ideology of professionalism. Qualifications also form the prerequisites and justification for merit-based systems of promotion (Sullivan, 1995; Evetts, 2000).

Professional practice is said to differ from the bureaucratic in that professional expertise is derived from a formalised training based on science, as well as the creation of a mystique among an elite and the dependence and disabling of those who come to the professional in the capacity as client (Hardill, 2002). The profession controls knowledge; it creates specialisations, celebrating depth rather than breadth. Professionals offer detached 'understanding' and the portrayal of a professional concern, such as an appropriate bedside manner for a doctor or keeping emotion at a distance. In addition to the older learned professions (medicine, law and the clergy), the professions include engineering and management and an expanding number of 'emerging' professions – including VMs, which we focus on later in this chapter.

The 'typical' female career trajectory in the UK, regardless of sector, has been non-linear, complex and dynamic, characterised by access to fewer choices/options (spatial and temporal) and fewer material resources in the woman's life than in the man's (Epstein et al, 1999). High-status, well-paid jobs tend to be organised as full time and are, therefore, generally incompatible with wanting to prioritise both home and work.

Driver (1980) describes four career concepts – 'steady state', 'linear', 'spiral' and 'transitory' – as underlying a person's thinking about their career. A steady-state career choice is made once and involves a lifetime commitment to an occupation, with few if any job changes within that occupation. Steady-state careerists value expertise and security and are most likely to be found in a structured but flat organisation. Linear career activity continues throughout life as one moves up an occupational ladder, usually within the same or similar organisation. A linear career is desired by those who value prestige, management skills, high income, power and achievement. This concept is consistent with a large, hierarchical structure with emphasis on performance and rewards of promotion, perquisites and status. Spiral careers evolve through a series of different positions entailing changes in the nature of the work performed and the skills required (seven to 10 years' duration), but where each new choice builds and extends on the past. The spiral career best fits an open system with low structure, entailing a semi-autonomous self. An emphasis on creativity and multiskilling provides further challenge and opportunities for self-development as the major rewards. Transitory careers entail almost continuous change: occupational fields, organisations and jobs change over one- to four-year intervals, with variety the dominant force. The transitory career structure requires fluidity and flexibility. Formal rules are unnecessary.

A number of geographers and sociologists have added a spatial dimension to understanding careers by examining the relationship between career advancement (sometimes termed 'social mobility'), especially for male workers within the internal labour markets of large organisations, and geographic migration (sometimes termed 'spatial mobility') between different branches of such multi-site organisations (Savage, 1988; Green, 1997). This work has placed emphasis on the way in which largely male managers and professionals have built a career, achieving social mobility through spatial mobility, typically involving inter-regional moves, with their female partners as 'trailing spouses'. This work makes clear that different organisational and career structures have different implications for the frequency and patterns of spatial mobility. Savage (1988) captured some of these main differences in his characterisation of three alternative social mobility strategies:

- *organisational strategy*: in which the individual pursues their career by moving upwards through the structure of an individual (often large) organisation;

- *entrepreneurial strategy*: in which a self-employed individual aims to become a small, or possibly large, employer of labour;
- *occupational strategy*: in which an individual continually invests in skills-based (often, but not always, occupationally specific) assets – typically gaining experience with a range of different employers – in order to pursue their career within their profession.

Each strategy has a different relationship to spatial mobility. Entrepreneurial strategies usually involve spatial immobility, largely because starting a business normally involves drawing on localised resources (Savage, 1988). Organisational and occupational strategies are more complex, but with a relatively high incidence of (interregional but increasingly international) spatial mobility. Such careers are often built on the foundation of heavy investments in cultural capital obtained within the increasingly internationalised higher education system (Hardill, 2002).

But the idea of the 'career' itself, however, has been subject to reassessment. Indeed, some writers argue that the career – implying a sustained narrative over a lifetime – is a 'traditional concept' that makes little sense in the present-day world of work in the private and public sectors. Since the 1980s, economic restructuring has affected the world of paid work as economic downturns have helped pressure the private sector in the UK into making longer-term adaptations to the competitive pressures of economies increasingly organised on a global scale (Sennett, 1998). The public sector in the UK has also undergone substantial changes and, as a result, men and women aspiring to careers in both the private and public sectors are pursuing careers in a very different working environment from that prevailing previously (Beck, 1992). Writing in 1998 about the US, Sennett (1998, p 31) remarked that today a career is no 'longer a well made road', with uncertainty 'woven into the everyday practices of … capitalism'.

Economic restructuring, especially through the forces of flexibilisation and globalisation, has resulted in other career strategies – in addition to occupational and organisational – including *portfolio careers*, in which each person builds their own individual career, often involving a range of employers/occupations/experience (Ackers, 1998; Hardill, 2002). Or returning to Driver's (1980; 1988) conceptualisation of careers, the linear career has been replaced by a spiral career. Both portfolio and spiral careers highlight non-work, including spells of working for wages or as unpaid volunteers in the VCS or making 'career' decisions for non-economic reasons. Writing about the US, Brooks (2000, pp 108-9) identified that non-economic motives of self-expression also shape people's career decisions: 'work … is a vocation, a calling … employees start thinking like artists and activists'. Career decisions may involve moving to the VCS, where in the last decade paid job opportunities have increased. These posts are often fixed term, part time and may involve working above contracted hours to get the job done, like jobs of a similar status in other sectors of the economy. We now turn to examine careers in the VCS.

Careers in the VCS

Careers in the VCS have been the focus of study in the US since the 1980s (Mirvis and Hackett, 1983; Mirvis, 1992). Mirvis (1992) identified three distinctive aspects of VCSOs that were likely to have an impact on employment. First, VCSOs may have legal restrictions on the distribution of organisational earnings, which limit individual earning capacity. Second, most VCSOs are purported to be 'value expressive' (Jeavons, 1992), to epitomise the ideals of selfless service and to be oriented towards social change (Drucker, 1990). Third, the nature of the organisational environment differs between the three sectors of the economy. Whereas for-profit organisations are subject to direct market control and public sector organisations are subject to direct political and bureaucratic control, 'by contrast, the relationship between providers of funds to non-profits and recipients of service is often distal and difficult to calibrate' (Mirvis, 1992, p 25).

The combined effect of these three VCS distinguishing characteristics led Mirvis (1992) to hypothesise that they may impact on employment profiles, with VCSOs more likely to recruit and retain those employees whose values and preferred modes of working are conducive to the VCS work culture. In turn, the conditions of employment within the VCS may serve to shape the career concepts of its employees. Mirvis found confirming evidence of consistent differences in employee attitudes towards work among the three sectors of the economy by drawing on US data – a large national sample of working adults for 1977 (Mirvis and Hackett, 1983) and 1990 (Mirvis, 1992). The findings from the two surveys undertaken by Mirvis (1992) confirmed that VCS employees brought to their jobs greater commitment and non-monetary orientations, found more challenge, variety and autonomy in their jobs and had more positive social values.

A decade and a half ago, Onyx and Maclean (1996) undertook an in-depth study of paid workers in the VCS in New South Wales, Australia. Their study was set against a background of a decade-long trend of VCS involvement in public service delivery – a very similar situation to that facing the VCS in the UK. But they noted that while there had been a growth in VCS funding, this growth was vulnerable to political changes and had generally not been translated into recognised (linear) career paths. Almost four out of five of Onyx and Maclean's (1996) respondents were women, almost half possessed a degree or higher qualifications and over two thirds were employed full time. Their job positions were varied from senior management roles, but almost half were in some sort of volunteer coordinating role.

Onyx and Maclean found a distinctive pattern of work orientation involving a preference for work that was both personally challenging and socially meaningful. Pragmatic career considerations were also found to be important for women with young children. This led them to conclude that most VCS employees pursued a career that more closely fitted Driver's spiral career model, a complex career shaped by both work and non-work, rather than the conventional linear career model.

More recently, Harrow and Mole (2005) undertook a study of the careers of chief executives of small- and medium-sized VCSOs.[2] We have included this work as some of the chief executives of the smaller VCSOs we have worked with also undertook volunteer management. The chief executives that Harrow and Mole (2005) surveyed worked in organisations covering a range of activities, but one third focused on 'social services' and a quarter on 'health'. Half the post holders were aged between 45 and 54 years and had held a variety of functional positions both inside and outside the VCS, including in public (academic, local government, health service, armed forces) and private sector organisations (Harrow and Mole, 2005, p 88). The women among the chief executives surveyed were more likely to have more than 10 years' service and one fifth of them had used the volunteer route as their career basis in the VCS, which none of the men had (Harrow and Mole, 2005, p 89). One half of the men and a quarter of the women had arrived at their current role as active career seekers; a fifth of the women said that their role was the result of 'chance' or 'just being in the right place'; interestingly, no men acknowledged this.

Harrow and Mole (2005) developed a typology for chief executives (see Box 4.5). The paid philanthropists ascribe their personal career paths as of secondary importance to their altruistic approach to their work in the sector, where their job is a way of life. They offer a dedicated outlook to their role and stress the importance of the work they do for reasons far beyond the salary. The careerists have a planned career, have made a conscious decision to join the sector, see their future within the sector and direct their personal development towards this

Box 4.5: Typology of careers for the VCS

Paid philanthropists: embedded in and committed to the VCS.

The careerists: those developing sets of skills or developing skills and abilities that they see as best deployed and developed further within the VCS.

The non-aligned: arrived in the sector by uncertain and unplanned routes, and feel they are doing a 'useful' job.

Source: Harrow and Mole (2005, p 92)

end. They have identified which organisations they may target in the future. Finally, the non-aligned chief executives describe their arrival in the sector as either unplanned (following other sectoral transitions, such as redundancy or early retirement) or planned, only to the extent that work and thus, careers in other sectors are uncongenial. They see themselves as possessing a wide range of managerial competencies and their future job search may not be confined to the sector.

Being a VM

We have worked closely with VMs on a number of our research projects and we now use empirical description to illuminate their career narratives. The VMs we have worked with have tended to be highly qualified (with managerial and professional qualifications), motivated middle-aged men and women, who have had work experience in the public sector (in various capacities, some as nurses/social workers, teachers and in community development) prior to taking up posts in the VCS. What unites them is how work and non-work have intertwined to shape their careers. Not all are in households with two incomes, but they have sought job opportunities in the VCS and while they know they can earn more elsewhere, they are motivated to work in the sector because of non-economic reasons. Finally, their careers are characterised by uncertainty. They tend to hold fixed-term contracts, work above contracted hours and their paid work spills over into formal and informal volunteer work for the organisation. Prior to working in the VCS, most have had experience of working in the public sector. The lived reality of being a VM is captured in Box 4.6. These employees work for a charity active across England, delivering help to older adults (Dwyer and Hardill, 2008; Hardill and Dwyer, 2011). We now examine the careers of six volunteer managers: two men and four women.

Box 4.6: The lived reality of being a VM

- '[T]hey theoretically work part-time ... a certain number of hours a week. They put an enormous amount more in.'
- '[Y]ou just give too much. I have to limit my time now because there is my own quality of life. So I now try to be more controlled. I've stopped doing the weekends. You don't get any overtime.'
- '[T]he worst thing about the job is the travel and the stress ... there was no back up, no admin help, I was on my own, I had a problem with excess hours, it was stressful and pressured and it made me feel ill. There were targets, lots of stats to collect.'
- 'I try to be very disciplined about what I do.'
- '[A] lot of my job is spent finding ... pots of money, building up relationships with trusts ... trying to find a way of keeping the service going.'
- '[T]here's no time to be strategic or time to develop. That's your problem. You are being reactive all the time and that's not really my natural style.'

Source: Hardill and Dwyer (2011, pp 166–8)

Malky (Box 4.7) heads a volunteer management team for a national charity. He is a qualified solicitor who "enjoyed my law degree but didn't really enjoy being a solicitor". As a result, he looked for something else to do:

> 'I saw an advert to be a volunteer in Africa carrying out conservation work. I had never done volunteering before. In fact at school, the option for community services was during the games period so it was carried out by people who didn't like playing sport, which left a bad impression.'

This spell of volunteer work completely changed Malky's career direction. He continued to volunteer for the organisation upon his return. "I started giving talks for the [charity] to future volunteers about my experiences and through that, heard they were looking for a volunteer manager. I applied and was successful." He then worked for them for four years as a VM in the UK and abroad until he was made redundant.

Since then, he has worked for three charities with a national reach in aspects of volunteer management, including 'good practice volunteer management'. "I became acting chief executive, which was my first experience of being involved in volunteering policy ... which I really

Box 4.7: Malky

Malky is married and in his early forties. He heads a department devoted to volunteer management for a charity active across the country. Malky is a qualified solicitor, who did not volunteer until after he graduated. His wife works as a senior legal researcher for a law firm.

While he enjoyed his law degree, he didn't really enjoy being a solicitor. He completed his one year at law school, two years as a trainee solicitor and became fully qualified as a solicitor. But six months after qualification, "I saw an advert to be a volunteer in Africa carrying out conservation work. I had never done volunteering before. In fact, at school, the option for community services was during the games period so it was carried out by people who didn't like playing sport, which left a bad impression. However, I always wanted to go to Africa and was passionate about environmentalism so applied and was chosen to be a volunteer in Africa....". When he came back to the UK, he started giving talks for the non-governmental organisation (NGO) to future volunteers about his experiences and through that heard they were looking were looking for a VM. He applied and was successful and since that post has worked for three other VCSOs in volunteer management.

enjoyed." It was at this time that he started to get involved in external activities and making contacts: "I joined the Make a Difference Day Annual Judging Panel, became a trustee of [the charity]." During this time, it became clear to Malky that while volunteering was moving up the agenda, there was nowhere for VMs to get together to discuss issues. He explained: "With another colleague, we got together a group of people we knew to meet up regularly, entirely self-run. This eventually evolved into the Association of Volunteer Managers." Malky then searched out other posts, "because they both entailed volunteering and volunteer management policy and strategy". Malky is a 'spiralist', but has become a 'careerist' within the VCS.

Dennis (Box 4.8) is a full-time volunteering development manager for a charity that works with and for older people in a northern English city. He is responsible for overall management of the charity's volunteer programme involving 300 volunteers. He works closely with other paid staff who support the volunteer programme. Dennis is in his fifties and he has had a varied career including nearly 20 years in the private sector. In addition to his job as a charity employee, he gives time and expertise unpaid to other VCSOs. He is chair of a charity based in Scotland and has also served on the board of a much smaller local charity. He has built a considerable reputation for his wealth of knowledge about volunteering. Having crossed the boundaries between

Box 4.8: Dennis

Dennis is a full-time volunteering development manager for a charity for older people, involving 300 volunteers. He worked for 19 years with British Telecom and for five years as a church minister. He has been employed in the VCS for 12 years. His responsibilities as volunteering development manager include the overall management of the volunteer programme, the recruitment, selection, induction, training and support of volunteers, as well as fulfilling an advocacy role on behalf of volunteers. He is responsible for compiling the quarterly *Volunteers' Newsletter* and running the Volunteers' Forum three times a year. In addition to his job based in the north of England, he is chair of a separate charity in Scotland that also involves volunteers working with older people. He has served in a voluntary capacity on the management committee of a separate, much smaller local charity with 36 volunteers, which offers befriending services for frail, older residents. He has a reputation as an expert on volunteering and managing volunteers and is often asked to lead seminars and workshops, particularly with regard to issues around older people.

sectors, his career pattern resembles the 'non-aligned' group identified by Harrow and Mole (2005).

Millie (Box 4.9) is a volunteering development officer in a northern English city whose current post is funded through a three-year project dedicated to increasing the diversity of volunteering. This job is part time and Millie is also employed by a private consultancy to provide training in diversity. She is in her early thirties and has built up a varied portfolio of skills from previous work in community development and mental health. She has worked in India and the UK. In common with Dennis, she gives time unpaid to another VCSO in a demanding governance role. She too crosses the boundaries of voluntary and private sector employment; in her case simultaneously as her income is derived

Box 4.9: Millie

Millie is a volunteering development officer based in a Community and Voluntary Services (CVS) centre in an urban area in the north of England. She is funded through a three-year Big Lottery project that aims to increase volunteering among non-traditional groups and people with support needs. The job is part time (three days a week) and Millie also has a part-time job in a consultancy that delivers diversity awareness training. Her background is in community development work and she has experience in international development NGOs and mental health organisations. She is also qualified as a mental health first aid instructor. In her spare time, Millie chairs a local voluntary youth group.

from the VCS and the private sector. She fits the 'non-aligned' profile according to the typology discussed above.

The next three women VMs all work in the East Midlands community of Brightville. Barbara (Box 4.10) has worked in the VCS for one organisation for over a decade. She is in her fifties, while her husband is considerably older and retired from paid work. Her children, from a previous marriage, are grown up and Barbara will soon become a grandmother. Her husband gets involved in the Community Project – when they are short-staffed he does 'help out' and he, along with her children and extended family, supports the charity by attending fundraising events. Barbara regularly works above her contracted hours. Part of her role involves managing volunteers, a 'needy' paid workforce and bid writing. In 2009, she was awarded an MBE in recognition of her work in the community through the Community Project.

The first post that Barbara held at the Community Project was part time, which she succeeded in getting after she had been made redundant from a public sector post in community education (she worked in Brightville): "When I came here they had funding starting to come in through SRB [Single Regeneration Budget][3] ... I applied

Box 4.10: Barbara

Barbara is in her early fifties and is the chief executive for a small VCSO, the Community Project, in Brightville, in the East Midlands. She has held this post since the mid-1990s and has a deep commitment to both Brightville and the Community Project, although she has never lived in Brightville.

Prior to working for the Community Project, Barbara worked in the public sector, including in community education in Brightville and she actually helped local residents set up the charity she now manages. But in the early 1990s there were cuts in community education.

"With the cuts in community education those projects throughout [the county] ceased. We had 101 groups affiliated to us and a good strong committee of residents. The residents wanted something to be in place when the education council disbanded. They worked then with some of the workers looking at what they could do and the first idea was to set up a luncheon club at the [centre]. And that's where it stemmed from. The paid workers ... County Council supported the residents in setting up what was called Community Project."

Today, Barbara manages a paid workforce of 12, as well as almost 100 volunteers. She has a diverse job remit from fundraising to managing paid staff and volunteers.

and came back to Brightville to job share. That was two and a half days a week as a community development worker." However, once she started working there, she realised that the organisation needed management structures for both paid staff and volunteers and she was able to convince the trustees that by changing her job focus, this would benefit the organisation, "because I've always been into the legal issues and looking at constitutions and finances and all sorts of things and systems, I realised that they needed support in a different way really … bringing it more into line with the regulations and all sorts of things … so that's why my role changed really." Her move to work at the Community Project coincided with a period of tremendous growth in opportunities for the sector. She started as an administrator, but recognised quickly that the organisation needed to make some key decisions. She introduced managerial systems and became the chief executive of the organisation. To help her with the role, she also acquired further professional qualifications, with the support of the organisation.

Barbara is totally committed to the Community Project: "I wouldn't swap it for the world … everybody in the organisation works in the same way, which is wonderful. You couldn't ask for a better place really." She has played a pivotal role in shaping the organisation, broadening its scope and scale. In bringing about these changes, she has developed professionally: "It's given me an opportunity to develop. I went on to do a law degree. I did a four-year law degree whilst working here and got a 2:1." In her interview, she stressed that the Community Project is 'professional': "People for years have always looked down on the voluntary sector as though we're amateurs. We're not. We are professional and we can compete." This professionalism is reflected in how the volunteering experience has changed within the organisation; it has become more formalised. So, while redundancy pushed her to seek employment, she has changed career direction, working for the Community Project, and developed professionally as the organisation has grown. According to Harrow and Mole's (2005) typology, Barbara is a 'paid philanthropist' and 'spiralist'.

One of Barbara's colleagues at the Community Project is Sheila (Box 4.11), who works part time as a volunteer coordinator. Sheila is divorced and has two teenage sons and her retired parents help her with childcare. She recruits, trains and manages the 100 or so Community Project volunteers. Immediately before taking the post, she had been undertaking a volunteering training course to enable her to switch career direction and she had identified managing volunteers as a job she was interested in:

Box 4.11: Sheila

Sheila is a divorced mother of two teenage sons, who has worked as the part-time volunteer coordinator at the Community Project for the past seven years. She is funded out of several projects and works 30 hours a week. In addition to being the volunteer coordinator, she volunteers herself for the Community Project.

> 'Before I started work ... I wanted to do basic skills volunteering, teaching and I started a training course to do that. I was about half way through when I got this job, so I had to stop that. But that's something I was interested in. Because I'd done it with children I wanted to do it with adults as well.'

Sheila works closely with Barbara, the chief executive. She represents the charity on the board of other organisations and regularly attends a local church. She is also very committed to the organisation and the community and works flexibly; this may include working evenings or attending events that publicise volunteering opportunities for the Community Project. She demonstrates her commitment to the organisation in a number of ways, for example "I take a dog a walk for somebody, do you count that as volunteering?" Sheila involves her sons in this work; she encourages them to get to know older people and wants them to develop a spirit of community engagement. She makes a regular commitment to an older lady, helping her – this commitment is informal, but the lady is one of the Community Project's clients.

> 'A lady that's one of our clients here at Community Project, she's not very well. [The Community Project] went to do some DIY work for her, knew the dog wanted to taking a walk ... I take her at the weekend. But that is exercise for me. I enjoy it because I haven't got a dog and it's good for kids, having a pet and responsibility. But with my two hours on Saturday, we go every Saturday and Sunday.'

Like Barbara, Sheila is a 'paid philanthropist' and 'spiralist'.

Deborah (Box 4.12) is a paid worker at the Government Project. Strictly speaking, this project does not fall within the VCS, but as it heavily involves volunteers and works closely with the VCS, we have included it in our work. The Government Project has volunteers and 'parent helpers'. Both groups give time to the organisation, but are differentiated by the degree of commitment they make to the

> ## Box 4.12: Deborah
>
> Deborah works as a training leader for Government Project. She is in her fifties and she and her husband live in Irontown. She has a grown-up family. She is very committed to Brightville and is very active in civil society; sitting on the committees of other VCSOs, as well as being an active member of the Labour Party and in the local Credit Union, "I sit on the Credit Union steering group that we're setting up". She was approached to get involved by a retired businessman who was also involved in the Credit Union.
>
> Deborah involves her whole family in supporting the fundraising activities for other charities in Brightville. Deborah is very committed to Government Project and the community. She regularly works above her contracted hours.

organisation. Parent helpers are seen as less committed and not as reliable as volunteers, who are climbing the ladder to get connected to the labour market.

Deborah's first career was as a school teacher and she has had a second career with adult learners: "I was a maths teacher but I was looking for other things to do. So that gave me the chance to try before I committed myself to another block of formal training. And I found I liked it, so I picked that up and moved on and had a career change." She has moved into working with volunteers at the Government Project through using her skills and experience with adult learners. She did indicate that this career switch from school to adult learning was facilitated by her undertaking volunteer work: "When I first started working with adults with poor basic skills, I started as a volunteer."

Deborah's role at the Government Project centres on working with the volunteer parents, using volunteering as a vehicle for empowerment and skill enhancement. When we interviewed her, she was attending car maintenance classes with some of the Government Project volunteer mothers:

> 'On Monday nights we're doing car maintenance for women (at a local college) … we're learning together on that one – because I'm going with them – four women and me. It's quite good fun, quite good fun. And I know as little as they know so we're learning together. So I think that's quite a positive thing as well that they see staff members that's not knowing everything.'

Part of her reason for giving up an evening was to raise the confidence of the four Government Project volunteers. She went on to say,

"The women find entering the college campus daunting, they lack confidence". By attending with them, she helped them overcome a barrier of entering unfamiliar buildings: "It's a bit of a psychological thing, that one." She went on to say: "I didn't mind what we went to as long as we went to something." She was not bothered what course they attended as long as it was one at the local college. Deborah is a 'paid philanthropist' and a 'spiralist'.

The search for a professional identity

In the remaining part of this chapter, we highlight the search for a professional identity among VMs themselves. A number of authors have mapped an expanding number of 'emerging' professionals, such as information technology (IT) specialists (Sullivan, 1995, p 27). There is more ambiguity in the public mind as to what other occupations are really 'professional'. The picture is complicated by the increasing tendency of managers to seek professional status; witness the explosion of the Master of Business Administration (MBA) degrees. Modern management clearly aspires towards a recognisable professional identity (Sullivan, 1995, p 4; Schoenberger, 1997, p 140). So the key question for us is whether volunteer management is an emerging profession.

In a number of countries, such as Australia, Canada, Ireland, New Zealand, Singapore and the US, professional associations exist for VMs. Since 1983, the journal *The International Journal of Volunteer Administration* has been published in the US and there is international recognition of 1 November as International Volunteers Manager Appreciation Day. Social identity theory (Tajfel and Turner, 1979) aids in the explanation of social cohesion, suggesting that individuals identify with, and behave as part of, a group, adopting shared attitudes and values. Thus, individuals' sense of who they are is defined in terms of the collective, which in the case of VMs prompts them to join associations for VMs.

Scotland did have an association, the Scottish Association of Volunteer Management (SAVM), for 12 years. It was launched in 1996 and gained charitable status in November 2005, but closed in 2008 when funding failed to materialise from the Scottish Government. In the 12 years that it existed, SAVM provided a range of support and mentoring services for VMs, but its funding was precarious.

There have been a number of attempts to establish a support network for VMs in England, including the National Association of Voluntary Service Managers (NAVSM). NAVSM was established in 1968 as the National Association of Voluntary Help Organisers (NAVHO). It was set up to provide support information and training to VHOs.

This development was strongly supported by the King's Fund, which organised training days and appointed a development officer for voluntary help organisers (VHOs). As the involvement of the King's Fund wound down, the emphasis shifted to the association itself to meet the developmental and training responsibilities of its members. In 1994, reflecting the development of its members' role into a more structured management position, NAVHO changed its name to NAVSM. It has over 160 members working in health and social care in England. Its website is maintained by Volunteering England (at the time of writing).

Another organisation was the National Volunteer Managers Forum (NVMF), which was set up by the National Centre for Volunteering (NCV) in the mid-1990s. While the forum grew and attracted members, it had few resources. Its London focus tended to prevent those in provincial organisations, who could not afford the travel costs to London, from being involved. Subsequently, the Professional Volunteer Managers Advisory Group was established to look at developing NVMF into a body independent of the NCV, with a working title of 'The Institute of Volunteering Management and Development'. Following project funding from the Lottery to look into setting up such a body, it concluded that there wasn't the capacity to do so and the group disbanded in 2003. This decision coincided with an awareness of the Excellence in Volunteer Management Project at Volunteering England (the successor to NCV), which aimed to take NVMF forward.

In 2004, a group of national VMs (including Malky; see Box 4.7), recognising the lack of peer support in the sector, set up their own peer support group. Their work represented a grassroots response to the specific challenges of the management roles in the VCS (Howlett, 2010). Their work resulted in the establishment of an Association of Volunteer Managers (AVM) in June 2007 (www.volunteermanagers.org.uk) (Box 4.13). It was set up 'to support, represent and champion

---

Box 4.13: The AVM

AVM aims to:

- facilitate and support effective peer-to-peer networking of those involved in volunteer management locally, regionally and nationally;
- campaign and speak out on issues that are key to people who manage volunteers;
- develop information and good practice resources on volunteer management.

Source: Association of Volunteer Managers (www.volunteermanagers.org.uk)

---

people who manage volunteers in England, regardless of field, discipline or sector'. The AVM says that it is 'a voice, a network, a resource' and represents both an individual and institutional response. Within a year, it had over 100 members, group support networks and a website with several hundred registered users (personal communication).

AVM peer groups are designed to facilitate and develop informal peer group networking and create support networks on a local level. These groups, the AVM hopes, will also enable it to develop its voice and to cascade information and obtain views of its membership. Each group is facilitated by an AVM peer group coordinator. They are responsible for organised regular group meetings, usually four times a year, and chairing each meeting. Groups have been formed across England in Bristol, Cheltenham, Cumbria/Lancaster, Northampton, Nottingham, Reading, St Albans and Staffordshire. There are also specialist peer groups for NHS service managers and VMs in animal welfare. The AVM also aims to facilitate skills sharing and there is a training calendar and specialist events that members can register to attend. Extensive use is made of digital technologies and there are blogs on the website as well as an e-newsletter (Howlett, 2010). In its first year, AVM joined forces with SAVM to conduct a short online survey of their members; 208 VMs participated, some of whom were members of other organisations, such as the Association of Hospice Managers and the National Association of Voluntary Service Managers (see Box 4.14).

Box 4.14: Survey of members of AVM/SAVM, 2008

- For 59% of them, managing volunteers was part of their job.
- For 41%, managing volunteers was the focus of their job.
- 78% worked full time, 22% part time.
- 39% expressed concerns about sustainability of funding for their role.
- 64% had organisational support for their role.
- 76% felt that they could not see a clear career path and 29% felt that was a strong issue for them.
- 57% felt volunteer management was a low status occupation.
- 64% felt that they had to recruit a given number of volunteers to satisfy the funder, which sometimes prevented them from looking for the 'right' volunteer.
- Of the 208 surveyed, 31% were a member of AVM, 9% of SAVM, 39% were non-members but were interested in joining, and 22% were non-members and not interested in joining AVM.

Source: Association of Volunteer Managers
(www.volunteermanagers.org.uk/about-us)

The AVM is working to influence how the tasks and skills of volunteer management are understood and evaluated by their members and non-members. In this sense, it represents an occupational group aspiring to emulate better-established professions (Scuilli, 2005). Professional standing for emerging occupational groups is sought through recognition of a body of specialist knowledge and the mechanisms of training and accreditation, especially within institutions of higher education. Such 'professionalisation projects' have been noted within feminised occupations such as nursing and social work, where they are sometimes contested and can be exclusionary (Exworthy and Halford, 1999; Bone, 2002; Hallam, 2002). The study of occupational change and professionalisation asks questions about how valued knowledge and skills are developed and their recognition negotiated and how they become incorporated (or not) into organisational and institutional arrangements (Marks and Scholarios, 2007; Montgomery and Oliver, 2007).

In addition to these grassroots developments, the professional training needs of VMs are increasingly being recognised by the higher education sector and other training providers. Within higher education, a number of institutions offer professional training (such as through the provision of specialist courses – diplomas, certificates, foundation degrees, Masters, MBAs and postgraduate research, as well as more general areas of study in management, law, finance and communication relevant to working in much of the voluntary sector (see www.volresource.org.uk/services. train_qua.htm).

Good practice guidance and training opportunities for VMs have expanded significantly. Online resources are available via organisations like the NCVO and the Charity Commission, both of which provide a plethora of documents for the VM. Since 2007, Excellence in Volunteer Managers (EVM) provides accredited learning modules on volunteer management, endorsed by the Institute of Leadership and Management and promoted via Volunteering England. Towards the end of New Labour's term in office the OTS allocated £1.45 million in grants to organisations to support VMs, £200,000 to Volunteering England to set up an online information bank and a £1 million bursary fund to support VM development needs. These needs are likely to continue rising.

Some initiatives have potentially significant implications for VMs because of the emphasis on volunteers with higher support needs. Examples include the DWP volunteer brokerage scheme initiated in April 2010 to give volunteering opportunities to jobseekers, and the

'National Citizen Service' for 16-year-olds, of which the first 12 pilots were announced in November 2010.

There are also local initiatives that support VMs. The Council for the VCS within Irontown supports and offers training for VMs (via a three-year award from the Big Lottery). The local council also works with other councils across the county to deliver VM training. Irontown's VM network alone has 80 members who meet monthly.

Conclusions

In this chapter, we have examined the VCS from the perspective of those paid staff who manage volunteers. Volunteering does not succeed in a vacuum and, anecdotally, the link between well-managed volunteers and more effective volunteers has been well rehearsed. VMs are largely invisible in published statistics as they are not recognised in the SOC, but the establishment of the AVM in 2007, in England, appears to point to a new occupational group who claim to be professional as well as being managers. The creation of the AVM represents both an institutional and an individual response to a changing environment and within some communities there are local support networks for VMs, as we have noted in Irontown.

Our understanding of the careers of VMs has been enriched by the use of TSOL, as the work decisions (and careers) of VMs have been shaped by work/non-work decisions. Non-work (volunteering) may precede paid work in the sector and, in some households, non-work (by a household member) may indirectly subsidise the VCSO, as some VM households make commitments to the VCSO (as volunteers, informal helpers, fundraisers). On the whole, the VMs we have worked with have been characterised by 'spiral' careers and as 'paid philanthropists'. Working in the VCS is shrouded with uncertainty, as illustrated by the preponderance of fixed-term contracts and precarious funding streams; but that said, VMs are dedicated and passionate about their work. They are drawn to the work as they find it personally challenging and socially meaningful. Most have had spiral/portfolio careers – their complex careers have been shaped by work and non-work. The six VMs we have profiled have attached importance to the need for professional standards in the volunteer experience and have an altruistic approach to their work in the sector.

Many of the comments we have heard from both volunteers and volunteer-involving organisations in our projects have related to the need for an effective infrastructure. Further investment in the volunteering infrastructure was seen as essential in order to ensure adequate management of volunteers. In particular, we were told by organisations that any more extensive involvement of volunteers in public services delivery would require careful management, support and training in order to ensure delivery of a consistent and high-quality service. Clearly, the issue of good management has major implications, both for service-providing organisations that need full cost recovery and for the volunteering infrastructure that needs to support and promote effective management. While there has been a growth in paid work opportunities in the sector, this may not continue with cuts to public services. It has been income from public service delivery that has been the catalyst for job growth.

Notes

[1] Growth in the use of volunteers in public services in the 1960s led to the creation of a professional association in 1968 (NAVSM) but in the VCS, the more formal role of VMs was not recognised until much later.

[2] Small VCSOs had an income below £500,000, and medium-sized VCSOs had an income between £500,000 and £3 million.

[3] The SRB was introduced in 1994. It combined a number of previously separate programmes designed to bring about economic, physical and social regeneration in local areas and its main purpose was to act as a catalyst for regeneration in the sense that it would work to attract other resources from the private, public and voluntary sectors in order to bring about improvements in local areas to the quality of life of local people.

FIVE

Voluntary and community sector organisations as enterprising care providers: keeping organisational values distinctive

'If we could do more, achieve more and be more effective with a model that did not involve volunteers then we would. Clearly this is unlikely to ever happen [but] whereas volunteering is, per se, a force for good in society, it isn't automatically so for every individual organisation.'
(Volunteer Manager, national charity working for older people)

Introduction: organisations that involve volunteers

Volunteers have been called the lifeblood of the VCS (NCVO, 2010). Volunteering occurs in all sectors of the economy but most volunteers in England and Wales (an estimated two thirds) give help through VCSOs (Low et al, 2007). The sector is fluid and diverse in the extreme. There are arguments about where its boundaries lie and, indeed, if it can reasonably be called a 'sector' (Halfpenny and Reid, 2002). It has been famously and picturesquely denoted as a 'loose and baggy monster' (Kendall and Knapp, 1995, p 67). More prosaically, it is 'complex in the sense that there are a great many types of organisations of different sizes and structures, doing many different things in many different ways' (Chapman et al, 2009, p 14). The recent momentum gained by 'social enterprise' and 'social entrepreneurship' has, controversially, expanded the category to include organisations that pursue social goals through practices and attitudes more usually associated with for-profit businesses (Shaw and Carter, 2007; Di Domenico et al, 2009; Dey, 2010). Our focus here is on organisations in the VCS, including social enterprises, that provide care. As the quotation above reminds us, even VCSOs that involve many volunteers and take their support and management very seriously exist for the sake of their beneficiaries, not their volunteers.

Over the past two decades in the UK, especially in England, local government and health services have been required to step up their engagement with charities, social enterprises and community organisations. Under New Labour, there were heightened expectations that VCSOs would advance government priorities, including citizen engagement, social cohesion, supporting employability through volunteering and improving public services. The role of VCSOs came to the centre of debates about public service reform and in the 2010 General Election all the major parties stressed the importance of VCSOs in public services (Alcock, 2010). The Big Society agenda of the coalition government promises continued recognition of the contribution that VCSOs make to the lives of individuals and communities. In this chapter, we examine recent and ongoing challenges facing VCSOs as they adapt to powerful imperatives to partner with the public sector and to generate income through business-like activities. We highlight trends towards more regulated and work-like volunteering and responses to policies on care that potentially offer new opportunities for enterprising VCSOs to develop services. The chapter is organised as follows. In the next section, we overview the size and variety of the sector, noting the different kinds of organisation that are considered to fall within it. In the following section, we highlight the recent history of the mainstreaming of VCSOs in public services, focusing mainly, but not exclusively, on England. After this, we recount arguments for and against the enrolment of VCSOs as service providers and review the small body of literature that has commented on this area of reform from the perspective of volunteers. We follow this by considering what it may mean to be an 'enterprising' VCSO, drawing on notions of entrepreneurship. The chapter then turns to evidence from research undertaken by the authors about how organisations offering care have adapted and responded to relationships with the statutory sector. This long section covers: entering into public service delivery; maintaining services and managing money; volunteers' responses to change; and cooperative enterprises in social care. Finally, we offer conclusions and reflections.

Size, scope and diversity of the voluntary and community sector

The VCS includes a host of organisations that deliver social and environmental benefits and are neither statutory agencies nor private enterprises. They include charities, community groups, faith-based organisations, social enterprises, cooperatives and infrastructure organisations that represent and support parts of the wider sector. Charities receive significant tax advantages and can access funds that other voluntary organisations cannot. In England and Wales, charity status is regulated by the Charity Commission on the basis that the bulk of a charity's activities or services must benefit the public in a way that the law agrees is charitable. Charities are run by 'trustees' who form the governing body. Most trustees are volunteers, and receive no payment except out-of-pocket expenses. Employees are deemed to have a conflict of interest that prevents them from acting as trustees but, since the 1990s, the Charity Commission has stated that it is possible for beneficiaries to become trustees (Ridley-Duff and Bull, 2011). The Charities Act 2006 consolidated earlier charity law to specify 'charitable purposes' and to require that all organisations wishing to be recognised as charities must demonstrate that their aims are for the public benefit. (See Box 5.1 for more information about charitable purpose and public

Box 5.1: Charitable purpose and public benefit under the Charity Act 2006

The following purposes are recognised as charitable:

- the prevention or relief of poverty;
- the advancement of:
  - education
  - religion
  - health and saving lives
  - citizenship or community development
  - the arts, culture, heritage or science
  - amateur sport
  - human rights, conflict resolution or reconciliation, the promotion of religious or racial harmony or equality and diversity
  - environmental protection or improvement
  - animal welfare;
- the relief of those in need by reason of youth, age, ill-health, disability, financial hardship or other disadvantage;
- the promotion of the efficiency of the armed forces of the Crown, the police, fire and rescue services or ambulance services;
- any other purposes, recognised as charitable under existing charity law.

All charities must exist for the public benefit. The Charity Act 2006 abolished the presumption that relief of poverty and advancement of education and religion were for the public benefit. Public benefit must be demonstrated and the Charity Commission carries out public benefit assessments. Public benefit is not defined but has been developed through case law.

benefit.) In terms of total income, the largest charitable sector is social services (Backus and Clifford, 2010).

There are approximately 171,000 registered charities in the UK (NCVO, 2009). How many voluntary and community groups exist that are not registered as charities is much harder to ascertain. So-called 'below the radar' organisations include small groups working at a local level or in communities of interest (such as refugee and migrant groups) that usually lack a regular, substantial annual income. They do not appear in national databases and have no need to engage with, or be known to, regulatory bodies. Estimates have suggested the presence of between 600,000 and 900,000 such groups throughout Britain (MacGillivray et al, 2001). A more recent review of the 'below the radar' sector suggests that small community organisations that are usually entirely reliant on volunteer efforts are some three to five times greater in number than the 'mainstream' voluntary sector (McCabe et al, 2010). Our focus in this chapter is on the more formal organisations that do have a relationship with statutory agencies. Some, however, have their origins in very small groups set up in response to a specific local need with no paid staff and no external funding.

According to the UK's national body for social enterprise, social enterprises are businesses that trade in the market with a social purpose and use business tools and techniques to achieve social aims (Social Enterprise Coalition, 2010a). Many trading organisations including commercial businesses espousing corporate social responsibility (CSR)[1] may be guided by values that impact on their business practices. Unlike a business with a strong CSR policy, however, the principal purpose of a social enterprise is to achieve social goals, such as creating employment for individuals excluded from the labour market or providing services lacking in disadvantaged communities (Pearce, 2003; Peredo and McLean 2006). There is a widely quoted estimate of the minimum number of social enterprises in the UK of 55,000 in 2005, rising to 62,000 in 2009 (Lyon et al, 2010). These figures are based on the Annual Small Business Survey UK, which included questions on social enterprise for the first time in 2004/05 (Lyon et al, 2010). According to the Small Business Service (2005), while some social enterprises start off as businesses, most are in transition from their beginnings as voluntary sector organisations, dependent largely on grants and volunteers.

By no means do all charities and voluntary groups that trade goods and services in order to meet their aims and objectives recognise themselves as social enterprises and some vehemently resist being associated with notions of business, enterprise and entrepreneurship (Bull, 2008; Parkinson and Howorth, 2008). Nevertheless, a national survey of 'non-profit distributing third sector organisations' undertaken in 2008 found that almost half of them identified as social enterprises, although only around 5% were classified officially as such (Teasdale, 2010). Teasdale (2010) notes that towards the end of the first decade of the 21st century, policy discourse in England increasingly elided 'social enterprise' with public sector contracts.

Some of the largest social care charities in the country gain most of their income through contracts with state agencies and have adopted the designation 'social enterprise'. Turning Point, for example, provides services to people with complex needs at 200 sites across England and Wales. It is one of the 100 largest charities in the country and, according to its website (www.turning-point.co.uk/Pages/home.aspx), is a social enterprise. Almost all (97%) of Turning Point's income comes from statutory sources. For some, this means it is neither an enterprise nor a genuine charity but a de facto agency of the state (Seddon, 2007). Lord Victor Adebowale, the chief executive of Turning Point, was one of 30 social enterprise ambassadors appointed under the Labour government in 2006 and has also been invited to advise the coalition government on social enterprise and the Big Society agenda (see Box 5.2 for more information about Turning Point).

With political attention now focused on social enterprises, clearer definition has been called for to prevent opportunistic misuse of the 'social enterprise' badge (Social Enterprise Coalition, 2010b). The social enterprise 'kite mark' proposed by the Social Enterprise Coalition, however, controversially excludes cooperatives that distribute surpluses to members (Teasdale, 2010). There are 4,800 cooperative businesses in the UK, owned by 11 million people and sustaining more than 200,000 jobs (Co-operatives UK, 2009). Recently, community ownership of enterprises such as local shops and renewable energy projects, using the cooperative model, has expanded (Woodin et al, 2010). Health and social care cooperatives are a growing phenomenon internationally (Girard, 2002). Cooperatives have a much longer history than 'social enterprises'.

The first successful modern type of cooperative was set up by the Rochdale Pioneers in 1844 and became the basis for cooperatives globally (Birchall, 1997). Cooperatives are distinctive because the way that they do business is driven by values and principles set at an international level and overseen by the International Co-operative Alliance (ICA) (see Box 5.3 for information on cooperative values and principles). The ICA embeds the idea that members should contribute to, and then share in, the economic surpluses generated by their enterprise. This and the ICA's commitment to democratic member

Box 5.2: Turning Point – one of the UK's largest social care charities

Turning Point is a registered charity that provides services for people with complex needs, including those affected by drug and alcohol misuse, mental health problems and those with a learning disability. It was founded in London, in 1964, as a single project working with street drinkers. Today, it operates around 200 specialist and integrated services across England and Wales, helping more than 130,000 people each year. Turning Point is one of the UK's 100 largest charities, with 1,600 employees and 450 volunteers. For 2009/10, it reported an income of £69 million for 'charitable activities'. Almost all this income came from statutory sources. Turning Point was castigated in a report for the think tank Civitas as one of the largest charities so dependent on government funding as to be de facto state agencies that should not be considered charities.

According to Turning Point's strategic plan, it wants to more than treble the number of people it helps, particularly providing a tailored response for those who are least engaged by existing services. The organisation is described on its website as a social enterprise reinvesting its surplus to provide the best services for vulnerable people (www.turning-point.co.uk/Pages/home.aspx). Cross-bench peer Lord Victor Adebowale has been chief executive since 2001. During his leadership, Lord Adebowale has steered the organisation in the direction of social business. He is one of 30 'social enterprise ambassadors' in a programme that aims to raise awareness and foster a culture of social enterprise in England. The programme is funded by the Office for Civil Society but the ambassadors give their time unpaid. In Lord Adebowale's words, 'competition is tough out there [but] we're good value and we offer credible outcomes. As a taxpayer, I would rather my money be put back into providing more services for people, so I would argue there should be a slight gradient towards commissioning social enterprises'.

Sources: Charity Commission (www.charitycommission.gov.uk/Showcharity/ RegisterOfCharities/CharityWithPartB.aspx?RegisteredCharityNumber= 234887&SubsidiaryNumber=0); Turning Point (www.turning-point.co.uk/ Pages/home.aspx); Seddon (2007); http://socialenterpriseambassadors.org.uk/ ambassador/victor-adebowale

control are in contrast to the charity system based on trustees and beneficiaries (Ridley-Duff and Bull, 2011). The ICA declaration on worker cooperatives states that members should be compensated for their work using an equitable system that evaluates their contribution and aims to reduce the gap between high- and low-paid workers (ICA, 2005). In producer cooperatives (manufacturing goods or delivering services) a share of profits and fair payment for work are the norm (Ridley-Duff, 2007). For some commentators, volunteering in the sense of working for the organisation without pay is contrary to these

Box 5.3: Cooperative identity and principles

A cooperative is an autonomous association of persons united voluntarily to meet their common economic, social and cultural needs and aspirations, through a jointly owned and democratically controlled enterprise. Cooperatives are based on the values of self-help, self-responsibility, democracy, equality, equity and solidarity. In the tradition of their founders, cooperative members believe in the ethical values of honesty, openness, social responsibility and caring for others. The following cooperative principles are guidelines by which cooperatives put their values into practice:

* voluntary and open membership;
* democratic member control;
* member economic participation;
* autonomy and independence;
* education, training and information;
* cooperation among cooperatives;
* concern for community.

Source: ICA 'Statement on the Co-operative Identity'
(www.ica.coop/coop/principles.html)

principles (Ridley-Duff and Bull, 2011). Many cooperatives, such as the new wave of community-owned shops, however, rely in varying degrees on voluntary labour.

We now turn from definitions and numbers to the involvement of VCSOs of many kinds in the provision of care.

State-sponsored VCSOs and the provision of care

In the UK, as in other Western states, voluntary groups initially pioneered the services that became part of statutory welfare in the 20th century. Although service delivery by VCSOs has become high profile in recent years, it is not essentially new (Blackmore, 2006). Indeed, there were examples of government contracting with charitable bodies 200 years ago (Blackmore, 2006). Our concern here is with more recent history. In the 1980s, governments on both sides of the Atlantic adopted neoliberal principles that included 'rolling back' the state, the strengthening of markets and a more pluralist system of welfare provision. All this was associated with New Public Management (NPM), which has been described as 'a desire to replace the presumed inefficiency of hierarchical bureaucracy with the presumed efficiency of markets' (Power, 1999, p 43). One of the claims of NPM is that public services fail or underperform without the disciplines of competition or profit.

NPM marks 'a shift in the way in which governments govern, from bureaucratic administration to the encouragement of numerous innovative and entrepreneurial forms of service delivery' (Curtis, 2008, p 277). In practice, this has meant that both private and voluntary organisations have been encouraged to provide welfare services through the application of competition; in other words, bidding for contracts to substitute for the state as provider. In England, the NHS and Community Care Act 1990 required contracting out of local authority social care services for disabled adults and older people and led to increased voluntary sector-provided social care (Osborne and McLaughlin, 2004). Provider organisations that took on service contracts had to demonstrate efficiency, value for money and a business ethos. As a result, voluntary organisations that participated in the 'contract culture' were said to become more regulated and more competitive (Tonkiss and Passey, 1999; Poole, 2007). Wolch (1990) introduced the idea of a 'shadow state' to emphasise the exertion of government power over those VCSOs that had come in to replace diminished state provision in both Britain and the US.

New Labour, elected in 1997, declared its intentions to boost the role of what it later began to call the 'third sector' in public services and to improve the funding relationship with government. The notion of the 'third sector' was not invented by New Labour but gained official acceptance, perhaps on account of its verbal echo of Third Way politics (Haugh and Kitson, 2007). The government used the term 'partnership' to describe the new form of engagement. The HM Treasury (2002) Cross-Cutting Review called on all government departments to partner more effectively with the voluntary sector. Short-term funding for services was identified as one of the barriers to the government's effective working with the sector (HM Treasury, 2002).

Compacts were introduced that called for longer-term funding to create stability for VCSOs. In return, VCSOs were expected to be beacons of financial management best practice and to recognise that public funding was received on the basis that it should contribute to government policy priorities. The Public Accounts Committee report, *Working with the Voluntary Sector* (House of Commons Committee of Public Accounts, 2006), criticised the government's modest targets for increasing the involvement of voluntary organisations in public service delivery. The perceived slowness of the sector take-up of public sector commissions was tackled on a variety of fronts. The Efficiency Review (Gershon, 2004) recommended longer-term funding and full-cost recovery as guiding principles. This is an aspect of VCS–government relations on which evidence from various sources indicates that official commitments from central government made little impact on the front line. Research by the National Audit Office (NAO, 2005) concluded that most VCSOs had not seen any general improvement in funding practices since 2002 and, in some cases, they were perceived to have worsened. The Charity Commission (2007) found that two thirds of all funding agreements with charities were for one year only. It also found that only one in eight charities delivering public services achieved full-cost recovery all of the time. According to the Audit Commission (2007), the debate on full-cost recovery created a false expectation within certain sections of the voluntary sector, that more money will be available for existing services.

The OTS, created in 2006 as part of the Cabinet Office, was tasked with bringing about a 'step-change' in the quality of interaction with government that VCSOs in England can expect. The OTS initiated a National Programme for Third Sector Commissioners, which aimed to improve their understanding of the potential of the third sector in designing, delivering and improving public services. Other solutions were in the form of guidance and training to address lack of expertise and produce more 'commission-ready' VCSOs, with skills to promote and sell their services (SCEDU, 2008).

By 2008, just under £13 billion, around 36% of total income for charities in England and Wales, was coming from statutory sources (Clark et al, 2010). Many VCSOs (and infrastructure organisations that speak for them) have welcomed opportunities to gain fee income, to improve services and to influence policy (Alcock et al, 2004; Blackmore, 2006). ACEVO (2007) has championed an ever-greater role in service delivery as an alternative to a bureaucratic state and a profit-oriented market. Some of the bodies representing smaller, more community-based organisations, however, have been critical of these developments, pointing to their potential to exclude these groups (Alcock, 2010).

VCSOs as service providers: innovation and trust

One plank in the argument for engaging the VCS in public service delivery is that it is close to service users and incorporates their needs into the shaping of services better than the statutory sector (Paxton et al, 2005; Blackmore, 2006). This form of closeness is captured in the notion of 'stakeholder ambiguity' (Billis and Glennerster, 1998; see Chapter Four). Stakeholder ambiguity refers to the lack of clear-cut differentiation between the various roles of employer, employee, provider, recipient and volunteer. This 'bewildering complexity of overlapping roles', Billis and Glennerster (1998, p 81) contend, implies a flexible, changing and informal structure capable of responding more sensitively than the state or the market to the disadvantage of service users. Claims about closeness to users are also linked to trust in the VCS by services users as well as the wider public. In an era of growing mistrust in many public institutions, there is still at least the perception of higher levels of trust in the VCS (Paxton et al, 2005). People, especially those from excluded groups, trust the VCS because it is not the statutory sector (Paxton et al, 2005).

Traditional social policy across the UK has emphasised the sector's advantages in being innovative as a pathfinder (Billis and Glennerster, 1998). A second set of claims for the advantages of VCS involvement in public services centres on the innovative capacity of the sector as public service providers. This has been described as the 'very crux of third sector distinctiveness' (Public Administration Select Committee, 2008, p 29). There have been some outstanding examples of new thinking and new ways of responding to unmet need since the establishment of the welfare state in the post-war period. Children's hospices, for example, were an innovation that grew from a voluntary sector response to the closure of long-stay hospitals (Jackson and Robinson, 2003). In the context of services for older people, VCSOs typically offer so-called 'low-level' services that fill in gaps between specialist and universal public services. Small-scale, local services can be innovative, especially in responding creatively to the importance that older people attach to support to care for themselves, rather than being recipients of care (Clark et al, 1998). Osborne et al (2008), however, argue that empirical research offers only limited support for assertions that innovation is an inherent strength of the VCS. According to their survey research in 1994 and 2006, the sector's record of innovative activity actually declined in that 12-year period. They explained this counterintuitive finding on the basis that innovation is not always possible when working to risk-averse public policy frameworks (Osborne et al, 2008).

There are concerns within the sector that in taking up contracts for services specified by public sector funders, VCSOs are likely to weaken their distinctive organisational values and become more like agencies of the state. Hodgson (2004) contrasts authentic civil society (characterised as complex, diverse and organically developing) with 'manufactured civil society', which is orchestrated by government (Hodgson, 2004, p 140). The notion of the 'shadow state' (Wolch, 1990) continues to be invoked in the first decade of the 21st century to signal the skewing of VCS activity to meet government targets and accepting government-defined frameworks of good practice (Milbourne, 2009). This can imply shifting the relationship between clients, employees and volunteers (Milbourne, 2009).

In the context of VCSO enrolment in public services, greater empirical attention appears to have been given to the concerns of staff than other stakeholders such as trustees, service users and volunteers (Macmillan, 2010). Nevertheless, a few studies have considered how adjustments associated with funding regimes and contracting can impact on the volunteer workforce (Russell and Scott, 1997; Davis Smith and Gay, 2005; Milligan and Fyfe, 2005). The NHS and Community Care Act 1990 assumed an untapped pool of volunteers ready to contribute to the provision of caring and other services at little additional cost (Wardell et al, 1992). There is some evidence that the workload, level of responsibility and skills required of volunteers all increased as a result of the development of contracts in the early 1990s. Russell and Scott (1997) reported that recruitment of volunteers, especially for management roles, became more difficult.

From the perspective of volunteers, more recent studies have shown that tighter service specifications and increased accountability bring new demands on workloads, responsibility and skills (Davis Smith and Gay, 2005; Jochum et al, 2005). These demands can be intimidating to the traditional volunteer base, who value the informality of voluntary work and do not wish to take on tasks that would, under state delivery of services, be performed by a paid professional (Milligan and Fyfe, 2005). Moreover, the increased professionalisation of volunteers can 'result in a disengagement from local communities and a disempowerment of citizens resulting in the emergence of increasingly passive forms of citizenship within these organisations' (Milligan and Fyfe, 2005, p 431).

Evidence from the US similarly suggests that contract competition increased focus on professional competency areas and devalued the work of volunteers (Eikenberry and Kluver, 2004). For small organisations, inner-city faith groups for example, that have been lately enrolled in service delivery in the UK, the burdens on a few overstretched volunteers have become hard to bear; and difficulties in recruiting new volunteers mean that longstanding volunteers have to work harder (Cairns et al, 2007). Moreover, lack of a broader volunteer base may make their longer-term participation in service delivery unsustainable (Cairns et al, 2007).

Making VCSOs more enterprising

There is a perception that, while the VCS is becoming more like the public sector as it takes on roles and responsibilities from the state, in other respects it is coming to resemble private sector businesses. 'Social enterprise' and 'social entrepreneurship' have become a high-profile policy agenda in health and social care. These terms are often used interchangeably, but 'social entrepreneurship' tends to put more emphasis on individual motivation and leadership (Birch and Whittam, 2008). Some influential writing on social entrepreneurship has concentrated on individual social entrepreneurs (for example Leadbeater, 1997). There is evidence, however, that the achievements in socially oriented business are rarely the product of the lone actions of heroic individuals (Amin, 2009a).

Parkinson and Howorth (2008, p 292) comment on a paradox that social enterprise with its roots in social movements might be 'more prone' to individualistic and economic presumptions than in the business 'mainstream ... where such perspectives have been questioned long ago'. Recent thinking on 'social enterprise', as noted in a thorough review by Peattie and Morley (2008), tends to focus not so much on individuals as on organisations and their trading activity, as well as the networks and institutional support that are often important factors for starting up and acquiring resources. For some commentators, there is a transition to more entrepreneurial language, mindsets and practices that is both desirable and inevitable (Zahra et al, 2009). Others are concerned that underfunded VCSOs are being tempted to reorient themselves from social to market goals in ways that weaken communitarian activity and volunteering (Coule, 2007; Haugh and Kitson, 2007). There is a danger, in the words of Westall (2009, p 6), that VCSOs will 'end up adopting and being forced to abide by practices and ideas that come from business and economics, which are ironically themselves being currently contested and altered'.

Becoming more entrepreneurial, in the context of the VCS, can be associated with being adaptable and responsive to changing demands and new opportunities; or it can seem to signal weakening of the social and voluntary ethos (Baines et al, 2010). Contemporary definitions of entrepreneurship centre on the pursuit of opportunity and effecting change (Stevenson and Jarillo, 1990). There has been a shift from seeing entrepreneurship in terms of the characteristics of individuals towards more emphasis on the processes of discovering and exploiting opportunities and the various contexts in which that happens (Down, 2010). Entrepreneurship and entrepreneurs have increasingly been identified as not only founders of businesses but also agents of change in other contexts, including public services (Sundin and Tillmar, 2008; Kearney et al, 2009). Opportunity seeking, risk taking and proactivity have been proposed as key dimensions of entrepreneurial orientation in public organisations, which must respond to frequent policy changes and pressure for quick results (Kearney et al, 2009). For example, Zerbinati and Souitaris (2005) invoke the work of entrepreneurship scholars Stevenson and Jarillo (1990), to explain how some local governments react to the fast-changing environment of competitive bidding for EU funds. 'Policy entrepreneurs' – a term coined by Kingdon (1995) – allocate time and resources to register issues on the policy agenda, or to promoting particular solutions to them (Kearney et al, 2008). Petchey et al (2008, p 28) claim that entrepreneurship in state organisations can result in the development of 'new and existing services, technologies, administrative techniques and new improved strategies, risk taking and pro-activity'. Such notions of entrepreneurship outside the private sector offer a potential theoretical resource for helping to think through unfamiliar expectations of VCSOs in an environment of competition, change and high expectations.

Evidence from the front line: changing organisations

In this section, we examine caring services and changing demands on organisations and volunteers. There are four interlinked themes:

- entering into public service delivery;
- maintaining services and managing money;
- volunteers' responses to change;
- cooperative enterprises in social care.

We draw on evidence from four separate studies in which one or both of the authors participated. These studies had different aims, scope and funding. The source of the first two subsections are two studies that focused on services delivered by VCSOs for older people.

The first study, 'Delivering public services in the mixed economy of welfare: putting research into practice' included 10 case studies of services, five in each of two English regions, the North East and the East Midlands. Data were collected through interviews with a key informant, usually the VCSO chief executive or in some cases the service manager, together with consultation of documentary evidence. We also held a series of workshops in which representatives of VCSOs (including some of the case study organisations) and commissioners participated together. The cases were not intended to be typical, but rather instances of service delivery that were thought to be successful and likely to offer useful learning material for others. The size and form of organisation and type of services varied widely. Some were independent local charities allied to a large national federation dedicated to working for older people. Others began as very small groups, sometimes initially without paid staff, working for people with particular needs or for a neighbourhood. One group, for example, was originally formed by a few local women to combat the isolation of older people in their community by providing them with company and a good meal. An organisation that now has an annual turnover of £4 million and 210 employees, started as a local authority-funded project for carers but became an independent charity, with carers and former carers as advisers. The largest organisation (by a long way) was established in 1990 as a not-for-profit company, became an employee-owned partnership in 1995 and a listed public limited company in 2007. It now has 4,000 employees. The smallest and newest was registered as a charity in December 2006 and has only three employees.

The second study sought to identify and evaluate existing effective practice in delivering services to excluded older people in remote rural communities across three English regions: the East and West Midlands and the East of England. Six services, two in each of these regions, were chosen as case studies.

In discussing volunteers' responses to change, we draw on a study involving 76 in-depth interviews with volunteers, former volunteers and service users of a charity dedicated to the welfare of older people in the north of England.

Finally, we report from a placement with Co-operatives UK to investigate opportunities for cooperative business models to deliver social care.

Entering into public service delivery

We look first at the rationales of VCSOs for entering into funding relationships with state agencies. Most typically, chief executive and other key informants we interviewed accounted for the origins of their public sector contracts by talking about how they first developed a service or services that addressed an unmet need. Often, they spoke with passion of being driven by a conviction that people in need were not provided for at all, or offered only poor-quality services by existing (usually public sector) suppliers. For example, the chief executive of a dementia charity told us "People with dementia were passed around like parcels; they and their carers felt powerless. Carers were frustrated with the lack of locally based services, leading to hospital and residential home admissions when what the people wanted was a 'home for life.'"

Initial sources of funding were often in the form of small, time-limited grants from charitable trusts to fund innovative services. There were several accounts of progression from charitable grants to public service contracts. The rationale for moving in this direction was that public sector contracts are much more reliable income sources that enable valuable work to continue. As one chief executive told us, "because one funding stream ends, does not mean the need has gone away". One organisation, for example, had started providing support for blind and partially sighted people via a small charitable grant and continued to develop this work, which filled a gap in available services, with a series of successful bids to other charitable trusts. But all these grants were time limited and the continuation of the work always precarious. As the chief executive noted, "We had spent time and energy building up expertise and it was stupid to wave all that goodbye when funding ended." The solution, she went on to explain, was seeking contracts from local authorities and health service sources. This was not a step to be taken lightly. Going for money from public sector contracts, she reflected, "looks opportunistic to some". But what some see as opportunistic can also be regarded as being adaptable and responsive to a fast-changing policy environment. "We are very aware of funders' criteria", she explained. "We can deliver to other issues, such as community cohesion, healthy living and obesity, as all these things affect people with low vision." Another case study organisation took on a local authority contract when a much longer-established VCSO withdrew because it could not provide the service at the price the authority paid. At this stage, the chief executive explained, the organisation was only five years old and very vulnerable so it was a difficult and risky decision.

An alternative path into delivering commissioned services was formalising an existing relationship between the VCSO and a local authority social service directorate, following legislation. In this case, the rationale for being a supplier to the public sector was the same as for those that had moved on from charitable grants: "It's where the money is – we need reliable sources of income and this is one despite the problems". At the same time, responsiveness to users was stressed: "Through the service we can demonstrate how it can be done well and provided in a way that people want."

Almost invariably, the VCSOs reported multifaceted and sometimes very close relationships with public sector personnel. Their chief executives and other senior officers sit on partnership boards and local fora; many of them are extremely proactive in being present at high-profile events. The interactions in the workshops for this project, nevertheless, highlighted particular strains between VCSOs and the public sector when VCSOs enter into service delivery. It was commented that the notion of the third sector as innovators – prevalent in rhetoric – does not sit well with a commissioning agenda because commissioners buy what they want and will not or cannot risk the new and untried. Volunteering and valuing volunteers was a fault-line around which mutual misunderstanding was particularly deep. One third sector chief executive told an anecdote about a council-run event where a council employee stood up in front of dozens of experienced senior officers from the VCS and lectured them about how to recruit volunteers – much to their annoyance. Public sector participants in one workshop pointed to a need for a clearer definition of volunteering and to a lack of robust datasets on numbers of volunteers and on the impact and sustainability of volunteering. They contended that the VCS perpetuates the idea that volunteering is cheap or free. VCS participants countered that they struggle to get funders to recognise the financial costs of managing, training and maintaining their volunteer workforce when negotiating contracts.

The VCSOs that participated in interviews and workshops had learned, changed and sometimes grown in response to opportunities in an environment of policy 'churn'. Interviewees did not use the term 'entrepreneurial' (although one of the chief executives we interviewed had received a voluntary sector 'Entrepreneur of the Year Award' in recognition of her pioneering work). However, almost all reported some behaviour that can be described as 'entrepreneurial' – actively seeking opportunities, offering new services, energetic networking and sometimes taking considered risks. Although income streams from public sector contracts were more reliable than alternatives, securing and maintaining them was demanding and time consuming. We now turn to struggles of managing financial resources and maintaining services.

Maintaining services and managing money

In this subsection, we concentrate mainly on six rural services and the annual funding dilemmas they faced. We also draw briefly on the case studies from the East Midlands and the North East discussed above. The rural services had various funding arrangements, including a fixed-term grant; an annual contract alongside service-level agreements; and annual contracts with multiple funders. The diverse mechanisms used to support them are illustrative of a wider complex jigsaw of funding sources on which charities often have to rely to support and deliver services (Alcock et al, 2004).

> 'A lot of my job is spent finding … pots of money, building up relationships with trusts … trying to find a way of keeping the service going. There is no long-term money … we just can't plan. You're getting some projects that are only for a year and it takes three or four months to get started, three months to wind down because the staff have to know what's happening.'

Those respondents delivering services with annually negotiated service-level agreements acknowledged that the statutory sector also faced recurrent annual budget problems as they juggled competing priorities while trying to maintain services that supported critical cases of serious, ongoing need. However, the routine reality of delivery of services for older people, particularly in the countryside, was one of annual cutbacks in budgets and/or the freezing of funding at the previous year's level due to increasing competition for scarce resources. For one rural project, the level of funding has remained the same for the last four years, while another project has experienced annual cutbacks of 10% for three years.

As grant income to run services is for a finite period, it also creates problems as demand for the service endures beyond the period of the grant. The manager of one rural service relayed how the maximum term of six years allowed by the grant funding body had elapsed and that the service was potentially in jeopardy unless a new long-term funder could be found. In the short term, the charity was allocating £12,000 of its own money to keep the service going. Unfortunately, the manager indicated that the funding shortfall would also mean that the contribution from older users of the service would also have to increase substantially from £4.50 per person per visit to £7.50. Other respondents also indicated that future funding for their services was uncertain and this necessitated drawing on the charity's core funds to maintain current levels of provision as initial, time-limited funding came to an end: "Once the funding finished and we saw the results and what a need it was, then yes it was decided that's not a service we can take away lightly. So now we're funding it through core funds, until we can find other funding streams."

Although aware of the costs of delivering a service, managers were routinely unable to achieve full-cost recovery (see Charity Commission

(2007) for discussion of this problem). Funding arrangements were underpinned by an inherent assumption that allocated money should be used to establish and maintain frontline service provision. Consequently, several projects received little or no money to cover project administration/management costs:

> 'The project was pared to the bone and as a consequence there were no funds for admin support ... just sufficient funds to cover her salary [of the worker delivering the service].'

> 'What we hadn't anticipated is that the funder wouldn't fund my salary [as a part-time paid worker]. So it was a moral obligation. We are a cheap option.'

A flavour of the financial pressures and compromises was captured by one chief executive from the North East of England:

> '[The city council] is able to exert some downward pressure on full-cost recovery because of the sheer size of the contracts. They [the council] make contributions to management costs through grant aid. In reality a price is negotiated to take into account the social services 'pot of money'; our overhead formula and differential payments for different categories of user.... We do subsidise our contacts because of our concern with quality. But if you can't make it pay you must complain, and we do.'

One of the most difficult challenges reported throughout the two studies was giving an account of the value of their services in ways that make sense to public sector agencies. Public sector stakeholders get exasperated when VCSOs try to win arguments about funding on the grounds that they do 'good work' (Chapman et al, 2007). VCSOs are increasingly required to gather quantitative and qualitative evidence to present to funders looking for evidence of service impact (Moxham and Boaden, 2007; Munoz, 2009; nef, 2009). Therefore, managing and delivering projects often brought additional administrative burdens for hard-pressed service providers. This included regular surveys of service users to gather qualitative and more holistic feedback on what the service meant to them and, in some cases, other household members. As they receive funding from a number of sources, they are likely to be subject to several regulatory regimes, with different approaches to performance management and reporting. The administrative burden of such record keeping was consistently noted:

> 'There were targets, lots of stats [sic] to collect … I looked at the contract and understood the implications so I collected stats … I did a monthly, six-monthly and final reports … on claims, visits, phone calls, surgeries, talks etc.'

> 'If we work for three days a week in the local community and for clients of over 50 we satisfy two of our funding bodies. If those clients also live in social housing we may also satisfy a third funding body. It is for me to monitor the work to ensure that our statistics are balancing, balancing all the way through.'

It is also necessary to communicate this complex information to paid workers and volunteers, as the same chief executive went on to explain:

> 'To demonstrate to the team the change from satisfying the requirements of one funding body to now satisfying several and each with their own client groups (geographically or by age), I have had to draw pie charts and Venn diagrams as illustrations to ensure that they have the full knowledge to develop a different way of thinking, working and dealing with the added pressure.'

Maintaining services and managing money demanded the entrepreneurial skills of networking and securing resources on the part of VCSO senior staff. It also, as the last quotation indicated, required the nature of change to be conveyed to workers and volunteers. We now turn to volunteers' responses to new funding regimes and associated pressures.

Volunteering in a local charity for older people

Age Concern North City is a registered charity that aims to improve the quality of life of older people living in a city in the north of England. It provides services for both frail and active older people and its mission statement is 'to promote the status and well-being of all older people in [North City] and to make later life a fulfilling and enjoyable experience'. The charity has been successful in recruiting and supporting a large and diverse volunteer 'workforce' consisting mainly of people over the age of retirement. Volunteer roles include governance, helping in its lunch club and leisure services, one-to-one support such as befriending and counselling and various activities based in the city centre office such as assisting at the computer help desk, serving in the cafe, general advice and financial services.

The research on which this subsection is based was undertaken in 2004–06 as a partnership between a university team and Age Concern North City, which was a member of the national Age Concern Federation. Age Concern has since merged with Help the Aged and the new organisation is known as Age UK. (The history of the two organisations and their merger are discussed in Chapter Seven.) The aim of the study was to draw on experiences at Age Concern North City to inform other organisations working with volunteers and to help VCSOs to understand and access the contribution of older people. The research process built upon an already innovative record in establishing mechanisms for including older people in policy implementation within the organisation. An advisory focus group was set up in order to draw on the knowledge and expertise of staff and volunteers and a self-completion questionnaire was sent to all the current volunteers and a sample of former volunteers – with questions about why they volunteered, the kinds of voluntary activities they undertook, use of time and the difficulties they faced as volunteers.[2] The most substantial part of the research was in-depth interviews with 76 volunteers. There is a full report of the study in Baines et al (2006). Lie and Baines (2007) address the theme of older volunteers' responses to organisational change. The data we report here are from interviews with Age Concern North City volunteers and former volunteers (in Chapter Seven, we return to the interviews with volunteers and refer also to some of the survey data).

Most typically, volunteers interviewed by the researchers spoke of the charity as "caring" and "very friendly" and of its city-centre head office as a place where there was a "family feeling" and "comradeship". In this subsection, however, we highlight perspectives on volunteers' changing roles and support needs within a context of short-term funding and constant innovation. In contrast to more general accounts we were given of the organisation and its support for volunteers, the experiences were often negative and, sometimes, quite painful. In common with many other charities, Age Concern North City has increasingly engaged in public service delivery (in its case, social care for older people) and income generation through trading (mainly selling financial services). Shortly before the research fieldwork, Age Concern North City had made changes to its services in response to new relationships with the statutory sector and the market economy.

The results included changes in volunteering roles, which were not well understood and often resented by volunteers.

Almost half of the 300 volunteers with Age Concern North City, at the time of the research, helped in its 'lunch and leisure club' service. There had been even more in that service before 2002 when the city council's social services directorate negotiated a new contract. Day care service users were reassessed according to their needs and two tiers of service provision were developed: one being a more supported environment with paid staff at every session and the other run by volunteers in community venues across the city. The title 'lunch and leisure' reflected Age Concern North City's partnership with the local further education college in providing activities such as glass painting and music making. Some of the community-based lunch clubs closed or changed venue after the revised funding. Some were able to offer only reduced services, for example, no longer providing transport. The number of volunteers in the service fell from 221 to 134. Apart from the distress and dismay of service users and staff, the impact on volunteer morale of these changes was significant and some volunteers were bitter and disillusioned. Here are extracts from interviews in which volunteers described how they saw the negative effects on service users and volunteers:

> 'Because of the way the funding was going ... they amalgamated so many into other clubs and some became core clubs, which is less able people, but what they do with them, which I didn't like, you had so many in the morning, they went home, then you had so many of an afternoon. Well to me that wasn't my intentions and that's not the way I wanted to run the lunch club.'

> 'Some of these old people loved it [the lunch club]. And they decided that four of them, if they couldn't be picked up, they'd be willing to get a taxi to come.... So they weren't [stopped from coming] because they were able to get their own taxi ... that is wrong. It's wrong. I mean it's a service ... we're giving a service. And we're giving our time free so who are they to come and say who's to come and who's not to come?!'

The increased emphasis on learning courses was also disliked by some longstanding volunteers who thought these were for the younger and more affluent older people and not for the older and more in need.

As one volunteer over 75 years of age saw it:

> 'The only thing I find about Age Concern North City is
> that it doesn't attract the people it was designed to attract in
> the first place. I mean, to be honest, most of the people that
> go to Age Concern North City for these things are quite
> well off. They're not, they're not very hard up, they're not
> very poor but I thought Age Concern North City would
> be more for the poor people, you know.'

Age Concern North City had a trading arm selling insurance and other
financial products to the general public. It used just seven volunteers
and, at the time of the study, had experienced structural changes as
a result of the Financial Services Authority (FSA) imposing new
requirements. As a result, both staff and volunteers had to undergo
retraining and skill learning. This coincided with staff sickness and led
to a particularly stressful period for staff and volunteers as they adjusted
to the new regulatory framework. Responsibilities falling on volunteers,
as a result of the new requirements from the FSA, were generally
unwelcome. Volunteers began to feel that the underlying reason for
their volunteering – the desire to provide a friendly, personal service
to older people – was under threat from the new formal requirements
mentioned at the start of the chapter. Most crucially, volunteers felt
that the service that was required of them went against the ethos they
wanted to adopt in helping older people. As a volunteer in this service
commented:

> 'But I think it's a bit onerous asking people to do this kind
> of thing because really it's what you expect from core centre
> staff, it's sort of like turning a voluntary organisation into
> a commercial profit-seeking, you know. And that's what I
> feel it is, to my mind, it isn't sort of doing things to help the
> older people, because you have to ask all of these intrusive
> questions and I'm not happy about it.'

This case study of one charity raises specific implications for the
management and support of volunteers in a particular organisation, but
many issues are of generic interest to all volunteer-using organisations
and confirm some of the difficult aspects of public service contracting
and extending business activity.

Cooperatives as care providers

We now turn from established organisations that contract with statutory agencies to small enterprises that have been created very recently on cooperative principles to respond to opportunities presented by changes in social care funding mechanisms. Reforms in the name of 'personalisation' promise more choice and new solutions that put individuals in control of the services they need. At least 40 cooperatives have been identified as actively delivering health and social care services across England – some owned and run by their employees but others involving a range of people, including services users, carers and the local community – known as the multi-stakeholder model (Co-operatives UK, 2009). Service provision is mainly within the home care sector (Co-operatives UK, 2009). The self-help business models of co-operatives seem closely aligned with the aspirations of personalisation for sustainable, equitable outcomes and new relationships between service providers and service users.

Personalisation has been described as a philosophy, underpinned by a shift in the balance of power, responsibility and resources from state agencies to individuals (Leadbetter, 2004; Dickinson and Glasby, 2010). It is enabled by mechanisms to devolve budgetary control to the individual. The most popular option for people in receipt of payments in lieu of services has been direct employment of personal assistants. This has been called a strange hybrid of 'citizen-as-consumer-as-service-user-as-employer' (Scourfield, 2005, p 481). There is potential for exploitation in the employer–employee relationship and the employee is isolated from opportunities for training, improved status and negotiation of working conditions. Tom Shakespeare, an academic and campaigner for disability rights, has acknowledged that while direct payments are important for the independence and empowerment of disabled people who need support, there are serious dangers for carers in 'an unreflexive reliance on a servant/employer solution' (Shakespeare, 2000, p 63). Not all service users are willing or able to take employment responsibilities for personal assistants.

The Department of Health-funded *Self-Managed Care – A Co-Operative Approach* programme was intended to explore cooperative ways to overcome such individual barriers to the uptake of direct payments and individual budgets. The programme aimed to achieve this by enabling service users to gain personal control over their care while the responsibilities of organisation, training, supervision and meeting quality standards would be managed through cooperatives that could also involve informal and/or paid carers. The programme was delivered by the cooperative consultancy, Mutual Advantage. It ran from 2006 to 2009, during which time Mutual Advantage assisted five pilot projects in England to develop cooperatives, involving service users, carers or both to facilitate mutual support and to meet aspirations to improve working conditions for paid carers. Working in close collaboration with Co-operatives UK, we were able to follow up the experiences of two of the pilots after the end of that programme (see Box 5.4 for more information).

Workers Co-operative was established in 2008, in Greater Manchester, by a group of four women home care workers employed by the local authority. They were concerned about the potential impact of personalisation on their clients and some clients suggested to them that they should set up as independent carers. They wanted to be able to influence the care they provided and also to enable employees to shape the organisation they worked for. One of the founders, Helen, had a wealth of experience as a community activist and was very confident of the support she and her colleagues could access. Since the end of the programme, they have achieved registration with the Care Quality Commission, the national regulatory body for social care providers. The establishment of the cooperative took a long time and suffered many serious setbacks. Helen states "It has been a challenging and hard

Box 5.4: New cooperative care providers

User Co-operative in South London is a social care cooperative for people wanting to have reliable and consistent quality services in their community. Its inspiration was Maria, who was diagnosed with multiple sclerosis and whose condition had deteriorated so that she was assessed as needing 24-hour care, which translated into 53 hours per week. It was Maria's vision that there must be a better way than the traditional agency as their staff were not motivated, properly trained, well paid or with sufficient time to care. User Co-operative provides a model of homecare based in small local clusters, giving practical support to unpaid carers, while training and employing local people as home and personal care assistants. Maria died in 2009. Her co-founder and friend, Vera, continues as secretary with the support of Maria's husband and 10 volunteer board members.

Workers Co-operative was founded in Greater Manchester by four women local government care workers in response to a radical restructuring of the council's in-house social care service. They wanted to be able to influence the care they provided and also to enable employees to shape the organisation they worked for. One of the founders, Helen, had a wealth of experience as a community activist and was very confident of the support she and her colleagues could access. Local councillors supported the organisation but the councillor responsible for social care was replaced after the General Election in 2010 and the relationship with his successor is uncertain. Workers Co-operative received a small grant from the local authority that enabled the organisation to set up an office. They minimised costs by painting and decorating the office themselves, with help from family members, negotiating cut-price rent through contacts in the community and acquiring free materials through family and friends.

Both these cooperatives were supported by the Department of Health-funded Self-Managed Care – a Co-operative Approach programme, to support its priority to extend the uptake of direct payments and individual budgets. In particular, it was intended to attract new users to these funding mechanisms from under-represented groups who may be deterred by the perception of associated risks and burdens. The programme aimed to achieve this by enabling service users to gain personal control over their care while the responsibilities of organisation, training, supervision and meeting quality standards would be managed through cooperatives that could also involve informal and/or paid carers. The programme was delivered by the cooperative consultancy, Mutual Advantage. It ran from 2006 to 2009, during which time Mutual Advantage assisted five pilot projects to develop cooperatives involving service users, carers or both to facilitate mutual support and to meet aspirations to improve working conditions for paid carers.

struggle throughout, everything including setting up the company has been difficult." Workers Co-operative received a small grant from the local authority (although this process was prolonged) that enabled the organisation to set up an office. They minimised costs by painting and decorating the office themselves with help from family members, negotiating cut-price rent through contacts in the community and acquiring free materials through family and friends.

Helen considers that the cooperative basis of the organisation is of particular importance to the employees and also attractive to older people in the area, where there is a strong tradition of the cooperative movement. This could potentially become a key marketing focus to attract new customers. A significant constraint, however, is the local authority's provider lists, as the cooperative is not a 'preferred' provider, thereby reducing its potential customer base. The organisation is isolated as it is unique in the town. If there were other cooperatives, there could be collaboration so that, for example, care assistants could be shared to cover staff absence. Despite this isolation, the networking skills of the directors, especially Helen (gained through a lifetime of community activism), are an important resource for Workers Co-operative.

User Co-operative was established by service users and carers in a London borough and the majority of board members are service users. It is registered with the regulatory body and has begun trading with customers who receive direct payments and some self-funders. The borough is much more affluent than the northern town where Workers Co-operative is based and it is easier to attract self-funders. The founders were two women – one of whom, Maria, had multiple sclerosis and died in 2009. Maria received care from her husband but she had a very poor experience in a care home when she needed help after her husband was injured and temporally unable to care. This episode gave her the idea for User Co-operative. She contacted her friend Vera and said she needed "a pair of hands". Maria was a committed socialist and political activist all her life and the cooperative model was in line with her personal ethos and values. Maria and Vera came into contact with Co-operatives UK through Mutual Advantage and were invited to be a pilot direct payment provider.

User Co-operative developed a cluster-based operational model, where care is provided by personal assistants for a group of service users within a very small geographical location. The 'cluster' idea developed as a result of Maria's experience of having a team of 10 people care for her. It was an innovation that was adopted by some of the other pilots and is strongly advocated by Mutual Advantage. Each cluster has a part-time support worker and overheads are kept low with support workers being home based. Benefits of the cluster model include a reduction in travel expenses and time, which is important in a large Outer London borough affected by heavy traffic congestion. The cluster facilitates development of a longer-term relationship between user and carer and flexibility to cover holidays and sickness. There are currently two clusters. In principle, the cooperative would grow by developing new clusters and they are interested in expanding into the neighbouring local authority.

User Co-operative held a high-profile launch in May 2010, with banners and flyers, and as a result received some very positive coverage in the national press. Vera reflected that it had been an extremely long haul to get to that point and the cooperative "has taken over our lives" including those of her family. All Vera's work is unpaid, as is that of Maria's husband who has continued to work hard for the cooperative since her death.

The self-managed care programme demonstrated that cooperatives already operational in the area of social care are providing a collective and community-based service. The central tenets of personalisation, choice, empowerment and involvement are firmly rooted in the origins of the case studies and inform their operation and values. Customers/ users who are members can shape the service provided according to their needs. Acting in a governance role as service users, however, is extremely demanding. Employees benefit from being able to influence the organisation and there are opportunities for working in innovative ways. The cooperative founders in the case studies have extensive contacts and excellent networking skills that in other contexts would be identified with proactive, entrepreneurial behaviour to garner important resources (Dubini and Aldrich, 1991; Chell and Baines, 2000). For cooperatives, networking skills gained as unpaid community activists could have very important and positive implications for the success of their enterprises. There was heavy dependence on unpaid work and family members' support in both the cooperative case studies. With regard to volunteering, unpaid work of any kind is more contested in the case of cooperatives than in charities, community groups and other VCSOs. The unpaid work was not referred to by the cooperatives as 'volunteering' – except for the contributions of board members – although it conforms with the definition indicated in Chapter Four. This unremunerated work seems to be rather a contradiction to some interpretations of the ICA's insistence on equitable compensation for each member's labour as a statement opposing uncompensated labour, which is seen as characteristic of much less business-like VCSOs (Ridley-Duff and Bull, 2011).

Conclusion: making sense of it

Strong claims are made by and on behalf of the private, public and voluntary sectors as providers of care to people in need. In this chapter, we have explored some of the ways in which VCSOs of various kinds have become increasingly engaged in taking on care services previously provided by the state. We have considered, in particular, their relationships with state agencies, which have often been uneasy and sometimes characterised by misunderstanding. Employees, beneficiaries and volunteers have all been affected by VCSOs being contracted by government to deliver services, as well as by a shift towards a social enterprise culture. The evidence from the VCSOs in our studies was that there is enormous creativity and resourcefulness in finding ways to do things differently, as Amin (2009a) has reported of the social economy more generally. There were some instances of innovation, for example, in finding new ways of involving carers in a pioneering dementia charity and a cluster model for working with social care users in a small, user-led cooperative. Some of their stories are inspiring, but it is important to recall their day-to-day struggles, with limited funding, unresponsive public sector agencies and ever-expanding need. We should beware of exaggerating expectations of what they can do, especially in an era of austerity.

With regard to volunteering, there are enormous variations in the significance of volunteering across different kinds of VCSO and, indeed, even within individual organisations. In charities, there is generally a much more positive attitude to developing a volunteer labour force than is the case in cooperatives, for example (Ridley-Duff and Bull, 2011). For some volunteers in a long-established charity working with and for older people, the experiences reported above are consistent with evidence from other research, that more professionalised, business-like organisations can become uncomfortable for traditional volunteers. In this sense, the expansion of volunteering and the uptake of more public service provision by the VCS seem to be working against each other. On the other hand, new enterprises that are entering into care provision, as in the case of recently formed cooperatives, are sustainable only through a raft of unpaid work that is not usually labelled as 'volunteering'.

Notes

[1] CSR can take the form of avoiding negative impact on suppliers, workers or residents in communities affected by the business activities; it can also extend to philanthropic action, for example making donations of money or executive time to community projects (Carroll, 1998). Some supporters of CSR reject the association with philanthropy and emphasise the business case, for example gaining competitive advantage by appealing to the ethical values of potential customers (WBCSD, 2000).

[2] Questionnaires were posted to 290 current volunteers and 322 former volunteers in summer 2004. This produced 134 responses (a 46% response rate) from current volunteers and 87 responses (a 27% response rate) from former volunteers.

SIX

Volunteering: an articulation of caring communities

Each day, in communities across the country, people act out their vision of Britain – rejecting selfishness and embracing community. (Blair, 1999)

Big Society is all about empowering people to become actively involved in their neighbourhoods and communities to bring about the changes they know are needed. (Nick Hurd, Minister for Civil Society; source: Brewis et al 2010, p 4)

Introduction

As we noted in Chapter Five, (formal) voluntary organisations are often established to serve the needs of neighbourhoods and communities (of place as well as interest). The spatially targeted nature of their activities has recently been the focus of attention by geographers and sociologists (such as Milligan and Fyfe, 2004, 2005; Sampson et al, 2005). This is because the community/neighbourhood has re-emerged in both policy and academic circles as an important setting for many of the processes that supposedly shape social identity and life chances, including local social relations, social cohesion and social capital (Forrest and Kearns, 2001; Galster, 2001). But 'community' – in common with volunteering – is not a simple descriptive word but one with a shifting and disputed meaning (Byrne, 1999; Galster, 2001; Sprigings and Allen, 2005). Subjectively, areas, neighbourhood and community mean different things to different people at different times; each individual's activities, networks and travel patterns shape their concept of neighbourhood and community (Massey, 1994).

Since the 1990s, policy measures in the UK (as elsewhere) have sought to address the contextual effects of neighbourhood; principally, the social consequences of an increasing concentration of disadvantaged people (Amin, 2005; Bauld et al, 2005) and 'the part that place and space play in exclusion' (Lee, 1999, p 483). Voluntary work is seen as contributing to community/neighbourhood regeneration through developing social capital (Putnam, 2000; Forrest and Kearns, 2001). In this chapter, we explore the role that volunteering plays as an articulation of caring communities – looking at the work of volunteers and voluntary organisations by presenting a case study of volunteering in a place-based community – Brightville. The case study community of Brightville has been beset by economic deprivation, but has retained a strong sense of community. After this brief introduction, the chapter is divided into four further sections. The next section explores what we understand as 'community'; and this is followed by a review of communities and public policy. The subsequent section examines volunteering and communities, highlighting the case study of Brightville (see Chapter One). The final section presents some concluding comments.

Community studies

Understanding communities has long enthralled both social scientists[1] and policy makers; but what we understand as community in post-war Britain has changed, from being place based with studies of spatially bound communities to recognising that communities can also be framed around identity and interest (Willmott, 1986, 1989; Chapter Seven); these imagined communities can be transnational (O'Reilly, 2000). In this section, we review the field of community studies, which remains contested, with both critics and advocates. In particular, we begin by focusing on studies of place-based communities, which were strongly influenced by the monographs of social anthropologists. In Chapter Seven, we focus on communities of identity and interest.

In a review of 50 years of community studies, Crow (2002) points to the 1950s and 1960s as the period in the UK that was dominated by traditional community studies; this approach went out of fashion in the 1970s. Since the 1980s, community studies have reappeared in a number of forms, including locality studies of spatial divisions of labour (Cooke, 1989). Community studies began in the US with the Chicago School. In the UK, they can be traced back to the work of the Institute of Community Studies,[2] which was founded by Michael Young and Peter Willmott in 1954 in Bethnal Green, East London (Crow, 2002).[3] Bethnal Green featured in three important studies undertaken by the Institute, which revealed the importance of the extended family (Townsend, 1957; Young and Willmott; 1957; Willmott and Young, 1960). Writing in 1985, Willmott commented that the Institute aimed to undertake research to understand society and social policy and publish in accessible, readable formats (Willmott, 1985). But unlike other community studies, the Institute focused on a single institution – the family – rather than exploring the inter-relationships of social institutions in a given locality (Young and Willmott, 1957).

The early studies were largely micro-sociological studies of mainly working-class communities. For example, the pioneering work of Young and Willmott (1957) in Bethnal Green focused on the extended family, embedded in a stable, predominately working-class community, with great neighbourliness and communal solidarity (Willmott, 1957; see also Frankenberg, 1969). Informal neighbouring and care were observed within kin groups by Young and Willmott in Bethnal Green and in a peripheral housing estate (Greenleigh in Essex) where Bethnal Greeners were relocated to. This informal neighbouring has traditionally been key to the wellbeing of communities. But Sprigings and Allen (2005, pp 398, 407) suggest that the inter-household cooperation and community care applauded by Young and Willmott took place because of self-interest and necessity rather than choice and reinforced gender stereotypes.

Frankenberg's (1969) book *Communities in Britain* consists of a detailed analysis of a series of community studies in urban and rural areas across the British Isles. His analysis highlighted the complexity of community life, of the importance of social networks and informal and formal voluntary work. Some community studies have provided a detailed description of the VCS in rural and urban areas. Williams' (1969) study of Gosforth in the Lake District, for example, included an examination of volunteer roles in formal voluntary organisations, which were deeply gendered and classed. He identified 31 formal voluntary organisations, which included the Agricultural Society, the Girl Guides, the British Legion, the Wrestling Academy and the Reading Room Committee; within them, there was a clear social stratification in volunteer roles, with trustees and chairs of organisations drawn from the 'gentry' who filled over half the posts of chair, vice chair or vice president.

In a very different community, a mining community in the West Riding of Yorkshire, which Dennis et al (1957) called Ashton, VCSOs were either connected to the colliery or run independently within the community and again participation in these organisations was very gendered. Those VCSOs linked to the colliery included the trade union, the rugby league club, the cricket team and St John Ambulance. The only voluntary association in which women participated fully was the Women's Section of the Labour Party that had a hundred members (see Frankenburg, 1969).

Local authority suburban housing estates, built to house families following slum clearance, have also been studied, with authors observing how families adjusted to life in their new neighbourhoods, along with their relationships with the residents of neighbouring communities, especially middle–class estates (such as Kuper, 1953; Durant, 1959). Durant (1959), for example, examined the households and the social networks and voluntary organisations that developed in Watling, London. The demographic profile of these new estates was very different from the communities that people had left, with very few older people. Most households comprised families with children, with one wage earner as job opportunities for women resident in the new estates were more limited (Young and Willmott, 1957; Durant, 1959).

Residents associations were formed and community centres were often built on these estates (Kuper, 1953; Durant, 1959). In addition to mapping the use of the community centre, Durant (1959) identified a large number of groups that developed on the estate, including an over-sixties club, which attracted most of the older people resident in Watling. Groups for children, women, sport and hobbies thrived and whist drives were a regular feature of Watling life (see also Kuper, 1953). Whist drives were popular in the 1930s: Priestley (1934, 2009) in his book *English Journey*, described attending one.

Kuper contributed to a book in 1953 on the residents of one road – Braydon Road – on a peripheral housing estate in Coventry, which he described as 'a working class suburb' (Kuper, 1953, p 7). Kuper used empirical description to map social relationships from the perspective of the street and the city. He was also concerned with the impact of the planning of urban neighbourhoods on social life. The physical environment, he thought, could impact on local ties, including the configuration of houses that were clustered in cul de sacs, impeding people seeing and interacting with their neighbours (Kuper, 1953, p 115). The residents who moved to Braydon Road were migrants to Coventry who moved from different parts of the UK in search of paid employment. Kuper (1953, p 43) looked at neighbouring – the sort of help people gave each other 'in times of need', associated with moving house or when someone was ill, for example. He noted that a number of churches had been built and some of the Blaydon Road residents sent their children to Sunday School (1953, p 120). Like Watling, there was a community centre and a social club, which had been established in 1950 (1953, p 115). At the time of the research, they had existed for a couple of years. The community centre was located in a converted farmhouse and it was essentially an adult club, but it had a youth centre annex (1953, p 123). The social club had 416 male members and about 100 affiliates and women accompanied their husbands (1953, p 125). Membership of the community centre was open to both men and women and there were 95 male and 199 female members (1953, p 123). Kuper concluded that the social club resembled more a community centre in the sense of providing channels to draw families together in the immediate locality, while the community centre was an adult club with more limited and specialised interests. Like Watling, there was an active Old Age Pensioners Association but because the residents of Braydon Road were of working age, they did not attend. The residents were, however, attracted to other associations; one in four were active in The Sick and Dividend, the British Legion, the Darts Club, the Angling Association or the Allotments Association – all were male dominated (1953, p 126).

The first occupants of these local authority estates found life very different to that in their former neighbourhoods; a number of authors noted that relocation brought with it increased living costs that in some cases put a severe strain on household finances because of increased rents. There was pressure to buy household items and travel expenses were incurred for the journey to work (see Young and Willmott, 1957; Durant, 1959). For some households, the costs proved prohibitive and they were forced to leave. That said, for these 'pioneer' households relocation to these estates was actively sought, in contrast to numerous – but not all – households who are placed on these estates today. For them, relocation is not always a choice but is forced on them because of their adverse circumstances; they do not choose to live there, their placement is a response to their demise.

In an article in 1969, Stacey argued for the abandonment of 'community', which she regarded as a non-concept. Instead, she appealed for the study of local social systems and connectedness in 'localities' (Stacey, 1969, pp 137, 140), which she undertook in Banbury (compare Wenger's work in North Wales: Wenger, 2001). Three decades later, two writers in the US – Putnam (2000) and Sampson et al (2005) – reignited the debate on community and social networks.

In the 1980s, the ESRC funded a research programme, the Changing Urban and Regional System (CURS), in the UK, which was coordinated by Professor Philip Cooke. Seven projects were funded, with a series of locality studies (rather than community studies), including Middlesbrough, Thanet and Swindon (Cooke, 1989). The object of study was the urban and regional system and a regional political economy approach was adopted; the spatial scale of study was larger than the community.

The community study method is used today and not necessarily with place-based communities (see Chapter Seven). Writing in 2002, Crow argued that the community study method was still of relevance in illuminating social life (see Box 6.1). Dennis et al (1969) also commented that the focus on social relationships within the community tends to obscure the fact that sets of relationships do extend beyond the community, in both space and time.

Box 6.1: Community study method

The community study method:

- has the capability of 'placing' sociological arguments;
- has the capacity to illustrate the meaning of macro-level trends for people's everyday lives;
- has the capacity to facilitate holistic treatments of social relations through its emphasis on context;
- is accessible, achieved through a narrative style.

Source: Crow (2002)

Community and public policy

Area-based programmes in the UK had their origin in the 1960s and were based on the idea that problems are local and social (Lupton, 2003, p 9). In 1969, the Community Development Project (CDP) programme was launched by the Home Office as an action-research project initially in 12 areas of social deprivation (CDP Information and Intelligence Unit, 1974). These were neighbourhoods of 3,000 to 15,000 people and included Benwell, in Newcastle upon Tyne. Each project involved a small group of professional workers and researchers. The emphasis in CDPs on research meant that they produced a range of important material, both about the nature of community work and about the social, political and economic condition of particular areas (see Benwell CDP, 1978). By 1974, the Home Office had largely given up on the projects and they were wound up in 1976.

Moving forward, it was under the New Labour administrations of 1997-2010 that the link between individuals, place and social exclusion was forcefully made (SEU, 1998, p 23). As a result, policy measures were introduced that sought to address the contextual effects of neighbourhood; principally, the social consequences of an increasing concentration of disadvantaged people (Lund, 1999; Kearns and Parkinson, 2001; Gripaois, 2002; Kearns and Parkes, 2003; Bauld, et al, 2005) and 'the part that place and space play in exclusion' (Lee, 1999, p 483). 'Community' was used to discuss poor or disadvantaged neighbourhoods rather than middle-class neighbourhoods (Taylor, 2002), for addressing problems rather than focusing on community assets.

As was noted above, under New Labour the concept of 'social capital' became enormously influential as an explanation for why some communities work better than others and it drew on the work of Putnam. Social capital, according to Putnam's (2000) much-cited analysis, consists of the networks, norms and trust that enable individuals and groups to engage in cooperative activity. In the UK, volunteering is seen by policy makers as an important indicator of social capital (Haezwindt, 2003; Ruston, 2003) and a key role was identified for community groups in community regeneration (Haezwindt, 2003). For some commentators, it is far from evident that collective capacity building is compatible with developing the capacities of excluded individuals (Shucksmith, 2000). Williams (2003) argues that a culture of engagement in groups is relatively alien to most people in deprived communities, unlike one-to-one aid.

Ideas of community rested on the notion that they offer resources, social glue, alternative ideas and knowledge, which are now seen as essential to society (Taylor, 2002). Putnam's approach was used by policy makers to justify their agenda of encouraging individuals to volunteer – especially the strategy to broaden the volunteer base – as seen in a series of New Labour policies, such as Public Service Arrangement (PSA) targets[4] (Williams, 2003) and spatially targeted schemes, such as New Deal for Communities and Sure Start, which aim to address the contextual effects of neighbourhood (see Chapter Three). Against Putnam, Sampson and colleagues (2005) argue that collective civic engagement has changed rather than declined and is organisational rather than interpersonal in nature. They place emphasis on conjoint capability; an active sense of collective engagement; residents of a community working through the VCS to solve problems.

As we have noted in Chapter One of this book, a strong and recurrent theme in the coalition government's emerging policies on the Big Society is neighbourhood and community, with the idea of 'your square mile' or community (www.thebigsociety.co.uk/square-mile.html). The theme is very much change from within and building on existing community assets. As services are cut, local communities will have to play a bigger 'mutual aid' role. In the following section, we present a case study of a community project that was undertaken during the New Labour administration.

Brightville: a case study

Introducing Brightville

In Chapter Three, we used empirical description from volunteers who gave time to help social welfare voluntary organisations active in Brightville to examine people's pathways into volunteering. Today, Brightville covers two wards: one aligns with the old village and the other is composed of two social housing estates constructed in the post-war period. It is made up of 3,696 households and 7,247 people. The population is overwhelmingly white working-class British (ONS, 2001 Census).

Had we been undertaking our study of Brightville in the 1950s, the lives of our working-class volunteers would have had much in common with the residents of Bethnal Green, Ashton or Watling, which we described earlier in this chapter. When we began undertaking research in Brightville in 2004, its economic base had been eroded. In common with so many smaller industrial towns, those industries and services that were once the cornerstone of urban living had been depleted and local residents had borne the brunt of social deprivation and unemployment. The raison d'être for its growth in the 19th century had gone. This economic base had been diverse but short lived. In the mid-19th century, Brightville comprised 'a hamlet and scattered village … principally occupied by colliers and framework knitters' (Kelly's Directory, 1855). D.H. Lawrence (2007, p 13) set his novel *The Rainbow* in the area, and he recorded that 'about 1840, a canal was constructed across the Meadows of Marsh Farm … a colliery was sunk on the other side of the canal'.

The economic growth that began in the 19th century resulted in people migrating to the area in search of job opportunities and the population increased from 2,129 in 1851 to 6,135 in 1931 (Harvey, 2005). Rows of terraced housing (two rooms downstairs, two bedrooms upstairs, with an outside lavatory) were constructed. These houses were originally rented but many are now owner occupied and have inside bathrooms (Figure 6.1). Kelly's Directory for 1936 lists that the community supported 29 general shops, 17 pubs, 14 off-licences, 13 butchers and three grocers in Brightville. The bulk of the housing stock in the old village is still terraced and it has been augmented by a limited number of inter-war and post-war semi-detached houses. The old village of Brightville still has some local shops (four takeaways, three off-licences, two general stores, two newsagents, a grocer and a chemist), four pubs and a number of employers who recruit from

Figure 6.1: Nineteenth-century Brightville

Irontown. One of our key informants, chief executive of the Economic Development Partnership, who is a board member of Community Centre and Community Project and once lived in the old village, described his old home as "A typical back-to-back terrace, no front garden, straight onto the street, and I knew all my neighbours ... very neighbourly place to live." He went on to comment that he thought that "that style of housing encourages neighbourliness, in a way".

The village was radically transformed in the post-war period by the construction of two large local authority housing estates on farmland on the eastern edge of the village (Irontown north ward) to serve Irontown. They were built by the local authority; one in the immediate post-war years (Figures 6.2, 6.3), the other in the 1970s and 1980s (Figure 6.4).

Figure 6.2: Post-war social housing estate Brightville

Figure 6.3: 1980s social housing Brightville

Figure 6.4: Post war social housing estate Brightville, derelict shopping centre

The houses were largely semi-detached properties with two reception rooms, a kitchen, three bedrooms, a bathroom and a large garden. When they were first built, they were much valued and the first estate had a parade of shops. By the 1990s, these shops were struggling and, by 2004, they were all boarded up (Figure 6.4) and have recently been demolished. The estate has a neglected feel. The new estate has one community building where the Community Project runs a luncheon club twice a week (Figures 6.5 and 6.6). The local authority no longer

Figure 6.5: Community Centre Brightville

Figure 6.6: Community Project offices in old Brightville

has direct responsibility for the housing stock; this now rests with a housing association. Today, 60% of Brightville's housing is owner occupied, 36% is public housing and 4% is private rented (Experian, www.business-strategies.co.uk). We now turn to hear firsthand about what it is like to live and work in the community.

Jean (Box 6.2) was not born in Brightville; she was born and raised on a farm some miles from Irontown and then "went to live in London and when I came back, I came here [Brightville]. That was a real culture shock. All the houses were boarded up and it looked terrible." When we interviewed Jean she reflected on the 12 years she had lived there; first as a tenant and then as an owner, through the Right to Buy scheme, which enabled council tenants to buy their homes for sums of money that reflected the total amount of rent they had paid for the property. She knows that the new estate has many problems; her house "is not much but it is mine." At the time of the interview with us, the housing association had a regeneration scheme under way to improve the newer houses and she had mixed views about the whole process: "Well, I'm a private owner, you see. It still concerns me the things that they're doing because obviously it takes away the value of my house." But she also said that "It's much better now. The whole estate is improving day by day" (Figure 6.4). While Jean appreciates how the housing stock is being improved, there remain virtually no shops, pubs or community facilities on the two estates except for a small community centre (see Figure 6.5).

Box 6.2: Jean

Jean is in her fifties, has lived in Brightville for over a decade and is embedded in active kin and community networks. She lives on the newer part of the estate. Jean is a 'doer'; she can be relied on to get things done. She knows a lot of people, and speaks to people – she has recruited neighbours to be volunteers while standing at the bus stop! Jean like many on the estate relies on public transport. She works (for wages) for the Community Project, as a team support worker, and as we noted in Chapter Three, she is a multiple volunteer, including volunteering for the Community Project. Her other unpaid work includes being an active member of the residents committee for the new estate and in local politics; she was elected a local councillor a couple of years ago. Jean is secretary of the over 50 forum for the whole of Irontown and Brightville. She therefore gives her time to the community – formally and informally – in a number of ways as she has been made to feel welcome, and she reciprocates by 'giving back' in the community.

However, she feels very positive about the people who live on the estate: "People are so nice. Most of them are so genuine. You get the odd ones that couldn't care less. But you get those anywhere." She then went on to say, "But it's not the area, it's not the majority, it's the minority. Just those few that just don't care. There's been all sorts of drug abuse. Some things have been stamped out. It's only a few." Other interviewees expressed resentment that the estate was being used as a 'sink estate' by the local authority. The estate residents in particular felt that this policy had negatively affected their lives (Hardill et al, 2010). Jean has been motivated to do something and for two and a half years she has been active in the Residents' Association: "Through the regeneration, there's been a lot of problems. And people don't know where to go or who to turn to. A lot of people have got problems."

On and off the map

Brightville, then, is very much a place-based community,[5] with low levels of in- and out-migration. Those who do migrate to the area are either 'placed' there from across the local authority district on the social housing estates, or they 'choose' to live in the old village largely because property prices are lower than in Irontown. The flows of people are overwhelmingly white. The chief executive of the Economic Development Partnership 'chose' to live in the old village when he bought his first house: 'I lived there actually when I left home because it's where I could buy a cheap house." He bought a derelict house and did it up (key informant interview). The property prices reflect the fact that Brightville is not a 'good address' (Box 6.3). Indeed, it has had a 'reputation' since Fred (aged 74) was a boy. People move out when they 'get on'. The chief executive of Irontown's Economic Development Partnership left when he was able to buy a better property: "When you make it, you leave Brightville. So when my job got better I bought a semi in Irontown."

There are families who have lived in Brightville for several generations. Lucy, the manager of the Community Centre, has lived in the old village of Brightville all her life, as do her daughter and grandchild: "I was brought up in Brightville. I know the people." She feels the area "is great. I think there is a great community spirit." She identifies with the people; she is one of them by birth but also by choice: "I choose to work here – and live here. I live five to ten minutes away [from work]."

Although Brightville and Irontown have coalesced to form a continuous urban area, interviewees resident in both Irontown and

Box 6.3: Brightville

"… had a bit of a stigma, but not as 'bad' as it is today." (Fred, aged 74 years, born in Brightville)

But stigma in the mind of "outsiders … [there is an] invisible line by Trinity Church." (key informant interview)

"This area is long established – it is very insular – and there are low expectations." (key informant interview)

"When I work in [county town] you sort of tell work colleagues where you live and they are horrified." (key informant interview)

Brightville thought of them as separate communities. There is "an invisible line by the Church" that is the boundary between Brightville and Irontown (Lucy, former volunteer and now manager of the Community Centre). Sally, who volunteers for the Family Centre in Brightville, commented that Brightville "is very closed". It is not always a good idea to highlight a Brightville address largely because of what 'outsiders' think. When Marie (local stakeholder) moved to Brightville she was told: "Don't put down that you live in Brightville else you'll never get a job. Leave Brightville off your address." Marie differentiates between the old village and the estates: "The estate was put down all the time."

Some of these feelings relate to the geography of Brightville, as it is the 'end of the line' so to speak; buses terminate there and there is no through road, so people do not pass through Brightville en route to other places. To the east and south of Brightville there is still farmland. It is 'off the map' and this helps to mould feelings of insularity. The Community Centre runs courses that are open to people beyond Brightville. Lucy, the manager, talked about people from outside the area having "preconceptions of what Brightville is like", which the Centre is "trying to knock down". There is reluctance on the part of some people wanting to come to Brightville: "We have problems sometimes getting people past the border of Irontown. If we can get them to the Centre it is fine and then the myth is dispelled."

Community engagement in Brightville

As we noted in Chapter Three, a number of social welfare VCSOs are active in Brightville and they attract volunteers from Brightville and

Irontown. Under New Labour, Brightville benefited from the resources of two national government regeneration schemes: one was a volunteer-using Government Project that we studied, which offers help to young families[6] (Box 6.4; Figure 6.6). This is located on the edge of the social housing estate. Of the four volunteer-using organisations, the two located in the heart of the old village of Brightville were established by residents (Community Project; Box 6.5) or former residents (Community Centre; Box 6.6). A former Brightville resident, who now runs the Irontown business-led Economic Development Partnership, has remained committed to the community. He was inspired to establish the Community Centre after he heard a lecture, 'Learning pays', and bid for funds from a coalfields community regeneration initiative. He thinks

Box 6.4: Government Project

- Assists families and young children to be successful and confident in their lives.
- Paid workers: 22.
- Volunteers: about 27, plus 'parent helpers' – those who cannot make the commitment demanded of volunteers.
- Funding: central government.
- Established: 2003.

"We are dealing with enhancing people's lives ... pick up skills and knowledge that will help ... get a reasonable job". (Government Project manager)

Volunteering as "a progression route." (Government Project manager)

Box 6.5: Community Project

- Community service organisation: luncheon club, befriending, shopping, gardening and DIY and so on.
- Paid workers: 12.
- Volunteers: 103 registered (43 male, 60 female), 45 active.
- Funding: diverse, including county council, primary care trust.
- Established: 1992.

"You listen to volunteers and board members and they have ... a kind of selfless classic Victorian philanthropic attitude." (chair of Community Project)

"Provides a support mechanism for people who have not been in paid work." (chief executive of Community Project)

Box 6.6: Community Centre

- Community adult education centre, with a crèche and out-of-school kids club.
- Paid workers: five (plus about 30 tutors, five to six paid support workers, some of whom used to be volunteers, and 5-6 crèche workers).
- Volunteers: pool of three to four, current manager was once a volunteer.
- Funding: European Social Fund.
- Established: 1997.

"We make learning the core and build around that." (chief executive of Economic Development Partnership, who is a board member of Community Centre and Community Project)

that the Community Centre has "become a bit of an institution really in Brightville", but the Community Centre's funding base is insecure, "We managed by the skin of our teeth to keep it open."

> 'Give people a chance and it's incredible what they can do. I think that's really what the centre's been about – providing a focus for that sort of activity. And really providing whatever it is that an individual needs to break out, really.' (chief executive, Economic Development Partnership)

Second, the Community Project began as 'fourth sector' community engagement (Williams, 2003) when Brightville women – including Laura – recognised a local need and began a luncheon club (for a fuller discussion, see Chapter Three; Box 6.5; Schervish and Havens, 2002). Two years later, core funding was secured and the luncheon club became a formal voluntary organisation. The Community Project aims to "nurture the willingness to help others and support those who need confidence to take their first steps into volunteering, training and employment" (Community Project manager). The Community Project has been successful in attracting funding from a number of sources, but in so doing has diversified its functions and geographical area of service delivery. As a consequence, it has changed its name from Community Project Brightville to Community Project Irontown, "to show that some of our services are accessible to people across Irontown" (chief executive, Community Project), but has retained the word 'community' in its title. The chair of the Community Project describes the volunteer work of the Community Project as "a kind of selfless classic Victorian philanthropic attitude".

The chief executive worked in Brightville before she ran the Community Project. She was employed by the county council delivering community education projects. Then, in 1994, that funding stream ended and she applied for and got a part-time post at the Community Project as a community development worker. Her post was funded by a SRB[7] project. She is totally committed to the community and said of her job at the Community Project: "I wouldn't swap it for the world. No. Not at all." When she described its work in Brightville, it was in terms of meeting an unmet need:

> 'We can offer services to people that need them and we have the passion and I think that's the difference. And we have the emotion and passion. Sometimes a bit too much emotion. We do get too involved. But I think having the passion and drive, you have to have it. And everybody in the organisation works in the same way, which is wonderful. You couldn't ask for a better place, really.'

That passion for making a difference was also expressed by other paid staff, trustees and volunteers. However, the Community Project has become more dependent on public service contracts (see Chapter Five).

A third organisation, the volunteer-using Government Project, began in rented premises on the western edge of Brightville and then moved to purpose-built accommodation in the heart of the most deprived part of the community, the oldest post-war social housing estate. The accommodation includes a range of community facilities. We interviewed Pauline before the Centre was built and she felt that "when their coffee shop opens, that will be the heart of the community". Since it has opened, for some residents on the estates it certainly plays an important social role in their lives (such as the Parents Club for women and the Bacon Butty Club for men).

That said, its remit is tightly centred on improving people's life chances by using volunteering as a vehicle for preparing people for paid work. The Government Project (see Box 3.2) is part of a national, large-scale, government-driven and-funded initiative started by New Labour that at the time of writing (autumn 2010) is still supported by the coalition government. The Government Project involves volunteers as one aspect of its main remit, in contrast to the three social welfare VCSOs in the study. Paid workers suggest "volunteering opportunities" to Government Project parents (local stakeholder interview; see Parsons and Broadbridge, 2004). Only those families with young children resident in certain postcodes are helped. One paid worker (Government

Project manager) commented that "some other Government Projects have not involved members of the community in the same way".

The fourth organisation, Family Charity (Box 6.7), is in freehold premises on the north-western edge of Brightville. It is the oldest of the four voluntary organisations and was established in 1989 by social work professionals new to Irontown, who identified a need in Brightville and Irontown. The work of the Family Charity is confidential, undertaken "in partnership with statutory organisations" (Family Charity volunteer organiser). It is invisible work as it takes place in people's homes and contrasts with the high visibility of the Government Project, which from the perspective of paid staff in the VCSOs seems to be awash with funds when compared with the limited resources of the Community Centre and Family Centre: "Our work is preventative and is therefore difficult for other organisations to understand and very hard to measure" (Family Centre volunteer organiser). An uncertain future because of funding issues was described by local stakeholders at the Community Centre and Family Centre and the paid workers at the Community Project stressed that their jobs were the result of successful grant applications written by the Community Project chief executive.

The volunteers

Volunteers active in Brightville are drawn from Brightville and Irontown, as we discussed in Chapter Three. They are active in the community for different reasons, but both groups discern a 'community spirit'; they recognise that there is a strong sense of belonging – of rootedness to place – to a village with a "bad address", with a "bit of a stigma" (Fred; Box 6.3), whether one is born there or moved there. This sense of belonging results in some locals giving time to the community by volunteering. Lucy (Brightville resident) now has a managerial job

---

Box 6.7: Family Charity

- Family support organisation offering volunteer home visiting support to families under stress where there is at least one child under five years of age.
- Paid workers: three.
- Volunteers: 63 (almost all are women).
- Funding: social services; the Community Fund.
- Established: 1989.

"Our work is preventative, and is therefore difficult for other organisations to understand and very hard to measure." (volunteer organiser)

at the Community Centre and could leave, but the "great community spirit" is part of the reason why she still lives there. Pippa (Brightville resident) recognises that there is a downside – nosey neighbours – but people do "look out for each other". When Claire (Brightville resident) started volunteering for the Family Centre, she specifically requested a family outside Brightville because "I know a lot of people. They'd see me going in and out, and it's confidential so I didn't want anyone within Brightville." One of her families has since moved to Brightville, but this is all right as "she knows nobody". Miranda, like a number of people who live in Irontown, is drawn to volunteer in Brightville. Miranda thinks the locals have "hearts of gold", and asks for Brightville families to visit.

For another Brightville resident, Laura, volunteering in the community represents a substantial time commitment for her and dominates her life; she spends four days per week undertaking formal voluntary work for three organisations and a club, all active in Brightville. Laura is not 'local' – she moved to Brightville when she married – but has a great sense of belonging to Brightville. She has been volunteering for the Family Charity for six years and takes on one family at a time, committing about two hours per week. She also helps with a local toddler group (linked to the Family Charity) for two hours per week, as well as being a befriender through the Community Project for a further two hours per week. Finally, she runs 'cooking on a budget' described as 'a voluntary group for the community' in a church hall in Brightville. She has also established a football club for young boys. She told us, "With me being classed as disabled, it gives me a bit of a boost to say that at least I can do something."

Conclusion

The focus of this chapter has been community, a subject that has been of interest to both academics and policy makers for some considerable time. Academics and policy makers have tended to focus on working-class communities, with academics observing everyday life, studying nuclear families and their wider kin networks and the neighbourhood social networks. As Crow (2002) noted, community studies as a methodological tool offers social scientists the capability of 'placing' sociological arguments, along with the capacity to illustrate the meaning of macro-level trends for people's everyday lives. In the largely white, working-class community of Brightville, despite socioeconomic change, the commitment to community, as evidenced by people giving time to others such as helping out neighbours, is still strong.

For the last decade, the community has been an important focus for public policy. Levitas (2000, p 191) argued that community became the central collective abstraction of New Labour, which had an increasingly communitarian mindset (Fyfe, 2005). Community under New Labour was seen as a space of 'opportunity, responsibility, employability and inclusion' (Levitas, 2000, p 191).[8] New Labour's Third Way was about renewing and reviving communities and voluntary work – active citizenship – was seen as playing an important role in bringing about civic renewal. Civil society became a useful tool for New Labour because it was seen as the arena that would enable individuals and by extension the community to improve their 'performance' (Hodgson, 2004, p 141). Voluntary organisations were seen as the seedbed of civic virtue and were placed at the heart of the decision-making process across a range of policy agendas, at a number of spatial scales (Hodgson, 2004).

With the coalition government, an important theme in the Big Society agenda is about making communities work better, in ensuring survival in times of economic austerity, with communities becoming more active in the co-production of services (see Chapter Eight). We noted at the beginning of this chapter that community studies was born in Chicago and it is therefore appropriate that we end by citing a recent study of community life in Chicago undertaken by Sampson et al (2005). They argued that collective civic engagement has changed rather than declined and is organisational rather than interpersonal in nature; perhaps indicating that in times of need, in some communities, 'helping out' survives. They place emphasis on conjoint capability; an active sense of collective engagement; residents of a community working through the VCS to solve problems.

Notes

[1] Both sociologists and anthropologists have undertaken community studies using both ethnography and participant observation.

[2] There was also a tradition of colonial anthropology with studies by colonial administrators in East Africa.

[3] The Institute of Community Studies was renamed the Young Foundation in 2005.

[4] PSAs detail the aims and objectives of New Labour departments for a three-year period. Such agreements also described how targets would be achieved and how performance against these targets would be measured. PSAs included 'building more cohesive, empowered and active communities'.

[5] We recognise that the notion of communities of place is contested (see, for example, Byrne, 1999; Sprigings and Allen, 2005) and communities are not just spatial but also can be constructed around identity and interest.

[6] From 2006 to 2010, the community received funding for a resident-led partnership group to lead the development and delivery of the funded Safer Stronger Communities Programme.

[7] The SRB was introduced in 1994. It combined a number of previously separate programmes designed to bring about economic, physical and social regeneration in local areas. Its main purpose was to act as a catalyst for regeneration in the sense that it would attract other resources from the private, public and voluntary sectors in order to bring about improvements in local areas to the quality of life of local people.

[8] Levitas highlighted the ambiguity and nebulousness of community within political discourse as different scales of geographic community are targeted, from local communities or neighbourhoods to rather wider constituencies of local government.

SEVEN

Volunteering: caring for people like me

One of the most important tasks for twenty-first century Britain is to unlock the talents and potential of all its citizens. Everybody has a valuable contribution to make, throughout their lives. Unless we encourage older people to remain actively engaged in socially valued activity, whether paid or unpaid, everybody in Britain will miss out on the benefits of their experience and social commitment. (Tony Blair, cited in Cabinet Office, 2000, p 3)

[O]lder volunteers are more likely to be involved in groups connected with religion, with hobbies and with the elderly, and less likely to be involved in those connected with children's education, youth activities and sport. (Davis Smith, 2000, p 92)

Introduction

In Chapter Six, we began looking at volunteering in communities and noted that 'community' can have meanings beyond designating individuals who share a particularly geographical space. In his seminal work *Bowling Alone*, Putnam (2000) highlights how a wide range of communities – the Brightville community (of Chapter Six) being one, but also the Scout community, the iPhone community, the Christian Aid community, the Peterborough United football supporting community and so on – give their members a sense of belonging. These communities are embedded to a greater or lesser extent in some geographic locality, but all share in common a sense of shared experience, shared norms and shared values among their members. Members of such communities may become active within them, give time and effort to support them, just as members of a village, town or suburban community may also do. Community can play a crucial symbolic role in generating people's sense of belonging (Crow and Allan, 1994, p 6); which resonates with Putnam's notion of social capital.

In order to understand these communities that coalesced around interest, we first go back to the work of Hillery, who in 1955 reviewed 94 different definitions of the term 'community'. In reviewing this, Hillery argued that they could be divided into two main groups: those that saw community as being largely a territorial term and those that saw community as being based on social network relations. In this latter group, we find the genesis of the notion of 'communities of interest'. This notion was further realised by urban theorist Webber, who in 1964 argued that in rapidly growing American cities, friendships and social groups were being created and maintained at a distance and that new communities were emerging on the basis of professional groupings and other interest-based themes. These newly urbanised Americans had access to transportation and communication technology, which made such communities viable prospects.[1] At the end of the 1960s in the UK, Stacey (1969) argued for the abandonment of community (of place), which she regarded as a non-concept. Instead, she appealed for the study of local social systems and connectedness in 'localities' (1969, pp 137, 140), which she undertook in Banbury (compare Wenger's work in North Wales: Wenger, 2001).

Lee and Newby (1983) consolidated Hillery's (1955) work to suggest a three-element conception of community – two of which are geographically constituted, to a greater or lesser extent. The final, though, considers community as a type of relationship, with no geographical meaning at all, where some sense of identity is shared between individuals who may have never met. For VCSOs embedded in communities of place, there is the chance for those giving their time and effort to the organisation to meet with the recipients of their care. While this may also be the case in a number of organisations embedded in both 'communities of interest' and identity, in many cases those that the volunteering is benefiting may be many miles, even continents, away from those giving their time and effort to support them, who themselves may be a group of individuals located in many different localities. The community is thus 'imagined' (Anderson, 1991), in that it is the shared sense of purpose and belonging that the volunteers have in common, rather than any shared locality.

This brings us back to the later work of Willmott (1986, 1987, 1989), on whose work with Michael Young at the Institute of Community Studies in Bethnall Green we highlighted in Chapter Six. Willmott argued that community entails individuals feeling that they have something in common with other individuals. Within this definition, he felt it useful to distinguish between the territorial community whose members live in a particular area and the interest community whose members have something in common that they wish to share. He felt that the two concepts of community were not mutually exclusive, although interest communities are often dispersed, as previous theorists suggested. Place and community groups can coincide, as in the case of mining villages (Dennis et al, 1969).

The term 'interest community' – or community of interest – has been adopted throughout the English-speaking world (Willmott, 1989). An alternative term – 'interest group' – is sometimes used. It is recognised that what is shared in such a grouping of people is more than 'interest', as that word is commonly understood; it can also cover characteristics as varied as ethnic origin, religion, politics, occupation, leisure pursuit and sexual propensity. It is applied, for instance, to the black community, the Jewish community and the lesbian community (Willmott, 1989, p 2).

Willmott (1986) also talked about 'communities of attachment'. Like Webber had for the US, he argued that modern communications and greater residential and personal mobility have encouraged the development of dispersed communities, or networks, at the expense of local ones (Willmott, 1986, p 87). People increasingly interact with others who do not reside in the same localities or neighbourhoods. Willmott went on to argue that these developments represent a greater choice of where to live, where to work, with whom to mix and that specialised interests and tastes can more readily be accommodated within larger catchment areas (and populations). He termed these spatially dispersed communities 'communities of attachment'. This third strand – communities of attachment – exists where there is interaction and a sense of identity. These communities are less personalised interest communities such as work communities. Work communities are dispersed in terms of their homes and residential areas – as can be self-help groups, which have a shared recognition of a problem and shared efforts to do something about it.

Dispersed interest communities in which people participate are fairly loose groupings; their membership changes and people's levels of participation fluctuate (Willmott, 1986, p 88), and the reinforcement of continuing contact is lacking. These groupings are loose-knit networks rather than communities of attachment and include a group that come together to play or watch sport – or as we argue in this chapter, volunteers who are drawn to help a spatially dispersed community of interest, like Age UK.

Writers exploring the sociology of identity have played an important role in illuminating non-place forms of community, which are a key feature of contemporary life. More recently, O'Reilly (2000) studied the British on the Costa del Sol. She argues that they represent the reconstitution of community in another context. This large and fluid group of expatriates is a community loosely formed around ethnicity. They have numerous British-run clubs and social groups, which tend not to have the word British in their title; indeed, the largest is the International Club. Most clubs and organisations are not affiliated to Spanish structures and are run by British people, with British volunteers. One organisation actively supporting the needs of older migrants on the Costa del Sol is Age Concern España (Hardill et al, 2005).

As we noted in Chapter Six, under New Labour, community/ neighbourhood re-emerged in public policy, including a more sensitive and precise understanding of the different types of 'community', with the interests of communities of 'identity' being considered alongside more traditional communities of 'place' (SEU, 1998, p 23; ODPM, 2003). Deeper understanding led to explicit concern to reach and engage groups that may otherwise be excluded, such as black and minority ethnic (BME) groups (Chouhan and Lusane, 2004), young people (Marshall, 2004), older people (South West Foundation, 2008) and groups with a particular viewpoint, such as faith communities (Farnell et al, 2003). With the Big Society agenda of the coalition government, the focus appears to be deeply spatial, based on place-based localities and neighbourhoods, but with an expectation that all communities (rich and poor) have to pull together.

Through a range of mechanisms, New Labour particularly sought to engage older people in its modernisation agenda. New Labour established the Better Government for Older People (BGOP) partnership in 1998, which was eventually replaced by an Advisory Forum (Groombridge, 2010). BGOP was first established to oversee 28 research projects on the engagement of older people (defined as those aged 50 and above) in a variety of services (Hayden and Boaz, 2000). When the initiative ended when the research projects were wound up, 'Network' was added and BGOP took into its membership 350 local member organisations to receive and share good practice. The members and subscribers included local authorities, health agencies and voluntary organisations (Groombridge, 2010). The Older People's Advisory Group (OPAG), an offshoot of BGOP, was established in 1999 to influence national and local policy and service provision for older people. OPAG engaged older people in service planning and BGOP also encouraged the establishment of senior citizens' forums across the country. Their scope increased under New Labour by legislative requirements for consultation and involvement including the National Service Framework for Older People (www.dh.gov.uk/en/

publicationsandstatistics/publications/publicationspolicyandguidance/ DH_4003066), which involved older people with primary care trusts. At the time of writing, the OPAGs still exist.

In the remaining part of this chapter, we look at a charity that supports older people to examine how a shared interest/campaign can be a powerful mobilisation for voluntary action. A number of studies of volunteers have identified specific age-related sets of motivations. There is evidence, for example, that organisations whose mission or purpose is to promote the wellbeing of older people have a considerable advantage in involving older people as volunteers (Rochester et al, 2002). Hogg (2010), in his study of older adults' pathways into volunteering, built on Davis Smith and Gay (2005) to suggest that there are three broad groups of volunteer pathway:

- *continuous volunteers* give lifelong commitment to an organisation and the volunteering they do in retirement is a continuation of that done during their paid careers;
- *serial volunteers* are those individuals who have volunteered while in younger and older age, but with a range of organisations and with different levels of engagement at different times;
- *trigger volunteers* are those who only start volunteering in older age, as a result of some change in their circumstances or that of their family.

An American review claimed that older volunteers are much less likely than younger ones to be motivated by material rewards or status (Fischer and Schaffer, 1993). The most usually reported age-related motive for volunteering is to fill the vocational void left by retirement and to manage increased free time (Barlow and Hainsworth, 2001; Barnes and Parry, 2004; Davis Smith and Gay, 2005). Young and Schuller (1991) described how the loss of the routine of the working day that comes with retirement need not condemn people to involuntary marginalisation, since many of their respondents had been able to use their freedom to good effect. For those older adults who still need to be connected or aspire to be reconnected to the labour market, volunteering can be a pathway into it, especially opening up new paid work opportunities (Brooks, 2000).

After a brief history of Age UK, we will examine the extent to which age-related motivations help explain why older volunteers are drawn to give time to help other older people.

Communities of interest: a case study of Age UK

Age UK, which is both a charity and a social enterprise (see Chapter Five), was created in April 2009 following the merger of Age Concern and Help the Aged. It is one of the UK's largest charities, which has a long history of serving the needs of older people – which they identify as being over 50 years of age (www.ageuk.org.uk/about-us/who-we-are/our-history/). The charity dates back to the Second World War, when the Old People's Welfare Committee was established to focus on the plight of older people. The committee quickly gained national recognition and, in 1944, it became known as the National Old People's Welfare Committee (NOPWC), taking under its umbrella many local organisations working to improve older people's welfare. These local organisations were based in geographical locations (Age UK, 2010).

After the Second World War, with the advent of the welfare state, government money became available to fund work with older people. The NOPWC coordinated and facilitated the work of an increasing number of committees. In 1971, the NOPWC became completely independent of government and was renamed Age Concern (Age UK, 2010). Many local groups took on the Age Concern name as time passed and together they benefited from a unified image and a name reflecting the fact that they were not just committees but active providers of direct services. So, groups of local people across the country became motivated to establish local organisations to help older people.

In July 2000, organisations sharing the name Age Concern came together to work in a federation: a structure that reflected their independence and autonomy but also their interdependence. Age Concern England, as the national federation member, worked alongside local Age Concerns and provided support and leadership in areas such as campaigning and policy, including volunteer management. The federation adopted a regional structure, with a regional manager and support team.

Help the Aged dates back to the 1960s, when the Help the Aged Refugees Appeal was set up in 1961 by businessman Cecil Jackson-Cole in response to the needs of older refugees following natural disasters abroad. The appeal raised £105,302 in its first year (Age UK, 2010). The nascent organisation, renamed Help the Aged, continued to raise money for emergency aid overseas. It also became involved with projects for older people in the UK; establishing day centres and pioneering the building of better housing for older people. HelpAge International was founded in 1983 by organisations including Help the Aged (Age UK, 2010). It created a worldwide network of organisations working to improve older people's lives. In 2001, Help the Aged merged with

Research into Ageing (Age UK, 2010). The charity continued to build on its research and policy work, and in 2005 it took a new strategic direction, shifting its focus to disadvantaged older people.

On 1 April 2009, Age Concern and Help the Aged joined to create a new charity – and together as Age UK – deliver services that align with their mission to promote the wellbeing of older people and to help make later life a fulfilling and enjoyable experience. Over recent decades, the proportion of services that are delivered under contract for the state by local Age Concerns has increased and this has brought with it a new set of challenges, relating to maintaining funding regimes and staffing (Hardill and Dwyer, 2011; see Chapter Five).

As can be seen from Box 7.1, Age UK relies heavily on the unpaid help of volunteers in the delivery of these services, about 70% of whom are older people. So, the demographic profile of volunteers aligns broadly with the demographic profile of service users (people over 50 years of age). Age UK needs volunteers to support 3,000 paid staff and volunteers fulfil a number of vital roles within the head office in London (including volunteer researchers), for local branches of the federation (trustees, administration and service delivery), in local shops and with fundraising committees (Mitchell, 2010).

Box 7.1: Age UK

Age UK is both a charity and a social enterprise. It has 8,000 volunteers and 60,000 volunteers across the federation (about 70% are older adults), and 3,000 paid employees and 513 shops. Turnover in 2009-10 was £160 million – £47 million from combined fundraising. There are approximately 340 local Age Concerns; each is a charity in its own right, but they vary in size and scope. Age UK is active in 70 countries.

Source: Michelle Mitchell, Age UK Conference, Nottingham, September 2010

While some service users access help from Age UK via national helplines and give their time by volunteering at headquarters, most volunteers and service users access and indeed identify Age UK more locally, via the federation. Age Concern Nottingham and Nottinghamshire (Box 7.2), for example, which is the largest local charity in the federation, has a physical presence across the county and, as such, operates across five local authority districts, from Mansfield in the north to Nottingham in the south. Over 200 volunteers support 180 paid staff in the delivery of services, offering advice and information and running coffee mornings (www.ageconcernnotts.org.uk/index.asp?getpage=true&sid=34).

Box 7.2: Age Concern Nottingham and Nottinghamshire

- Age Concern Nottingham and Nottinghamshire covers both the city and the county, a total of five local authority districts.
- The largest local independent charity working with older people, it was established in 1942, with only a handful of committed volunteers.
- Today, its employs over 180 staff, has over 200 dedicated volunteers and helps over 50,000 people every year.
- It provides a number of direct support services to local older people in a number of areas in the city and the county.
- Services include: advice and information; a direct payment support service; advocacy and support in hospitals and care homes; housing services; an accredited traders register; support following a stay in hospital, such as day care and luncheon clubs; visiting and befriending services; carers' support; support at home; emergency alarm systems; coffee mornings and activities; and signposting to other services.

Source: Age Concern Nottingham and Nottinghamshire
(www.ageconcernnotts.org.uk/index.asp?getpage=true&sid=34)

Volunteering for Age UK, wherever it takes place, occurs within clear structures, with selection criteria, training and ongoing support – an indication that the volunteering experience has been 'professionalised' (see Chapters Three and Four). It has a department, at its headquarters in London, devoted to volunteer management, where policies are developed. In addition to this national function, local organisations provide training and support and have induction and training packages for volunteers. Some of the larger organisations have staff who have a specific responsibility for the management of volunteers (see Chapter Four).

In the remaining part of this section, we draw on the findings from two projects undertaken before the merger (Baines et al, 2006; Dwyer and Hardill, 2008). The first study was undertaken between 2004 and 2006, focused on older people's volunteering and was commissioned by the Big Lottery. The second study was undertaken during 2007–08 and was commissioned by Age Concern East, East Midlands and West Midlands to identify and evaluate existing effective practice in delivering services to older people aged 70 plus in remote rural communities (see Chapter One).

The services that these organisations provide, whether in urban or rural areas, align with the charity's mission to promote the wellbeing of older people and to help make later life a fulfilling and enjoyable experience (Box 7.3; Robson et al, 2004). The type of services provided includes information and advice services, day centres and lunch clubs. Some of these activities are 'low-level services'. These services give 'that little bit of help' and are highly valued. They can help sustain self-confidence and identity (Baldock and Hadlow, 2002, p 3). In common with many other VCSOs, these surveyed organisations rely on the unpaid contributions made by largely older volunteers for service delivery (Raynes et al, 2006).

Box 7.3: Helping older people

- The older person is the beneficiary (KI15).
- We close the door to nobody. The doors are open (KI1).
- Our work is about changing people's lives (KI23).
- The approach we have with old people may be different from the statutory [sector]. It is much more supportive and low key. And that mistakenly is sometimes taken as being not specialist. It isn't, it's actually working with what people need. And actually giving them the service that they will find most useful (KI7).

Source: Dwyer and Hardill (2008)

Baines et al's (2006) case study organisation covered a large local authority in a former industrial city with a population in excess of 259,000 people. Their survey respondents[2] were asked to indicate their reasons for volunteering from a series of options. The three most prominent reasons for volunteering were 'to put my spare time to good use' (53%), 'to improve the lives of older people' (42%) and because 'someone asked me to help' (40%). 'To put my time to good use' was more often reported by volunteers aged over 55 (56% as opposed to 40% of the younger groups). 'Someone asked me to help' was also much more characteristic of older volunteers (reported by 45% of those aged 55 and over and by only 20% of their younger counterparts). 'To improve the lives of older people', on the other hand, was reported by 50% of the volunteers aged under 55 and only 42% of those over that age. A few of the less popular reasons were most typical of younger volunteers. Of the nine who volunteered to improve their job prospects, eight were under the age of 44 and one was between 65 and 74 years of age. Two young volunteers described their reasons for volunteering as being a requirement for the further studies that they intended to pursue.

In analysing how volunteers perceive their experiences within the formal structures outlined above, it is useful to start with what they know of the aims of organisation.

> 'I think it's to look out for the older people. To make sure that they get all that they're due. To fight for what they think they should be due. Facilities for them to do these things because they cater for everything, the blind and everything.'(Mrs Burn)

Mrs Burn had a clear perception of the importance of recognising the dignity of older people, defending their rights and getting them a better deal so that they would have a better life, very much in line with the organisation's aims. In general, however, volunteers were vague and unsure about the wider aims of the organisation in promoting the needs and welfare of older people. Just a few interviewees referred to some of its aims. This included a handful who recognised the role of the organisation in lobbying on behalf of older people and having access to the government because of its status as a national charity.

> 'I mean they act as a sort of voice at higher levels, at government levels you know, to sort of put forward the case for older people. They kind of defend older people, you know, where older people wouldn't have, when you're working you've got a voice.' (Mrs Hetherington)

Some interviewees also made reference to the organisation's aims to change attitudes and to combat the social exclusion of older people.

In contrast, many were aware and informed about the service provision aspect of the organisation. Most interviewees spoke about its role in "helping" older people and more practical aspects such as "looking after older people", supporting them with advice and guidance, making life more comfortable for them – especially those without family – providing services and classes and encouraging older people's participation and activity. It is the various services provided such as 'leisure and learning', 'information and advice' and the 'involving older people' strategy that are most visible to volunteers and which inform their perceptions of organisation. It is interesting to note that when asked what they knew about the organisation before they joined it as a volunteer, many said that they knew little. This was particularly the case for volunteers around the city in the lunch clubs, which is discussed below.

Baines et al (2006) identified four main categories of volunteer roles. The largest group were those involved in the lunch and leisure clubs serving neighbourhoods dispersed throughout the city. They could volunteer a few times every week or once every three to four weeks on a rotation basis and these lunch and leisure clubs were located in church halls rather than in the premises of the charity. A number of lunch clubs were started as a church activity that later drew support and funding from the charity. For such volunteers, their allegiance tended to be to the church or neighbourhood rather than to the charity as an organisation as their volunteer work preceded financial support from Age UK.

The next largest group of volunteers were those based at the main offices of the charity and in the leisure and learning department. Their volunteer work included helping in the cafe, providing assistance at the computer help desk or assisting or leading leisure and learning activities. Other volunteers were involved in miscellaneous work such as office, reception, transport, advice and sales work. Some volunteers tended to be involved in more than one activity. These volunteers were more likely to have actively sought out the charity.

'Befriending' covered visiting and bereavement support services. These volunteers tended to work very independently from the charity and their role was particularly 'individualised' on a one-to-one basis, specifically catering to housebound and frail older service users, sometimes over a long period of time. The management volunteers were the trustees and others who were involved in ad-hoc committee or project work, who met at various times through the year. Table 7.1 shows comparisons between the different types of volunteers according to gender, age and retirement.

The management volunteers stand out as being distinct from the other volunteers on a number of counts: they have a more equal ratio of male to female volunteers, a younger age profile and are more likely to be in paid employment. None of them reported an income below

Table 7.1: Volunteer profiles by volunteer role

Type of volunteer	N	Male: female	% over 65	% retired or 'other'	% earning <£15,000	% in deprived neighbourhood
Management	10	1:0.7	40.0	55.6	0.0	25.0
Lunch club	71	1:9	67.0	89.6	66.0	42.6
Befriending	12	1:5	42.0	68.3	67.0	33.3
City centre office	40	1:3	50.0	78.4	67.0	32.4

Source: Baines et al (2006)

£15,000 per annum and only a quarter live in neighbourhoods classed as deprived. In contrast, the lunch club volunteers have the smallest ratio of men to women, are most likely to be over the age of 65 and either retired or 'other'. The gender composition of volunteers in lunch clubs can perhaps be explained by the nature of luncheon clubs, which is such that the large majority of service users are women. Lunch club volunteers are also most likely among the other categories of volunteers to live in a deprived neighbourhood. The befriending and main office volunteers were quite similar except on certain measures. The main office volunteers were more likely to be over the age of 65 and to be retired than the befriending volunteers and the proportion of men in this group was higher.

The second study was in rural England, and fieldwork took place in areas characterised by an ageing population (Wenger, 2001). Demographic change is more advanced in rural than in urban England; in part the result of rural in-migration (HM Government, 2009) – making 'rural England the pioneer in terms of the nation's population ageing' (Atterton, 2008, p 20). One fifth of England's population live in rural areas – that is, settlements of 10,000 or less (Champion and Shepherd, 2006). In recent decades, the number of older rural residents has been boosted by the in-migration of people in middle age and older age (Hardill, 2006) and 'ageing has become a powerful factor in shaping rural areas ... 1 in 12 is over 75' (Lowe and Speakman, 2006, p 9).

The rural organisations we worked with had a broadly similar age profile of volunteers and service users (Hardill and Dwyer, 2011), which meant that some clients became volunteers:

> 'befriending project leaders ... encourage some older men who have been referred as a recipient of befriending to become befrienders ... meets a need for them as well. I think especially post bereavement side of things.' (John, manager)

By the same token, volunteers also became clients. Hardill and Dwyer (2011) found that one service user (Mrs Smith, aged 76 years), who played a critical role in the establishment of one project through negotiating for the project to use a village hall, had become a service user. She now benefits from the service as a client – as does another service user (Mrs Brown, aged in her late seventies), who helped establish another project and now enjoys lunches and the social contact provided by that project. Other volunteers talked about the service users they met as providing positive role models of how to cope with getting older:

'I enjoy meeting the people – there's some characters [at the luncheon club]! It's given me a lot of hope for my future ... some of them are in their late eighties and early nineties and you think "My goodness me!"' (Barry, retired accountant, volunteer driver)

All the organisations they surveyed made extensive use of (usually older) volunteers; without them the services would have ceased to function: "I have 187 volunteers in [service name] ... without those 187 volunteers ... it would not exist" (Eddy, manager).

Some volunteers were engaged in an advisory capacity or undertook committee work that utilised managerial or professional skills; others undertook clerical duties, including raising money and administrative and organising work. However, most were engaged in service delivery, including visiting or befriending isolated older people in their own homes and driving users to and from the various village halls and so on where luncheon clubs were held (see also Murphy et al, 2005).

In the rural areas where Hardill and Dwyer (2011) undertook their fieldwork, some of the public service commissioners they interviewed indicated that they were looking for organisations with a wide geographical spread to work with:

'County-wide structures rather than an organisation that would just service a small part of [county]. What we wanted [was] to go out to all parts of [county] and Age Concern have the infrastructure to do that and they also understand the sort of structure of society. They are the biggest provider of services to older people in the county. So they have a very good understanding of the nature and background of who they are working with.' (Tina, part-time service manager)

In this case, the local authority commissioner valued a provider who can serve clients over a large geographical area. But while the geographical reach of the organisation is crucial in winning such contracts, the dispersed character of the population in the more remote parts of rural England meant that "[i]t can be difficult to get workers and volunteers. Simply providing the service is difficult ... you can be talking about a farm track a mile and a half off the next tarmac road" (Joan, manager). "It's always an issue getting volunteers [in rural areas]. And we do particularly targeted work to try and get volunteers in an appropriate area" (Janet, manager).

Indeed, the availability of volunteers in the right location (with the requisite skills) determines the capacity of some projects:

> 'We match a volunteer to a befriender ... they tend to live physically closer to the people that they befriend.... But it is quite time consuming as well, for people that volunteer. It can be emotionally draining work befriending.' (Janet, manager)

With spatially targeted schemes in rural areas with dispersed populations, the availability of potential volunteers is borne in mind when planning services:

> 'At the same time as we were looking at the venue suitability, we were also looking at the availability of volunteers in that area. And they came together as they say.' (Paul, manager)

> 'Wherever possible we recruit volunteers from the area we're targeting.' (Oliver, manager)

As the above quotations highlight, often the pool of volunteers with the right skills, in broadly the right location and with access to a private car to allow them to serve a geographically dispersed population was finite. Those charged with managing and delivering identified this as a key constraint when planning rural services.

Conclusion

In this chapter, we have examined volunteering via organisations that could be perceived of as spatially dispersed communities of attachment or interest. Authors such as Willmott have described how the advent of information and communication technologies (ICTs) and greater residential and personal mobility have encouraged the development of dispersed communities, or networks, at the expense of local ones (Willmott, 1986, p 87). As a result, people increasingly interact with others who do not share the same residence with them in localities and neighbourhoods; we have argued that this could explain why people volunteer for organisations serving special interests or specific sections of the population, such as charities that support the wellbeing of older people.

But as we have shown in this chapter, territorial communities, whose members live in a particular area and the interest community, whose members have something in common that they wish to share, represent two concepts of community that are not mutually exclusive (see Willmott, 1986).Volunteering for organisations such as Age UK, with a national reach that champions a group of the population, is complex, as it both appeals to some volunteers who identify with truly local needs and those who want to help older people in their neighbourhood, such as by helping out at luncheon clubs (Hogg, 2010). Some of these services are run in partnership with other organisations, such as a local church, or community group, as we noted with the organisation active in a northern city, and therefore volunteers identify with both an interest group and a locality. So place and community groups can coincide, as was noted in the case of mining villages in Chapter Six (Dennis et al, 1969).

Others volunteer their time more directly to the organisation; they want to help older people in general and they are determined not just to help older people resident in one particular community of place, such as a neighbourhood. Perhaps the notion of mutual aid can help explain such voluntary work. 'Mutual aid', as the term suggests, concerns voluntary activity in which individuals or groups undertake voluntary work for mutually beneficial reasons (Gerard, 1983). Beveridge's own definition makes explicit the self-help impulse that drives mutual aid, based around a 'realisation that since one's fellows have the same need, by undertaking to help one another, they may also help themselves' (Beveridge, 1948, cited in Davis Smith and Gay, 1995, p 28). This reciprocity need not be bipolar and may indeed be deferred over long periods, but it is integral to mutual volunteerism that there is an obligation and an expectation for reciprocation (Kidd, 1996). For core members, it is likely that social networks have been strengthened, political activism encouraged and their inclusion in civil society boosted by their involvement (Gorsky, 1998).

Notes

[1] It is fascinating to note that this is to blame for Milton Keynes' car-friendly and neighbourhood-stifling design.Webber was influential in the layout of Milton Keynes and argued that the grid layout facilitated ease of transportation – vital for the growth of communities of interest.

[2] In the study, older volunteers were identified as those over the age of 55.

EIGHT

The big issue of the Big Society: mobilising communities alongside fiscal austerity

Introduction: the Year of the Volunteer

The year 2011 has been declared the 'European Year of Volunteering' to recognise over 100 million European volunteers active across member states and the contribution they make to society. This initiative of the European Commission marks the 10th anniversary of the UN 'International Year of the Volunteer 2001', which aimed to highlight the achievements of volunteers worldwide and to encourage more people to engage in voluntary activity. Such celebratory cross national events reflect the high profile of volunteering and political imperatives to celebrate and expand it. We have looked throughout this book at volunteering with organisations that provide care in England, in the first decade of the 21st century. In the next section of this final chapter, we review that context and the scope of the book and summarise the organising framework and key concepts we have deployed. Then we turn to the landscape for volunteering, VCSOs and care in the UK in 2011. We highlight elements of change and of continuity and consider what the empirical findings and conceptual lenses from the book can contribute to ongoing analysis. We recall the ways in which we set about research and knowledge exchange (KE) with volunteers and organisations that involve them and comment on some lessons we have learned. Finally, we end with a few comments on the Big Society.

Reflections on the scope and context of the book

In this book, we have reported and reflected on volunteering from research we undertook between 2003 and 2010. Our topic was volunteering through organisations (large and small) involved in care. The mainstreaming of the VCS in delivering public services within England has been an important policy context for our work – but during New Labour's administrations, devolution has seen the devolved governments and parliaments of Scotland, Wales and Northern Ireland increasingly adopting different approaches to the delivery of care and engagement with the VCS (Danson and Whittam, 2011). With more powers and responsibilities, Scotland has been leading the moves to divergence in social and economic policies across the UK (Keating, 2005; Mooney and Scott, 2005; Danson and Whittam, 2011), not least in the role of the VCS. Danson and Whittam (2011) argue that the US/UK ('Anglo-Saxon') welfare model (Esping-Andersen, 1990, 1999) continues to dominate and set the agenda at Westminster – restricting and corrupting the role of the VCS in public service delivery – while in Scotland, these tendencies have been tempered by the government and civil society.

The sites of our research were in urban and rural England, where health services and local authorities throughout that period were required to work more closely with VCSOs, especially registered charities, cooperatives and social enterprises. These organisations have experienced a shift in their resource base towards competitive contracts with the public sector. Sensitive to the often-expressed notion that VCSOs need to be more 'enterprising' in a mixed economy of care, we drew on academic debates in literature about social enterprise and from the longer-established genre of small business and entrepreneurship.

'Care', as we discussed in Chapter Two, is a significant and contested concept. In public policy, it is framed as an overwhelming problem in the context of expanding need and budgetary constraint. From the perspective of disability activists, care usually implies the disempowering actions of professionals and bureaucracies (Barnes et al, 1999; Kröger, 2009). Some feminists have seen care as the burden that traps women in unpaid and low-status service work (for a discussion, see Folbre, 1995; Himmelweit, 1995). The increasingly influential feminist ethic of care, however, proclaims, on the contrary, that care should be celebrated as an ethic or moral orientation, placing emphasis on collective welfare through doing things for others (Williams, F., 2001, 2005; Sevenhuijsen, 2003). For that reason, we identified the 'ethic of care' as a useful concept for thinking about volunteering as one of the practices of caring citizenship operating within communities (of place and identity/interest). Another key concept was 'TSOL', which offers a robust and subtle set of tools to make sense of how work is undertaken on different socioeconomic bases (market and non-market, formal or informal, paid or unpaid) and how value attributed to work on those bases changes in response to factors including national welfare policies (Lyon and Glucksmann, 2008; Williams, 2011). (See Figure 8.1 for examples of how a TSOL approach positions some of the activity discussed in the book.)

Figure 8.1: Typology of labour practices in the 'total social organisation of labour' with examples from this book in the shaded areas

PAID

(1) Formal paid job in private or public sector	(2) Formal paid job in voluntary sector	(3) Informal employment	(4) Reimbursed favours	(5) Paid family/ household work
Care workers in a local authority (prior to starting Workers' Co-operative) (Chapter Five)	VMs who enable volunteering (Chapter Four)			

INFORMAL

Volunteering at the Government Project (Chapters Three and Seven)	Volunteering in frontline services and governance roles (Chapters Three, Five, Six and Seven)	The organisers of the Brightville lunch club (before it grew and formalised) (Chapters Three and Four)	The help of family and friends to support new cooperative enterprises (Chapter Five)	Unpaid domestic work (discussed in Chapter Three as sometimes constraining time for volunteering)
(6) Formal unpaid work in private and public sector	(7) Formal unpaid work in VCS	(8) 'Below the radar' unpaid labour in groups	(9) One-to-one unpaid labour	(10) Self-provisioning

UNPAID

Source: Adapted from Williams (2011)

Volunteering through care-providing organisations does not include all possible sites and kinds of volunteering and we do not, therefore, claim to encompass the full breadth and variety of volunteering and volunteers, as do Rochester et al (2010) in their comprehensive recent volume. In contrast, we worked with VCSOs (charities, cooperatives and social enterprises) whose activities are exclusively or mainly dedicated to the delivery of care. All the organisations that participated in the research we report in this book involved volunteers and also employed paid staff, but the proportion of paid staff to volunteers varied at the level of the organisation and even within an organisation at the level of each project/service. Some had, however, begun as what are now often referred to as 'below the radar' informal voluntary organisations/ community groups, without paid employees or regular income. That focus has enabled us to offer an empirically grounded exploration of the multiple ways in which volunteering and care intersect and overlap.

For some individual volunteers, giving care means helping in frontline services, for example providing meals in community venues for isolated older people or counselling young parents in their homes. These activities are enabled by people in governance roles (who are also themselves unpaid volunteers), as well as paid employees who organise volunteer-delivered services and, in some cases, volunteer themselves. So although the book is about volunteering, it is not exclusively about volunteers. We included in Chapters Two to Seven the voices of a wide range of people who touch, and are touched by, volunteering, including paid workers and community stakeholders. As an organising framework for this book, we used the approach of Omoto and Snyder (2002), who conceived of volunteering at three spatial scales: individuals, organisations and communities of place, identity and attachment.

Many individual volunteers and employees who enable volunteering, appear in the book in vignettes and case studies. We recognise a body of research that is mainly concerned with enumerating and classifying volunteering and assessing volunteer motives. In our work, in the spirit of TSOL, we have taken a more holistic approach in which we consider the ways in which actions, choices and constraints for individuals are embedded in household, kinship and friendship networks, as well as organisations and communities. Such an approach has enabled us to illuminate the blurring of volunteering with other forms of work. For example, over time a volunteer can become the recipient of care and a paid worker can become a volunteer (or vice versa). These fluid boundaries also mean that a paid worker for a VCSO can be a volunteer at the same time, as their paid work spills over into unpaid voluntary work.

In Chapter Three, we considered the pathways by which people entered volunteering for organisations present in the community of Brightville. Following Hardill et al (2007), we proposed that cultural theory (often referred to as Grid and Group) can be used as a conceptual resource to move beyond list-based research on individuals' rationales for volunteering. We noted that historical accounts of volunteering talk of the impulses to philanthropy and mutual aid, and these resonated strongly with what Brightville volunteers told us about their lives and concerns. In Grid and Group terminology, most Brightville volunteers were located in the high grid–high group quadrant ('hierarchy') or the low grid–high group quadrant ('egalitarian') (Figure 3.2). We equated these positions respectively with philanthropy and mutual aid. Both philanthropy and mutual aid are characterised by forms of altruism but with very different ways of thinking about and responding to others. The people who were drawn to volunteer in Brightville included local residents, as well as people who lived further afield in the neighbouring Irontown. Based on the evidence of Brightville volunteers, we join Amin (2009a) in questioning the policy of advancing engagement with the formal economy through volunteering, yet recognising its power to help build capacity for some excluded individuals.

At the organisational level, we considered careers in the VCS focusing on the increasingly visible group of employees who have developed professional expertise in supporting and enabling volunteering (Chapter Four). Organisations that participated in the studies had changed and grown and, in some cases, taken on services previously provided by local authorities such as domiciliary care. Some had developed innovative responses to unmet needs following consultation with service users, for example for carers of people with dementia. These dynamics were explored in Chapter Five.

Recognising that community is both a target for voluntary effort and a context that shapes much volunteering, we revisited the rich classic tradition of community studies to think about communities as sites of voluntary action. Communities can be defined as territorial (communities of place). That is the sense in which community is usually used in public policy, including policy focused on expanding volunteering. But under New Labour, the policy context shifted to recognise communities of identity/interest, ranging from diasporic communities to older people. We returned to Brightville in Chapter Six, to consider what volunteering can mean as a response to local needs. Community implies both similarity and difference, and communities can also be seen as a 'space' (physical as well as imagined) where people have something in common other than place. Chapter Seven turned the spotlight to older people and ways in which VCSOs espousing their interests can galvanise voluntary action, both at the very local level and at larger spatial scales.

What next? The Big Society and fiscal austerity

The VCS and volunteers are more visible now (spring 2011) in Britain than ever and it is the higher expectations of them that place them in the limelight. Alcock (2010) feels that this is an important legacy of New Labour. The coalition government is reimagining volunteering and the VCS in the Big Society. The central themes of the Big Society philosophy – compassionate conservatism, devolution of responsibility and empowerment of citizens – have been central to David Cameron's political ideology from before his election as Conservative Party leader in December 2005 (BBC, 2005). Kisby (2010, p 486) has commented that while David Cameron regards the Big Society as being novel, it does not represent a significant break with New Labour with regard to the emphasis on volunteering, rather 'a continuation, albeit with greater intensity, especially ... in the context of the country's dire financial position'.

The idea of the Big Society was articulated in the Conservative Party Green Paper, *A Stronger Society: Voluntary Action in the 21st Century* (Conservative Party, 2008). In that document, New Labour's use of the term 'third sector' was denounced as demeaning to the sector, which should more accurately be called the 'first sector' (Conservative Party, 2008). In March 2010, theologian Philip Blond's *Red Tory* book was published in which he argued that there had been a wholesale collapse of British culture, virtue and belief because of decades of emphasis on personal choice, with the loss of the conception of the common good. This demise was the result of an uncritical alliance of the state and the market in the Anglo-American economies of the UK and the US (Blond, 2010, p 4). Blond's remedy is a combination of cultural conservatism and anti-market radicalism. By joining together this conservative brand of anti-capitalism with policies aiming to strengthen social and moral bonds, 'broken Britain' can be repaired and a more cohesive, organic society restored. He argues for the reshaping of tax structures to re-localise the economy and make life in small towns and villages more sustainable. Blond has redefined the centre ground, and his ideas have influenced the agenda around the Big Society (see below).

In the introduction to the 2010 Conservative election manifesto, David Cameron argued: 'a country is at its best when the bonds between people are strong' (Conservative Party, 2010, p viii). One of the first acts of the coalition government was the launch of a strategy for *Building the Big Society* by the Prime Minister and Deputy Prime Minister in May 2010 (Cabinet Office, 2010a). That short document encompasses volunteering as well as local democracy, revising planning laws, the publication of government data, the abolition of regional spatial policy and giving public sector workers a right to bid to take over the services they deliver (Cabinet Office, 2010a). (See Box 8.1 for the Prime Minister's words on the Big Society.)

Alcock (2010) observes that the Big Society is intended to be contrasted with the big state of New Labour (see also Smith, 2010b) and (among other things) to be an endorsement of the positive and

Box 8.1: The Big Society

The success of the Big Society will depend on the daily decisions of millions of people – on them giving their time, effort, even money, to causes around them. So government cannot remain neutral on that – it must foster and support a new culture of voluntarism, philanthropy, social action. Second, public service reform. We've got to get rid of the centralised bureaucracy that wastes money and undermines morale. And in its place we've got to give professionals much more freedom, and open up public services to new providers like charities, social enterprises and private companies so we get more innovation, diversity and responsiveness to public need. And third, community empowerment. We need to create communities with oomph – neighbourhoods who are in charge of their own destiny, who feel if they club together and get involved they can shape the world around them.

Source: Cameron (2010a)

proactive roles that voluntary action and social enterprise could play in promoting improved social inclusion and 'fixing Britain's broken society'. It also represents a redefining of the relationship between the state, the market and the individual (Diamond, 2011). According to Scott (2011, p 830) the Big Society speaks to a Tory tradition of public duty and social responsibility of the well-off to the disadvantaged, and sits within an idea of welfare being provided by an organic civil society. The Big Society agenda focuses on England and not the devolved administrations (Alcock, 2010; Danson and Whittam, 2011; Hogg and Baines, 2011), and so will result in a widening policy gap towards volunteering, the VCS and public service delivery between the constituent parts of the UK.

In November 2010, Jesse Norman, the Conservative MP for Hereford and South Herefordshire, published a book-length account of the political and philosophical rationale for the Big Society (Norman, 2010). He draws heavily on the work of Michael Oakeshott to propose that the Big Society is both a driver and a product of a connected society, where institutions exist between the individual and the state. The Big Society is both an idea and a political programme, 'a series of interlocking ideas ... a concerted and wide-ranging attempt to engage with the twin challenges of social and economic decline and move us to a more connected society' (Norman, 2010, p 210). The Big Society, then, is certainly more than volunteering. Volunteering, charitable giving and social action, however, lie close to its heart (Norman, 2010). So do neighbourhood and community, with an emphasis on building on existing community assets, as we noted in Chapter Six.

The Green Paper entitled *Giving* (Cabinet Office, 2010b) begins by highlighting the three key elements to the government's role in building the Big Society: empowering communities (via the Localism Bill); opening up public services (via public service reform for more local involvement in shaping services); and encouraging social action (which is the focus of the Green Paper). The Green Paper explores how levels of giving and mutual support can be fostered, and as a consultation document it has generated comment.

The Localism Bill, which is being led by Eric Pickles (Secretary of State for Communities and Local Government), proposes radical changes to the planning system via decentralisation to give neighbourhoods far more ability to determine the shape of the places where people live (Cabinet Office, 2010b). In terms of the Bill's implications for the VCSO at the local level, there are plans for significant changes in the commissioning and procurement of local public service contracts (mainly local authorities) and Community Right to Buy public or private assets of community value, with powers to delay the sale of local assets to allow community groups time to get a bid together to buy them (Cabinet Office, 2010b).

At the time of writing (spring 2011) policies to bring about the Big Society are operating at three spatial scales: at the level of the individual, the organisation and the community. First, individuals are being encouraged/'nudged' to volunteer via specific programmes. Second, social action at the level of the organisation is being rewarded, and organisations facing cuts in their budgets can apply for financial help. Third, mutualism is being nurtured at the level of the community.

Like New Labour, the coalition government is placing a particular emphasis on behaviour change, inspired by the work of US psychologists Thaler and Sunstein (2009), who argue that people need 'nudging' to change habits, and Professor Thaler is advising the government. The Behavioural Insights Team in the Cabinet Office (led by David Halpern) is working with the Office for Civil Society to encourage voluntary work (see the *Giving* Green Paper cited above: Cabinet Office 2010b). Since 2010, the National Citizen Service has been giving 16-year-old school leavers the chance to get involved with their local community, learn how to be active citizens and mix with people from different backgrounds (Cabinet Office, 2010b).

VCSOs have the Big Society Awards, which have been introduced to showcase excellent examples of such action. The recipient of the first such award is a social enterprise providing community nursing and therapy services (see Box 8.2). The Big Society idea goes alongside deep cuts in public spending in 2010, which have brought a harsh

Box 8.2: Big Society Award Winner, Central Surrey Health

The first Big Society Award winner was Central Surrey Health (CSH). CSH is a social enterprise providing community nursing and therapy services in mid-Surrey. It was established in October 2006, following a review of services by Elmbridge and Mid Surrey Primary Care Trust (PCT). The review considered various options, including partnership arrangements with local general practitioners and private sector companies. It recommended that patients would be best served through the establishment of a not-for-profit, limited liability company owned by – and employing – nurses and therapists who formerly delivered services within the PCT. CSH has around 770 co-owners, who are also employees. It has been hailed as an example of how public services can do more with less, and it claims to 'combine the values and principles of the NHS with the "can do" culture of a successfully run business (NHS Central Surrey Health, 2010).

According to the Department of Health, as a social enterprise, CSH creates a higher 'social value' than if it were a public sector organisation or private company. In March 2010, CSH started a 'Telecare' pilot in partnership with social care, the ambulance service and borough councils. The pilot uses equipment, such as community alarms and pressure mats, to monitor patients at home who have a history of frequent falls.

The Prime Minister said of CSH when he launched the new award: 'They are an excellent example of people on the front line taking a stake in their organisation, driving real improvements and shaping the service they provide. Their innovation and commitment has made a real difference to their community nursing and therapy services'

Sources: NHS Central Surrey Health (2010); Cabinet Office (2010c); Big Society Awards launched, London: Cabinet Office http://www.cabinetoffice.gov.uk/news/big-society-awards-launched

financial environment for those VCSOs that derive income from statutory sources. As part of the Comprehensive Spending Review of October 2010, George Osborne, the Chancellor of the Exchequer, announced a £100 million Transition Fund (www.biglotteryfund.org.uk/transitionfund) to help VCSOs in England, which deliver public services, to adapt to declining funds from statutory sources. It is being administered by the Big Lottery Fund (BIG),[1] and in the first round a total of 183 VCSOs were awarded grants totalling about £15 million, a fraction of those VCSOs delivering public services.

The Big Society in communities began in summer 2010 when the Prime Minister announced four 'vanguard communities' – Cumbria,

Liverpool, Windsor and Maidenhead, and Sutton – where community initiatives to support a range of activities (a community buy-out of a pub, increasing volunteering at museums to keep them open, developing youth projects) started receiving organisational and civil service support. But after six months, Liverpool withdrew because the government's cuts had seriously undermined the ability of community organisations to improve the quality of life of residents (*The Independent*, 2011).

Liverpool's decision coincided with the launch of the Big Society Community Organisers Programme by Nick Hurd, Minister for Civil Society. This programme is one of the flagships of the Big Society in England. This 'new generation' of community organisers is to 'help bring communities together and support neighbourhood groups to address common problems' (Conservative Party, 2010, p 6). The remit is to recruit and train 5,000 independent community organisers across England over the lifetime of the current Parliament. The aim is to host community organisers within existing community organisations. The first cohort of 'kickstarter' hosts are rooted in communities of place with a strong focus on under-represented and disadvantaged communities. The programme has been influenced by the Brazilian educationalist Paulo Freire (1921-97) and Saul Alinsky (1909-72), the American organiser and activist (Locality, 2010). Freire focused on raising consciousness through dialogical encounter and the praxis of action-reflection. Liberation theology in South America combined Christianity and Marxism to empower the dispossessed, but it had some unintended consequences, which Cassidy (1977), for example, wrote so movingly about in the 1970s. Alinsky called for action to directly challenge the powerful. He established the community organising movement in poor neighbourhoods in the US and thousands of Americans, including President Obama, trained as community organisers. In his autobiography *Dreams of My Father*, Obama (2007) wrote about being drawn to be a community organiser in 1983 because of the need to change: 'I'll organise black folks. At the grass roots. For change ... communities had to be created, fought for, tended like gardens' (2007, pp 133-4). His idea of organising was 'a promise of redemption ... organisers didn't make money; their poverty was proof of integrity' (2007, p 135).

The Community Organisers Programme differs in a number of respects from David Cameron's pre-election call for a 'neighbourhood army' of 5,000 full-time, professional community organisers (Cameron, 2010). The programme provides funds for 500 'senior community organisers' to receive payment, while training, in the form of a learning bursary. Four and a half thousand 'mid-level community organisers' will be unpaid volunteers. So like the community organisers in the US that Obama joined, the Big Society community organisers will certainly not make money! While the vision is of community organisers throughout the whole of England, the Community First areas will be a particular focus; these are the 100 areas with the highest levels of deprivation and lowest levels of social capital.

Community organising is expected to leverage existing local networks and create new ones. The biggest challenge is sustainability. The funding from the Office for Civil Society is intended only as pump priming. After that the organisers and their hosts will be expected to secure funding for their activities. Community organising, as understood by the programme, 'has a strong flavour of mutual enterprise' (Locality, 2010, p 8).

The Comprehensive Spending Review of October 2010 added cuts in welfare spending, amounting to £7 billion to the £11 billion already announced in the June 2010 budget. Councils, for example, can expect a 27% cut in their grant funding in the period until 2014-15. From the perspective of VCSOs and the people who work with them, the prospects are gloomy. Some anticipate sharper competition and even a divide-and-rule approach by government (nef, 2010). The Chartered Institute of Public Finance and Accountancy (CIPFA) and the Society of Local Authority Chief Executives and Senior Managers (SOLACE) in a joint publication warn that '[i]n the short term, there are real fears that spending cuts will impact adversely on the capacity of the charitable/not-for-profit sector. Far from taking on more and providing capacity to enable a shift away from the state, it may be able to do rather less' (SOLACE, 2010, p 8).

As we noted in Chapter Five, for charities in England and Wales, more than a third of overall income is from statutory sources (Clark et al, 2010). This figure masks enormous variations within the charity sector (see Milligan and Fife, 2005; Seddon, 2007). Some large social care charities derive almost all their income from statutory sources. Seddon (2007) expressed concerns about the degree of dependency of some charities on the state. He argued that charities that derive more than 70% of their income from the state have reached a level of dependency that makes them more part of the state than civil society. While the VCSOs we studied had not reached such a level of dependency, the proportion of their income from statutory sources had increased.

One of the big tasks for both government and the VCS will be responding to the pressures to cut spending within a climate of public sector austerity (Alcock, 2010). Box 8.3 illustrates these debates from

> ## Box 8.3: Big Society and questions about the funding of VCSOs
>
> Malcolm Wicks (Croydon North): Given that one of the building blocks of the Big Society, which I believe in, is the voluntary sector, will the Minister comment on the decision by Croydon council to axe the grants to more than 20 voluntary organisations? Those organisations form the great majority of those that the council has been funding, and they include the Croydon rape and sexual abuse support centre. Does he agree that if the same thing happens nationwide, that will not be about building the good society – or, if he prefers, the big society – but will put us on a slippery slope towards a painful and bad society?
>
> Greg Clark (Minister of State, Department for Communities and Local Government): The Right Hon. Gentleman and I agree, I think, that it is highly desirable that we should transfer power from the centre to local communities, and that involves councils, too. I do not expect them to pull up the drawbridge in the town hall when we decentralise power and resources to them. I look to councils to increase their contacts with the voluntary sector as part of the decentralisation initiative, which affects everyone.
>
> *Source:* House of Commons (2010)

an exchange in the House of Commons about local authority cuts. An argument emerging from some exponents of the Big Society is that the VCS will step in to replace a reduced public welfare provision. This is based, at least in part, on the analysis that public sector provision has historically tended to 'crowd out' voluntary provision. Alcock (2010) disputes the crowding-out theory with evidence from the Third Sector Research Centre's (TSRC) long-term analysis of charity registrations, which reveals that the post-war welfare state heralded a growth, not a decline, in charitable formation.

Big Society reform of the mixed economy of welfare is intended to recast relationships between the state and the individual. According to Steve Johnson, corporate director of Capital Ambition (London councils' public service improvement body), cited in Smith 2010a '[w]e need to realise that people aren't passive consumers ... cost savings come in because the users are doing things for themselves'. To explain the benefits of these innovations in public sector delivery models, Johnson invokes as an analogy the shift from a market counter to a supermarket: '[w]hereas someone else used to fetch all our goods for us, now we're happy with getting it ourselves. The time cost is transferred to the consumer, who is empowered by more freedom and ownership'

(Smith, 2010a).This is fiercely contested of course and many arguments can be and have been made about such claims around consumers, empowerment and ownership. The obligations of the state for care will certainly diminish but it is not clear how they will be distributed between the market, household and the VCS. Many of the accounts from our work reported in this book, under the themes of individuals, organisations and communities, have demonstrated some of the extent to which the different sectors collaborate and overlap.

As a conceptual framework, TSOL has proved a rich resource for thinking about changes in work, volunteering and care.The Big Society and the impact of reduced public spending are likely to diminish the scope for providing care through formal governmental channels, while more is expected of volunteering, self-help and informal efforts. We turn again to Figure 8.1 and think about some early examples of events related to volunteering and the voluntary sector in spring 2011. There are certainly some early indications that withdrawn funding has affected VCSOs, as in the example of a community and voluntary service that closed with several job losses (Box 8.4). In this case, work in the form of formal paid jobs in the voluntary sector (segment 2 in Figure 8.1) were removed. It is unclear where, if at all, this work will be undertaken.The other example of policy change in Box 8.4 is a likely direct transfer of paid work in a publicly funded body (segment 1 in Figure 8.1) to formal unpaid in the VCS (segment 7).This reconfiguring of the boundaries between sectors of the economy, and economic bases, seems set to increase self-help, mutual aid and the complex of activity that Gibson-Graham (2006) talk of as the submerged part of the iceberg (see Chapter One).

Box 8.4: Examples of change in 2010

Stockport Community and Voluntary Services closed in October 2010 with the loss of eight jobs when the trustees decided to wind up the support organisation after Stockport Metropolitan Borough Council withdrew £127,000 of funding (Third Sector, 2010).

In October 2010, it was reported that the energy watchdog Consumer Focus was to be scrapped as part of the government's 'bonfire of the quangos'. Citizens Advice, a network of independent UK charities staffed mostly by volunteers, would instead take on responsibility for advice to consumers and handling complaints against energy companies (*The Guardian*, 2010).

Approach to research: co-produced knowledge

The research we have reported on in this book has been 'co-produced' in partnership with volunteers and VCSOs. Such research partners are increasingly referred to as 'research users' (Nutley et al, 2007; ESRC, 2009b). Research that aims to engage with research users and have an impact is not new. Indeed, within the social sciences, there are a number of epistemological traditions – feminism, participatory research, disability studies and the more recently emerging field of sustainability science – that foreground user engagement, while mainstream social scientists have traditionally preserved their 'distance' from their research subjects (Hardill and Baines, 2009). We have a strong commitment to feminist methods and in recent years we have increasingly embraced participatory methods (Hardill and Baines, 2009).

As we mentioned at the outset of this book, in Chapter One, our interest in volunteering and the voluntary sector began in 2003 with a standard ESRC response-mode research grant and since that award our research has been funded in a number of ways: as evaluation work commissioned by a VCSO, which was both a charity and a social enterprise; a project jointly designed by a VCSO (which was both a registered charity and a social enterprise) and a research team that was funded by BIG; and a series of KE[2] grants from the ESRC, again designed in partnership with a diverse range of VCSOs. The bulk of the research we have reported on in this book, therefore, was co-produced, undertaken as KE (see below) – research *with* organisations and individuals, not *on* them.

Although our initial work was funded as a standard response-mode research grant, it was participatory, undertaken in the spirit of interactive social science (see below; Caswill and Shove, 2000; Robinson and Tansey, 2006) with an emphasis on two-way dialogue. Interactive social science is where 'researchers, funding agencies and user groups interact throughout the entire research process, including the definition of the research agenda, project selection, project execution and the application of research insights' (Woolgar, 2000, p 165). Such a view of social science research is not supported by all social scientists as it can be seen as compromising the detached pursuit of knowledge and raises questions about 'the complex interconnection between objectivity, adequacy, relevance and utility in social science research' (Woolgar, 2000, p 165). Interactive social science brings about a realignment of the relation between the 'producers' and the 'consumers' of social science research, which has long been a concern of those researching the sociology of knowledge (Woolgar, 2000, p 166). That said, there are strong rationales for user engagement, including 'methodological efficiency' (improving the quality of the resulting research), 'egalitarian ideal' (the co-production of knowledge) (Gibbons et al, 1994) and the 'imperative of accountability' (which demands that publicly funded research demonstrates an account of its value in terms of a return on the original investment) (Woolgar, 2000).

Interactions between academic researchers and non-academic research users are not new (Robinson and Tansey, 2006). Indeed, it has been an evolving, political and contested process since the publication of the White Paper *Realising Our Potential* in 1993 (HMSO, 1993), when the importance of a thriving academic knowledge base was most clearly tied in to economic prosperity and enhanced quality of life. We have reported in the book the need since we began the research to demonstrate that the wider benefit of publicly funded social science has increased rapidly (Hardill and Baines, 2009). Since the Warry Report (Warry, 2006), governments across the UK have placed increasing emphasis on the need to provide evidence of the economic and social returns from its investment in research. So, the principles of demonstrating a wider relevance of research are being asked of all social scientists due to changes in public policy.

The major funder of UK social science research, the ESRC, which funded much of the research discussed in this book, has therefore become increasingly concerned with the 'double hurdle' of scholarly and practical impact of the research it funds (see Cave and Hannay, 1996; Pettigrew, 2001; Davies et al, 2005; Molas-Gallart and Tang, 2007; ESRC, 2009a). The 'double hurdle' now has a wider resonance for UK social science (Martin and Tang, 2007; Tam, 2007; LSE Public Policy Group, 2008) as the Research Excellence Framework (REF) continues to take shape (see www.hefce.ac.uk/research/ref/impact/). An element of the next evaluation of research quality will include case studies of research impact; with 20% of a unit of assessment grade resting on the degree to which the wider benefit to the economy and society can be demonstrated in the impact case studies. We now raise questions about academic and non-academic interaction in the context of current initiatives for the promotion of KE.

For effective user engagement and KE, trusting, established, ongoing relationships between academics and research partners are important. But research partners do change. For example, during 2007, we worked with the Disability Rights Commission (DRC), providing them with case studies of volunteers and voluntary organisations, which they placed in a guidance document, *Recruiting, Retaining and Developing Disabled Volunteers: Guidance for Volunteer Opportunity Providers* (DRC,

2007). The DRC has since been subsumed within the new Equality and Human Rights Commission. We also developed a web-based toolkit for voluntary organisations to support inclusive volunteering (especially for older and disabled volunteers), which was launched during the National Volunteering Week in 2007 by Ed Miliband MP when he was Minister for the Third Sector (Figure 8.2). Since 2007, the OTS has been renamed the Office for Civil Society by the coalition government and Ed Miliband MP now leads the Labour Opposition.

For some kinds of ESRC-sponsored KE activity (CASE studentships, partnerships and placements), user organisations are required to make a financial commitment to the research. In this sense, KE aligns with the third stream activity that, it has been argued, has transformed the research university into the 'entrepreneurial' university (Etzkowitz, 2003). However, what used to be called 'reach out to business' has become 'reach out to business and the wider community' (Duggan and Kagan, 2007). We suggest that there is still a need for reflective approaches to the multiple and contradictory constructions of the non-academic 'user', including the rhetorically powerful, but difficult to realise, notion of the 'wider community'.

The issue of co-funding invites hard questions about resources. Civil society and VCSOs made a disproportionate contribution to

Figure 8.2: National Volunteering Week, House of Commons, 2007

ESRC-sponsored KE in the form of CASE studentships as 33% of CASE studentships awarded in 2007-08 were with the third sector/ civil society, 28% were with the business and social enterprise sector and 39% were with the public sector (communication with ESRC).[3]

How can the 'research–practice gap' be bridged? Academia and its sponsors nurture too many assumptions that users are ready and waiting for academically generated knowledge (Woolgar, 2000). Researchers and the 'users' of research belong to different communities with very different values and ideologies (Beyer and Trice, 1982). Conflicting perspectives on problem-solving styles, timeframes and desired outcomes are among the many tensions between academics and practitioners (Badham and Sense, 2006). Methods that can be employed by social scientists for KE include seminars, media relations exercises, placements and partnerships (ESRC, 2009b). There is evidence, however, that routes from research to policy and practice follow more various and untidy paths of interaction, interpretation and influence than are usually articulated in KE models (Shove and Rip, 2000; Mesman, 2007). A research agenda that takes seriously the need to engage with non-academic stakeholders in all their diversity, including the more disadvantaged and 'hard to reach' parts of the VCS, will need to work with a variety of culturally and subculturally relevant means of getting people from different communities to work together (Kagan, 2007). In some instances, the tried-and-tested repertoire of placements, partnerships, media relations exercises and seminars work well. But there is also a need for more imaginative or innovative ways of supporting sense making and dialogue across boundaries.

Back to communities

Finally, we end by making three concluding comments. First, the vision of the Big Society of the coalition government, as expressed by Prime Minister David Cameron (2010) is about 'fostering and supporting a new culture of voluntarism, philanthropy and social action' and, as such, marks a significant break from the view of a former Conservative Prime Minister, Margaret Thatcher, who argued that 'there is no such thing as society. There are individual men and women and there are families' (Thatcher, 1987). Indeed, in some respects, the Big Society is more aligned to the politics of the Third Way. Giddens (1998, p 78) argued that 'fostering an active civil society is a basic part of the politics of the Third Way'. But that is where the comparison ends because the Big Society is being accompanied by unprecedented cuts in public spending; economic austerity on a scale not seen in post-war Britain.

Second, the Big Society will mark out a distinctive route for England from the devolved administrations of the UK and, indeed, European nations (Danson and Whittam, 2011). Danson and Whittam (2011) argue that among the devolved administrations, Scotland, in particular, is embarking on a different trajectory of how to address economic austerity, with a healthy volunteering tradition and VCS sector operating in a context of a continuing attachment to the collective provision of public services. In autumn 2010, Scottish First Minister Alex Salmond launched the Christie Commission to examine how Scotland's public services could be delivered in future to secure improved outcomes for communities across the country. The Commission's remit included a vision of public services delivered in partnership, involving local communities and the third sector (www.scotland.gov.uk/About/publicservicescommission).

Third, the Big Society envisages change at a number of spatial scales: the individual, the organisation and the community, as noted above, but perhaps its most enduring theme is communities ('strengthening communities', 'empowering communities', 'communities with oomph', 'vanguard communities'). A particular emphasis is placed on the local rather than the regional, as seen in the abolition of the regional tier of government, and the Localism Bill, which is due to become law in late 2011.

Ideas about communities and how to understand them have run throughout this book and we have taken a historical overview of various ways in which policy makers have sought to enrol communities. But is the re-energising of communities as envisioned in the Big Society new? At the outset of the book we mentioned that while we were working in Brightville we participated in helping the community bid for funds as part of the Local Alchemy scheme run by emda and nef. For a limited period, Brightville community groups could access support and advice from a part-time community organiser. In Chapter Six we highlighted the Home Office's CDPs of the 1960s to 1970s. For a 12-year period, the CDPs involved professional workers and researchers working in deprived communities. The Big Society's community organisers will not be in post for 12 years, and most will be unpaid.

It is also important to remember that communities are gendered. Looking at the Big Society through the feminist lens that has also informed this book, there are well-founded concerns that more reliance on communities (with fewer professional public services) means in practice increased demands on women's unpaid work within the home and wider kin networks, and formal and informal unpaid work outside the home and a reinforcement of traditionally gendered roles and responsibilities.

In the Big Society, public expenditure cuts will see an increased demand for practising community spirit and community self-help on a scale far greater than that captured by the authors of the community studies of the 1950s (see Chapter Six). Sprigings and Allen (2005, pp 398, 407) offered a different reading of 'helping out' to that of Young and Willmott (1957) by suggesting that the inter-household cooperation and community care applauded by Young and Willmott (1957) took place because of self-interest and necessity. So, as public services are being cut, whether they are delivered by public, private or VCS providers, it will be because of necessity that households will have to rely on informal help. In Chapter One, we described the birth of the cooperative movement, with the 'Rochdale pioneers', which formed part of a wider visible shift during the 19th century from informalised to formalised philanthropic and voluntary associations and to a differentiation between 'volunteers' and 'unpaid helpers' (see Taylor, 2005). Will the seismic shifts being heralded by the pronouncements of the Big Society also reconfigure what we understand as volunteering in the 21st century?

Notes

[1] The Big Lottery Fund (BIG) is responsible for the delivery of some of the funds raised by the National Lottery to VCSOs.

[2] KE emphasises interaction and conversation, that is, the two-way flows of people, knowledge and ideas between universities and external organisations, allow the knowledge generated from research to be fully utilised beyond academe.

[3] In 2011, the ESRC changed the system of postgraduate funding for studentships, and the CASE studentship scheme ended.

Bibliography

6, P., Leat, D., Selzer, K. and Stoker, G. (2002) *Toward Holistic Governance: The New Reform Agenda*, Basingstoke: Palgrave.

ACEVO (Association of Chief Executives of Voluntary Organisations) (2007) *The Future of Commissioning: Leadership Challenges*, London: ACEVO, http://icn.csip.org.uk/_library/Future_of_Commissioning leadership_challenges.pdf

ACEVO (2010) *The ACEVO Pay Survey 2010/11*, London: ACEVO, www.acevo.org.uk/Document.Doc?id=1119

Ackers, L. (1998) *Shifting Spaces: Women, Citizenship and Migration within the European Union*, Bristol: The Policy Press.

Age UK (2010) 'Our history', www.ageuk.org.uk/about-us/who-we-are/our-history/

Alcock, P. (2010) 'Building the Big Society: A New Policy Environment for the Third Sector in England', *Voluntary Sector Review*, 1(3), pp 381-91, www.tsrc.ac.uk/LinkClick.aspx?fileticket=PwhvBXnPGAU%3D&tabid=716

Alcock, P., Brannelly, T. and Ross, L. (2004) *Formality or Flexibility? Voluntary Sector Contracting in Social Care and Health*, London: NCVO and The Countryside Agency.

Amin, A. (2005) 'Local Community on Trial', *Economy and Society*, 34(4), pp 612-33.

Amin, A. (2009a) 'Extraordinarily Ordinary: Working in the Social Economy', *Social Enterprise Journal*, 5(2), pp 30-49.

Amin, A. (2009b) *The Social Economy: International Perspectives on Economic Solidarity*, London: Zed Books.

Amin, A. and Roberts, J. (2008) 'Knowing in Action: Beyond Communities of Practice', *Research Policy*, 37, pp 353-69.

Anastacio, J., Gidley, B., Hart, L., Keith, M., Mayo, M. and Kowarziki, U. (2000) *Reflecting Realities: Participants' Perspectives on Integrated Communities and Sustainable Development*, Bristol: The Policy Press.

Anderson, B. (1991) *Imagined Communities: Reflections on the Origin and Spread of Nationalism* (2nd edition), London and New York, NY: Verso.

Anheier, H. and Salamon, L. (2006) 'The Non-Profit Sector in Comparative Perspective', in W. Powell and R. Steinberg (eds) *The Non-Profit Sector: A Research Handbook*, New Haven, CT: Yale University Press, pp 89-116.

Arai, S. and Pedlar, A. (2003) 'Moving Beyond Individualism in Leisure Theory: A Critical Analysis of Concepts of Community and Social Engagement', *Leisure Studies*, 22(3), pp 185-202.

Archambault, E. (2001) 'Historical Roots of the Non-profit Sector in France', *Non-Profit and Voluntary Sector Quarterly*, 30, pp 204-20.

Arthur, M.B. (2008) 'Examining Contemporary Careers: A Call for Interdisciplinary Inquiry', *Human Relations*, 61(2), pp 163-218.

Arthur, M.B and Rousseau, D.M. (1996) (eds) *The Boundaryless Career: A New Employment Principle for a New Organizational Era*, Oxford: Oxford University Press.

Atterton, J. (2008) 'Demographics of the Ageing Rural Population', *Working with Older People*, 12(3), pp 19-22.

Audit Commission (2007) *Hearts and Minds: Commissioning from the Voluntary Sector*, London: Audit Commission.

Backus, P. and Clifford, D. (2010) *Trends in the Concentration of Income among Charities*, Birmingham: TSRC.

Badham, R. and Sense, A. (2006) 'Spiralling Up or Spinning Out: A Guide for Reflecting on Action Research Practice', *International Journal of Social Research Methodology*, 9(5), pp 367-77.

Bailyn, L. (1989) 'Understanding Individual Experiences at Work: Comments on the Theory and Practice of Careers', in M.B. Arthur, D.T. Hall and B.S. Lawrence (eds) *Handbook of Career Theory*, Cambridge: Cambridge University Press, pp 477-89.

Bailyn, L. (1993) 'Individual Constraints' Occupational Demands and Private Life', in L. Bailyn, *Breaking the Mould*, New York, NY: Free Press.

Baines, D. (2004) 'Caring for Nothing: Work Organization and Unwaged Labour in Social Services', *Work, Employment & Society*, 18(2), pp 267-95.

Baines, S. and Hardill, I. (2008) '"At Least I Can Do Something": The Work of Volunteering in a Community Beset by Worklessness', *Social Policy and Society*, 7(3), pp 307-17.

Baines, S., Bull, M. and Woolrych, R. (2010) 'A More Entrepreneurial Mindset? Engaging Third Sector Suppliers to the NHS', *Social Enterprise Journal*, 6(1), pp 49-58.

Baines, S., Lie, M. and Wheelock, J. (2006) *Volunteering, Self-help and Citizenship in Later Life*, Newcastle upon Tyne: Newcastle University, www.ncl.ac.uk/gps/assets/documents/ACN%20Volunteering%20Report.pdf

Baines, S., Lie, M. and Wheelock, J. (2007) *Volunteering, Self-Help and Citizenship in Later Life*, Newcastle upon Tyne: Age Concern Newcastle and Newcastle University, www.worldvolunteerweb.org/fileadmin/docdb/pdf/2006/newcastle_senior_volunteer.pdf

Baines, S., Wilson, R. and Hardill, I. (2008) 'How Can Voluntary Organisations Help to Transform Care? Articulating Social Value', Paper presented at the Transforming Elder Care Conference, Copenhagen, June, www.socialwelfareservicedelivery.org.uk/files/Transforming%20Care%20Paper.pdf

Baldock, J. and Hadlow, J. (2002) *Housebound Older People: The Links between Identity, Self Esteem and the Use of Care Services*, Research Findings 4, Sheffield: GO Programme.

Barlow, J. and Hainsworth, J. (2001) 'Volunteerism among Older People with Arthritis', *Ageing and Society*, 21(2), pp 203-317.

Barnes, C., Mercer, G. and Shakespeare, T. (1999) *Exploring Disability: A Sociological Introduction*, Cambridge: Polity Press.

Barnes, H. and Parry, J. (2004) 'Renegotiating Identity and Relationships: Men and Women's Adjustment to Retirement', *Ageing and Society*, 24, pp 213-33.

Bauld, L., Judge, K., Barnes, M., Benzeval, M., Mackenzie, M. and Sullivan, H. (2005) 'Promoting Social Change: The Experience of Health Action Zones in England', *Journal of Social Policy*, 34(3), pp 427-45.

BBC (2005) Cameron chosen as new Tory leader, 6th December, http://news.bbc.co.uk/1/hi/uk_politics/4502652.stm.

Beck, U. (1992) *Risk Society: Towards a New Modernity*, London: Sage Publications.

Beck, U. (2000) *The Brave New World of Work*, Cambridge: Polity Press

Beechey, V. (1987) *Unequal Work*, London: Verso.

Beneria, L. (1999) 'The Enduring Debate Over Unpaid Labour', *International Labour Review*, 138(3), pp 287-309.

Benwell CDP (Community Development Project) (1978) *Slums on the Drawing Board: Final Report No. 4*, Newcastle: Benwell CDP.

Beveridge, W. (1948) *Voluntary Action*, New York, NY: Macmillan.

Beyer, J. and Trice, H. (1982) 'The Utilization Process: A Conceptual Framework and Synthesis of Empirical Evidence', *Administrative Science Quarterly*, 27(4), pp 591-622.

Billis, D. (1993) *Organising Public and Voluntary Agencies*, London: Routledge.

Billis, D. and Glennerster, H. (1998) 'Human Services and the Voluntary Sector: Towards a Theory of Comparative Advantage', *Journal of Social Policy*, 27, pp 79-98.

Birch, K. and Whittam, G. (2008) 'The Third Sector and the Regional Development of Social Capital', *Regional Studies*, 42(3), pp 437-50.

Birchall, J. (1997) *The International Co-operative Movement*, Manchester: Manchester University Press.

Blackburn, R. and Kovalain, A. (2009) 'Researching Small Firms and Entrepreneurship: Past, Present and Future', *Journal of Management Reviews*, 11(2), pp 127–48.

Blackburn, R. and Ram, M. (2006) 'Fix or Fixation? The Contributions and Limitations of Entrepreneurship and Small Firms to Combating Social Exclusion', *Entrepreneurship and Regional Development*, 18(1), pp 73–89.

Blackmore, A. (2005) *The Reform of Public Services: The Role of the Voluntary Sector*, London: NCVO.

Blackmore, A. (2006) *How Voluntary and Community Organisations Can Help Transform Public Services*, London: NCVO.

Blair, T. (1999) Keynote speech, NCVO Annual Conference, February, www.number10.gov.uk/Page8072

Blond, P. (2010) *Red Tory: How Left and Right Have Broken Britain and How We Can Fix It*, London: Faber and Faber.

Bone, D. (2002) 'Dilemmas of Emotion Work in Nursing under Market-Driven Health Care', *International Journal of Public Sector Management*, 152, pp 140-50.

Bradley, H., Erikson, M., Stephenson, C. and Williams, S. (2000) *Myths at Work*, Cambridge: Polity Press.

Brewis, G., Hill, M. and Stevens, D. (2010) *Valuing Volunteer Management Skills*, London: Institute for Volunteering Research.

British Academy of Management (2009) *REF Consultation and the Measurement of Impact*, London: BAM.

Brooks, D. (2000) *Bobos in Paradise: The New Upper Class and How They Got There*, New York, NY: Simon & Schuster.

Brophy, J. (1994) 'Parent Management Committees and Pre-School Playgroups: The Partnership Model and Future Management Policy', *Journal of Social Policy*, 23(2), pp 161-94.

Brown, E. (1999) 'Assessing the Value of Volunteer Activity', *Non-Profit and Voluntary Sector Quarterly*, 28(1), pp 3-17.

Bruegel, I. (2000) 'Getting Explicit: Gender and Local Economic Development', *Local Economy*, 15, pp 2-8.

Bull, M. (2008) 'Challenging Tensions: Critical, Theoretical and Empirical Perspectives on Social Enterprise', *International Journal of Entrepreneurial Behaviour and Research*, 14(5), pp 268-75.

Byrne, D. (1999) *Social Exclusion*, Buckingham: Open University Press.

Cabinet Office (2000) *Winning the Generation Game: Improving Opportunities for People Aged 50-65 in Work and Community Activity*, London: Cabinet Office.

Cabinet Office (2007) *The Future Role of the Third Sector in Social and Economic Regeneration: Final Report*, London: Cabinet Office.

Cabinet Office (2010a) *Building the Big Society*, London: Cabinet Office, www.cabinetoffice.gov.uk/media/407789/building-big-society.pdf

Cabinet Office (2010b) *Giving: Green Paper*, London: Cabinet Office, www.cabinetoffice.gov.uk/resource-library/giving-green-paper

Cairns, B., Harris, M. and Hutchison, R. (2007) 'Sharing God's Love or Meeting Government Goals? Local Churches and Public Policy Implementation', *Policy & Politics*, 35(3), pp 413-32.

Cameron, D. (2010a) 'Big Society Speech', July, www.number10.gov.uk/news/speeches-and-transcripts/2010/07/big-society-speech-53572.

Cameron, D. (2010) 'The Big Society', *The Independent*, 20 July, p 1.

Campbell, K.H. (2004) *A Unified National Response to the 2004 Volunteer Management Capacity Study*, Washington DC: National Human Services Assembly.

Carroll, A. (1998) 'The Four Faces of Corporate Citizenship', *Business and Society Review*, 100(1), pp 1-7.

Cassidy, S. (1977) *Audacity to Believe*, Glasgow: Collins.

Caswill, C. and Shove, E. (2000) *Postscript to the Special Issue on Interactive Social Science*, Science and Public Policy, 27(3), pp 220-2.

Cave, M. and Hannay, S. (1996) *Assessment of Research Impact on Non-Academic Audiences: Consultants Report*, Uxbridge: Faculty of Social Sciences, Brunel University.

CDP Information and Intelligence Unit (1974) *Inter-Project Report*, London: CDP Information and Intelligence Unit.

Champion, T. and Shepherd, J. (2006) 'Demographic Change in Rural England', in P. Lowe and L. Speakman (eds) *The Ageing Countryside: The Growing Older Population of Rural England*, London: Age Concern England, pp 29-50.

Chapman, T., Forbes, D. and Brown, J. (2007) 'They Think They Have God on Their Side: The Impact of Public Sector Attitudes on the Development of Social Enterprise', *Social Enterprise Journal*, 3(1), www.sel.org.uk/docs/3rd%20volume%20SEJ.pdf

Chapman, T., Robinson, F., Brown, J., Shaw, S., Ford, C., Bailey, E. and Crow, R. (2009) *Mosaic, Jigsaw or Abstract? Getting a Big Picture Perspective on the Third Sector in North East England and Cumbria*, Northern Rock Foundation Third Sector Trends Study, Newcastle upon Tyne: Northern Rock Foundation, www.nr-foundation.org.uk/thirdsectortrends

Charity Commission (2007) *Stand and Deliver: The Future for Charities Providing Public Services*, Liverpool: Charity Commission.

Chell, E. (2007) 'Social Enterprise and Entrepreneurship: Towards a Convergent Theory of the Entrepreneurial Process', *International Small Business Journal*, 25, pp 5-26.

Chell, E. and Baines, S. (2000) 'Networking, Entrepreneurship and Microbusiness Behaviour', *Entrepreneurship and Regional Development*, 12(3), pp 195-215.

Chell, E., Haworth, J. and Brearley, S. (1991) *The Entrepreneurial Personality: Concepts, Cases and Categories*, London: Routledge.

Chouhan, K. and Lusane, C. (2004) *Black Voluntary and Community Sector Funding, Civic Engagement and Capacity-Building*, York: Joseph Rowntree Foundation.

Churchill, W.S., www.brainyquote.com/quotes/quotes/w/winstonchu131192.html

Clark, H., Dyer, S. and Horwood, J. (1998) *'That Bit of Help':The High Value of Low Level Preventative Services for Older People*, Bristol: The Policy Press.

Clark, J. (2007) *Voluntary Sector Skills Survey 2007: England*, London: The UK Workforce Hub.

Clark, J., Kane, D., Wilding, K. and Wilton, J. (2010) *UK Civil Society*, London: NCVO.

Cochrane, A. (2007) *Understanding Urban Policy: A Critical Approach*, Oxford: Blackwell.

Cockburn, C. (1981) 'The material of male power', *Feminist Review*, 9, 41–58.

Collin, A. and Watts, A.G. (1996) 'The Death and Transfiguration of Career – and of Career Guidance?', *British Journal of Guidance and Counselling*, 25(4), pp 435-46.

Commission on the Future of Volunteering (2008) *Report of the Commission on the Future of Volunteering and Manifesto for Change*, London: Volunteering England.

Conservative Party (2008) *Voluntary Action in the 21st Century*, London: Conservative Party.

Conservative Party (2010) *Big Society Not Big Government*, London: Conservative Party, www.conservatives.com/news/news_stories/2010/03/~/media/Files/Downloadable%20Files/Building-a-Big-Society.ashx

Cooke, P. (1989) (ed) *Localities*, London: Unwin Hyman.

Co-operatives UK (2009) *Co-operative Review 2009*, Manchester: Co-operatives UK, www.uk.coop/sites/default/files/Review09_0.pdf

Coule, T. (2007) 'Developing Strategies for Sustainability: Implications for Governance and Accountability', *13th Researching the Voluntary Sector Conference*, University of Warwick, www.ncvo-vol.org.uk/uploadedFiles/NCVO/What_we_do/Research/Research_Events/Coule_T_PDF.pdf

CRESR (Centre for Regional Economic and Social Research) (2002) *Hidden Unemployment in the East Midlands*, Sheffield: CRESR, Sheffield Hallam University, www.eastmidlandsobservatory.org.uk

Crow, G. (2002) 'Community Studies, Fifty Years of Theorisation', *Sociological Research Online*, 7(3), www.socresonline.org.uk/7/3/crow.html

Crow, G. and Allan, G. (1994) *Community Life: An Introduction to Local Social Relations*, Hemel Hempstead: Harvester Wheatsheaf.

Curtis, T. (2008) 'Finding the Grit that Makes a Pearl', *International Journal of Entrepreneurial Behaviour and Research*, 14(5), pp 276-90.

Daly, M. (2002) 'Care as a Good for Social Policy', *Journal of Social Policy*, 31(2), pp 251-70.

Daly, M. and Lewis, J. (2000) 'The Concept of Social Care and the Analysis of Contemporary Welfare States', *British Journal of Sociology*, 51(2), pp 281-98.

Danson, M. and Whittam, G. (2011) 'Scotland's Civic Society v England's Big Society? Diverging Roles of the VCS in Public Service Delivery', *Social Policy and Society*, 10(3), pp 353-63.

Davies, H., Nutley, S. and Walter, I. (2005) *Assessing the Impact of Social Science Research: Conceptual, Methodological and Practical Issues*, London: ESRC Symposium on Assessing Non-Academic Impact of Research.

Davies, H., Nutley, S.M. and Smith, P.C. (2000) *What Works? Evidence-Based Policy and Practice in Public Services*, Bristol: The Policy Press.

Davis Smith, J. (1995) 'The Voluntary Tradition: Philanthropy and Self-Help in Britain 1500-1945', in J. Davis Smith, C. Rochester and R. Hedley (eds) *An Introduction to the Voluntary Sector*, London: Routledge, pp 9-39.

Davis Smith, J. (1996) 'Should Volunteers be Managed?', in D. Billis and M. Harris (eds) *Voluntary Agencies: Challenges of Organisation and Management*, Basingstoke: Macmillan, pp 187-99.

Davis Smith, J. (1998) *1997 National Survey of Volunteering*, London: National Centre for Volunteering.

Davis Smith, J. (2000) 'Active Participation Beyond Employment', in D. Hirsch (ed) *Life After 50: Issues for Policy and Research*, York: Joseph Rowntree Foundation.

Davis Smith, J. and Gay, P. (2005) *Volunteering in Retirement*, York: Joseph Rowntree Foundation.

DCLG (Department for Communities and Local Government) (2008) *Citizenship Survey April-December 2008, England*, Cohesion Research Statistical Release 4(2), London: HMSO, www.communities.gov.uk/ publications/corporate/statistics/citizenshipsurveyq3200809

DCSF (Department for Children, Schools and Families) *Every Child Matters*, www.dcsf.gov.uk/everychildmatters/earlyyears/surestart/ whatsurestartdoes

Deakin, N. (1995) 'The Perils of Partnership: The Voluntary Sector and the State 1945-1992', in J. Davis Smith, C. Rochester and R. Hedley (eds) *Introduction to the Voluntary Sector*, London: Routledge, pp 40-65.

Dean, H. (2003) 'Re-Conceptualising Welfare-to-Work for People with Multiple Problems and Needs', *Journal of Social Policy*, 32(3), pp 441-59.

Dennis, N., Henriques, F. and Slaughter, C. (1957, 1969) *Coal Is Our Life: An Analysis of a Yorkshire Mining Community*, London: Tavistock.

Devine, F. (2003) *A Qualitative Study of Democracy and Participation in Britain: ESRC award L215252023*, Swindon: ESRC.

Devine, F. and Roberts, J. (2003) 'Alternative Approaches to Researching Social Capital: A Comment on Van Deth's Measuring Social Capital', *International Journal of Social Research Methodology*, 6, pp 93-100.

Dex, S. (1991) *Life and Work History Analysis: Qualitative and Quantitative Development*, London: Routledge.

Dey, P. (2010) 'The Politics of Narrating Social Entrepreneurship', *Journal of Enterprising Communities: People and Places in the Global Economy*, 4(1), pp 85-108.

DH (Department of Health) (2001) *The National Service Framework for Older People*, London: DH, www.dh.gov.uk/en/publicationsandstatistics/ publications/publicationspolicyandguidance/DH_4003066

DH (2008) *Towards a Strategy in Health and Social Care: Consultation*, London: DH.

Di Domencio, M., Tracey, P. and Haugh, H. (2009) 'Social Economy Involvement in Public Service Delivery: Community Engagement and Accountability', *Regional Studies*, 43(7), pp 981-22.

Diamond, J. (2011) 'The Big Society and the Regional Studies Agenda: Why the Connections Matter', *Regions*, 281, pp 4-5.

Dickens, C. (1976) *Bleak House*, London: Pan Books.

Dickinson, H. and Glasby, J. (2010) *The Personalisation Agenda: Implications for the Third Sector*, Third Sector Research Centre Working Paper 30, Birmingham: TSRC.

DirectGov (2010) *The New Deal*, www.direct.gov.uk/en/Employment/ Jobseekers/programmesandservices/DG_173717

Dolnica, S. and Randle, M. (2007) 'What Motivates Which Volunteers? Psychographic Heterogeneity among Volunteers in Australia', *Voluntas*, 18, pp 135-55.

Douglas, M. (1992) *Risk and Blame: How Institutions Think*, London: Routledge.

Down, S. (2006) *Narratives of Enterprise: Crafting Entrepreneurial Self-Identity in a Small Firm*, Cheltenham: Edward Elgar.

Down, S. (2010) *Enterprise, Entrepreneurship and Small Business*, London: Sage Publications.

Down, S. and Reveley, J. (2004) 'Generational Encounters and the Social Formation of Entrepreneurial Identity: "Young Guns" and "Old Farts"', *Organization*, 11(2), pp 233-50.

Doyle, M.E. and Smith, M.K. (1999) *Born and Bred? Leadership, Heart and Informal Education*, London: YMCA George Williams College/ The Rank Foundation.

DRC (2007) *Recruiting, Retaining and Developing Disabled Volunteers: Guidance for Volunteer Opportunity Providers*, Manchester, Disability Rights Commission

Driver, M. (1980) 'Career Concepts and Organizational Change', in C. Derr (ed) *Work, Family and the Career*, New York, NY: Praeger.

Driver, M. (1988) 'Careers: A Review of Personal and Organizational Research', in C. Cooper and I. Robertson (eds) *International Review of Industrial and Organizational Psychology*, New York, NY: Wiley, pp 237-69.

Drucker, P.E. (1990) *Managing the Nonprofit Organization*, New York, NY: HarperCollins.

du Gay, P. (1996) *Consumption and Identity at Work*, London: Sage Publications.

du Gay, P. (2000) *In Praise of Bureaucracy: Weber, Organisation and Ethics*, London: Sage Publications.

du Gay, P. (2007) *Organizing Identity: Persons and Organizations after Theory*, London: Sage Publications.

Dubini, P. and Aldrich, H. (1991) 'Personal and Extended Networks are Central to the Entrepreneurial Process', *Journal of Business Venturing*, 6, pp 305-13.

Duggan, K. and Kagan, C. (2007) *We Don't Believe You Want a Genuine Partnership: Universities Work With Communities*, RIHSC Working Paper, Manchester: Manchester Metropolitan University.

Durant, R. (1959) *Watling: A Survey of Social Life on a New Housing Estate*, London: P.S. King.

Duryea, M., Hoffman, M. and Parfitt, A. (2007) 'Measuring the Impact of Research, *Research Global*, 9, pp 26-7.

DWP (Department for Work and Pensions) (2006) *A Guide to Volunteering While on Benefits*, London: DWP.

Dwyer, P. and Hardill, I. (2008) *Older People and Village Services: Exploring the Impact on Community Based Services in Rural England*, London: Age Concern, www.ageconcern.org.uk/AgeConcern/Documents/53_0508_Village_Services.pdf

Edwards, R., Franklin, J. and Holland, J. (2003) *Families and Social Capital: Exploring the Issues*, London: South Bank University.

Eikenberry, A. and Kluver, J. (2004) 'The Marketization of the Nonprofit Sector', *Public Administration Review*, 64(2), pp 132-40.

Ellis Paine, A., Ockenden, N. and Stuart, J. (2010) 'Volunteers in Hybrid Organizations: A marginalised majority?' in D. Billis (ed) *Hybrid Organizations and the Third Sector: Challenges for practice, theory and policy*, Basingstoke: Palgrave Macmillan.

Epstein, C.F., Seron, C., Oglensky, B. and Saute, R. (1999) *The Part-Time Paradox: Time Norms, Professional Life, Family and Gender*, New York, NY: Routledge.

Erikson, R. and Goldthorpe, J.H. (1992) *The Constant Flux: A Study of Class Mobility in Industrial Societies*, Oxford: Clarendon Press.

Erlinghagen, M. and Hank, K. (2006) 'The Participation of Older Europeans in Volunteer Work', *Ageing and Society*, 26(4), pp 567-84.

Esping-Andersen, G. (1990) *The Three Worlds of Welfare Capitalism*, Princeton, NJ: Princeton University Press.

Esping-Andersen, G. (1999) *Social Foundations of Postindustrial Economies*, New York, NY: Oxford University Press.

ESRC (Economic and Social Research Council) (2009a) *Taking Stock: A Summary of the ESRC's Work to Evaluate the Impact of Research on Policy and Practice*, Swindon: ESRC.

ESRC (2009b) *Approaches to Assessing the Non-Academic Impact of Social Science Research*, Swindon: ESRC, www.esrc.ac.uk/ESRCInfoCentre/Images/non-academic_impact_symposium_report_tcm6-16593.pdf

Etzkowitz, H. (2003) 'Research Groups as "Quasi-Firms": The Invention of the Entrepreneurial University', *Research Policy*, 32(1), pp 109-21.

Evers, A. (2003) 'Social Capital and Civic Commitment: On Putnam's Way of Understanding', *Social Policy and Society*, 2, pp 13-21.

Evetts, J. (2000) 'Analysing Change in Women's Careers: Culture, Structure and Action Dimensions', *Gender, Work and Organizations*, 7(1), pp 57-67.

Exworthy, M. and Halford, S. (1999) (eds) *Professionals and the New Managerialism in the Public Sector*, Buckingham: Open University Press.

Farnell, R., Furbey, R., Shams, S., Hills, A., Macey, M. and Smith, G. (2003) *Faith in Urban Regeneration? Engaging Faith Communities in Urban Regeneration*, Bristol: The Policy Press.

Fischer, L.R. and Schaffer, K.B. (1993) *Older Volunteers: A Guide to Research and Practice*, Newbury Park, London and New Delhi: Sage Publications.

Folbre, N. (1995) '"Holding Hands at Midnight": The Paradox of Caring Labour', *Feminist Economics*, 1(1), pp 73-92.

Forrest, R. and Kearns, A. (2001) 'Social Cohesion, Social Capital and the Neighbourhood', *Urban Studies*, 38(12), pp 2125-62.

Frankenburg, R. (1969) *Communities in Britain: Social Life in Town and Country*, Harmondsworth: Penguin.

Frazer, E. (1999) 'Unpicking Political Communitarianism: A Critique of "the Communitarian Family"', in G. Jagger and C. Wright (eds) *Changing Family Values*, London: Routledge, pp 150-64.

Fyfe, N.R. (2005) 'Making Space for "Neo-Communitarianism"? The Third Sector, State and Civil Society in the UK', *Antipode*, 3(3), pp 536-57.

Galster, G. (2001) 'On the Nature of Neighbourhood', *Urban Studies*, 38(12), pp 2111-24.

Gartner, W. (2010) 'A New Path to the Waterfall: A Narrative on a Use of Entrepreneurial Narrative', *International Small Business Journal*, 28(1), pp 6-19.

Gaskell, E. (2003) *North and South*, Harmondsworth: Penguin Classic.

Gay, P. (2000a) *Delivering the Goods: A Report of the Work of Volunteer Managers*, London: Institute for Volunteering Research.

Gay, P. (2000b) 'Delivering the Goods: The Work and Future Direction of Volunteer Management', *Voluntary Action*, 2(5), pp 45-67.

Gerard, D. (1983) *Charities in Britain: Conservatism or Change?*, London: Bedford Square Press.

Gershon, P. (2004) *Releasing Resources for the Frontline: Independent Review of Public Sector Efficiency*, London: HM Treasury.

Gibbons, M., Limoges, C., Nowotny, H., Schwartzman, S., Scott, P. and Trow, M., (1994). *The new production of knowledge: the dynamics of science and research in contemporary societies*, London: Sage.

Gibson-Graham, J.K. (2006) *A Postcapitalist politics*, Minneapolis, MN: University of Minnesota Press.

Giddens, A. (1991) *Modernity and Self-Identity*, Cambridge: Polity Press.

Giddens, A. (1998) *The Third Way: The Renewal of Social Democracy*, Cambridge: Polity Press.

Gidley, A., Hart, B., Keith, L., Mayo, M. and Kowarziki, U. (2000) *Reflecting Realities: Participants' Perspectives on Integrated Communities and Sustainable Development*, Bristol: The Policy Press.

Gilligan, C. (1982) *In a Different Voice*, Cambridge, MA: Harvard University Press.

Girard, J.P. (2002) 'Social Cohesion, Governance and the Development of Health and Social Care Co-operatives', *Review of International Cooperation*, 95(1), pp 58-64.

Glucksmann, M. (1995) 'Why Work? Gender and the Total Social Organisation of Labour', *Gender, Work and Organisation*, 2(2), pp 63-75.

Glucksmann, M. (2000) *Cottons and Casuals: The Gendered Organisation of Labour in Time and Space*, Durham: Sociology Press.

Glucksmann, M. (2005) 'Shifting Boundaries and Interconnections: Extending the "Total Social Organisation of Labour"', in L. Pettinger, J. Parry, R.F. Taylor and M. Glucksmann (eds) *A New Sociology of Work?*, Oxford: Blackwell, pp 19-36.

Glucksmann, M. (2009) 'Formations, Connections and Divisions of Labour', *Sociology*, 43(5), pp 878-95.

Glucksmann, M. and Lyon, D. (2006) 'Configurations of Care Work: Paid and Unpaid Elder Care in Italy and the Netherlands', *Sociological Research Online*, 11(2), www.socresonline.org.uk/11/2/glucksmann. html

Gorsky, M. (1998) 'Mutual Aid and Civil Society: Friendly Societies in Nineteenth-Century Bristol', *Urban History*, 25(3), pp 302-22.

Green, A.E. (1997) 'A Question of Compromise? Case Study Evidence on the Location and Mobility Strategies of Dual Career Households', *Regional Studies*, 31, pp 643-59.

Gripaois, P. (2002) 'The Failure of Regeneration Policy in Britain', *Regional Studies*, 36(5), pp 568-78.

Groombridge, B. (2010) 'Better Government with Older Citizens: A Test of Democracy', *Political Quarterly*, 81(1), pp 131-40.

Haezewindt, P. (2003) 'Investing in Each Other and the Community: The Role of Social Capital', in C. Summerfield and P. Babb (eds) *Social Trends*, London: HMSO, pp 19-27.

Halfpenny, P. and Reid, M. (2002) 'Research on the Voluntary Sector: An Overview', *Policy & Politics*, 30(4), pp 533-50.

Hallam, J. (2002) 'Vocation to Profession: Changing Images of Nursing in Britain', *Journal of Organizational Change Management*, 15(1), pp 35-47.

Handy, C. (1995) 'Trust and the Virtual Organization', *Harvard Business Review*, May-June, pp 40-50.

Hardill, I. (2002) *Gender, Migration and the Dual Career Household*, International Studies of Women and Place series, London: Routledge.

Hardill, I. (2006) '"A Place in the Countryside": Migration and the Construction of Rural Living', in P. Lowe and L. Speakman (eds) *The Ageing Countryside: The Growing Older Population of Rural England*, London: Age Concern England, pp 51-68.

Hardill, I. and Baines, S. (2003) 'Doing One's Duty? Voluntary Work and the "New Economy"', *Local Economy*, 18(2), pp 102-8.

Hardill, I. and Baines, S. (2009) 'Active Citizenship in Later Life: Older Adults in a Deprived Community', *Professional Geographer*, 61(1), pp 36-45.

Hardill, I. and Dwyer, P. (2011) 'Growing Old in Rural England: Some Challenges of Delivering Village Services in the Mixed Economy of Welfare', *Journal of Social Policy*, 40(1), pp 157-72.

Hardill, I., Baines, S. and 6, P. (2007) 'Volunteering for All? Explaining Patterns of Volunteering, Identifying Strategies to Promote it', *Policy & Politics*, 35(3), pp 395-412.

Hardill, I., Mackenzie, H. and Burnett, T. (2010) *Engaging Parents*, An unpublished report to Derbyshire County Council.

Hardill, I., Spradbery, J., Arnold-Boakes, J. and Marrugat, M.L. (2005) 'Severe Health and Social Care Issues among British Migrants who Retire to Spain', *Ageing and Society*, 25, pp 769-83.

Harrow, J. and Mole, V. (2005) '"I Want to Move Once I Have Got Things Straight!": Voluntary Sector Chief Executive Career Accounts', *Non-Profit Management and Leadership*, 16(1), pp 79-100.

Harvey, S. (2005) *Ilkeston (Pocket Images)*, Stroud: NonSuch.

Haugh, H. and Kitson, M. (2007) 'The Third Way and the Third Sector: New Labour's Economic Policy and the Social Economy', *Cambridge Journal of Economics*, 31(6), pp 973-94.

Hayden, C. and Boaz, A. (2002) *Making a Difference: The Better Government for Older People Evaluation Report*, Coventry: Local Government Centre, University of Warwick.

Hibbitt, K., Jones, P. and Meegan, R. (2001) 'Tackling Social Exclusion: The Role of Social Capital in Urban Regeneration on Merseyside', *European Planning Studies*, 9(2), pp 141-61.

Hill, M., Russell, J. and Brewis, G. (2009) *Young People, Volunteering and Youth Projects: A Rapid Review of Recent Evidence*, London: Institute for Volunteering Research.

Hillery, G. (1955) 'Definitions of Community: Areas of Agreement', *Rural Sociology*, 20(1), pp 111-23.

Himmelweit, S. (1995) 'The Discovery of "Unpaid" Work: The Social Consequences of the Expansion of "Work"', *Feminist Economics*, 1(2), pp 1-19.

HM Government (2009) *Building a Society for all Ages*, Cm 7655, Norwich: The Stationery Office, www.hmg.gov.uk/buildingasocietyforallages. aspx

HM Treasury (2002) *The Role of the Voluntary and Community Sector in Service Delivery: A Cross Cutting Review*, London: HM Treasury, www.hm-treasury.gov.uk/spending_review/spend_ccr/spend_ccr_ voluntary/ccr_voluntary_report.cfm

HMSO (1993) *Realising Our Potential: A Strategy for Science, Engineering and Technology*, Cm 2250, London: The Stationery Office.

Hochschild, A.R. (1983) *The Managed Heart: Commercialization of Human Feeling*, Berkeley, CA: University of California Press.

Hodgson, L. (2004) 'Manufactured Civil Society: Counting the Cost', *Critical Social Policy*, 24(2), pp 139-64.

Hogg, E. (2010) 'The Demographic Opportunity: Volunteering in Older Age', Paper presented at the VSSN Day Conference, London, 1 December.

Hogg, E. and Baines, S. (2011) 'Changing Responsibilities and Roles of the VCS in the Welfare Mix: A Review', *Social Policy and Society*, 10(3), pp 341-52.

Hood, C. (1998) *The Art of the State*, Oxford: Oxford University Press.

House of Commons (2006) *Select Committee on Public Accounts: Thirty-Second Report*, London: HMSO.

House of Commons Committee of Public Accounts (2006) *Working with the voluntary sector, Thirty–second Report of Session 2005–06*, London: HMSO.

House of Commons (2010) 21 October, www.publications.parliament. uk/pa/cm201011/cmhansrd/cm101021/debtext/101021-0001. htm#10102141000918

Howlett, S. (2010) 'Developing Volunteer Management as a Profession', *Voluntary Sector Review*, 1(3), pp 355-60.

Hyatt, J. and England, J. (1995) *Investing in the Heart of Change: The Case for Resourcing the Support and Development of Self Help Activities*, London: NCVO.

Industry Commission (1994) *Charitable Organisations in Australia: An Inquiry into Community Social Welfare Organisations*, Canberra, Australia: Industry Commission.

Institute for Volunteering Research (2009) *A Gateway to Work: The Role of Volunteer Centres in Supporting the Link between Volunteering and Employment*, London: Institute for Volunteering Research.

ICA (International Co-operative Association) (undated) 'Statement of Co-operative Identity', www.ica.coop/coop/principles.html

ICA (2005) *Co-operative History: The Rochdale Pioneers*, Geneva: ICA, www.ica.coop/coop/history.html

IVR (Institute for Volunteering Research) (2009) *A Gateway to Work: The Role of Volunteer Centres in Supporting the Link between Volunteering and Employment*, London: IVR, www.ivr.org.uk/evidence-bank/evidence-pages/A+Gateway+to+Work.+The+role+of+Volunteer+Centres+in+supporting+the+link+between+volunteering+and+emp.htm

Jackson, P. and Robinson, C. (2003) 'Children's Hospices: Where Do They Fit?', *Critical Social Policy*, 23(1), pp 103-12.

Jarvis, H. (1999) 'The Tangled Webs We Weave: Household Strategies to Co-ordinate Home and Work', *Work, Employment & Society*, 13(2), pp 225-47.

Jayne, M. (2003) 'Too Many Voices, "Too Problematic to be Plausible": Representing Multiple Responses to Local Economic Development Strategies?', *Environment and Planning A*, 35(6), pp 959-81.

Jeavons, T. (1992) 'When Management is the Message: Relating Values to Management Practice in Nonprofit Organizations', *Non-Profit Leadership and Management*, 2(4), pp 403-17.

Jochum, V., Pratten, B. and Wilding, K. (2005) *Civil Renewal and Active Citizenship: A Guide to the Debate*, London: NCVO.

Kagan, C.M. (2007) Working at the Edge: Making Use of Psychological Resources through Collaboration, *The Psychologist*, 20(4), pp 224-27.

Kanter, R.M. (1995) *World Class: Thriving Locally in the Global Economy*, New York, NY: Simon & Schuster.

Kearney, C., Hisrich, R.D. and Roche, F. (2009) 'Public and Private Sector Entrepreneurship: Similarities, Differences or a Combination?', *Journal of Small Business and Enterprise Development*, 16(1), pp 26-46.

Kearney, C., Robert, D. and Hisrich, F.R. (2009) 'Public and Private Sector Entrepreneurship: Similarities, Differences or a Combination?', *Journal of Small Business and Enterprise Development*, 16(1), pp 26-46.

Kearns, A. and Parkes, A. (2003) 'Living in and Leaving Poor Neighbourhood Conditions in England', *Housing Studies*, 18(6), pp 827-51.

Kearns, A. and Parkinson, M. (2001) 'The Significance of Neighbourhood', *Urban Studies*, 38(12), pp 2103-10.

Keating, M. (2005) *Policy Making and Policy Divergence in Scotland after Devolution*. Devolution Briefing No. 21, University of Edinburgh. www.devolution.ac.uk/pdfdata/Briefing%2021%20-%20Keating.pdf

Kelly's Directory, *1855*, London: Kelly & Co Ltd.

Kelly's Directory, *1936*, London: Kelly & Co Ltd.

Kendall, J. (2003) *The Voluntary Sector: Comparative Perspectives in the UK*, London: Routledge.

Kendall, J. (2010) *Volunteering in Europe in the Noughties: What Would Beveridge Have Thought?*, Birmingham: TSRC, www.tsrc.ac.uk/LinkClick.aspx?fileticket=LI7Q0POrU0c%3D&tabid=596

Kendall, J. and Knapp, M. (1995) 'A Loose and Baggy Monster: Boundaries, Definitions and Typologies', in J. Davis Smith, C. Rochester and R. Hedley (eds) *An Introduction to the Voluntary Sector*, London: Routledge, pp 66-95.

Kendall, J. and Knapp, M. (2000) 'Measuring the Performance of Voluntary Organisations', *Public Management*, 2, pp 105-32.

Kidd, A. (1996) 'Philanthropy and the "Social History Paradigm"', *Social History*, 21(2), pp 181-92.

Kingdon, J. (1995) *Agendas, Alternatives and Public Policy*, New York, NY: HarperCollins.

Kisby, B. (2010) 'The Big Society: Power to the People?', *The Political Quarterly*, 81(4), pp 484-91.

Knapp, M., Vasiliki, K. and Davis Smith, J. (1995) *Who Volunteers and Why? The Key Factors which Determine Volunteering*, London: The Volunteer Centre.

Kröger, T. (2009) 'Care Research and Disability Studies: Nothing in Common?, *Critical Social Policy*, 29(3), pp 398-420.

Kuper, L. (1953) *Living in Towns*, London: Cresset Press.

Lawrence, D.H. (2007) *The Rainbow*, Harmondsworth: Penguin.

Lawson, V. (2007) 'Geographies of Care and Responsibility', *Annals of the Association of American Geographers*, 97(1), pp 1-11.

Leadbeater, C. (1997) *The Rise of the Social Entrepreneur*, London: Demos.

Leadbeater, C. (2004) *Personalisation through participation: A new script for public services*, London: Demos.

Lee, D. and Newby, H. (1983) *The Problem of Sociology: An Introduction to the Discipline*, London: Hutchinson.

Lee, P. (1999) 'Where are the Socially Excluded? Continuing Debates on the Identification of Poor Neighbourhoods', *Regional Studies*, 33(5), pp 483-6.

Leete, L. (2006) 'Work in the Non-Profit Sector', in W. Powell and R. Steinberg (eds) *The Non-Profit Sector: A Research Handbook*, New Haven, CT: Yale University, pp 159-79.

Levitas, R. (2000) 'Community, Utopia and New Labour', *Local Economy*, 15(3), pp 188-97.

Lewis, J. (2005) 'New Labour's Approach to the Voluntary Sector', *Social Policy and Society*, 4(2), pp 121-31.

Lie, M. and Baines, S. (2007) 'Making Sense or Organisational Change: The Voices of Older Volunteers', *Voluntas*, 18(3), pp 225-40.

Lister, R. (2002) 'The Dilemmas of Pendulum Politics: Balancing Paid Work, Care and Citizenship', *Economy and Society*, 31(4), pp 520-32.

Little, J. (1997) 'Constructions of Rural Women's Voluntary Work', *Gender, Place and Culture*, 4(2), pp 197 209.

Locality (2010) *Tender to Provide a National Partner for the Community Organisers Programme*, www.dta.org.uk/Resources/Development%20 Trust%20Association/Documents/Final-Locality-CO-public.pdf

Locke, M., Sampson, A. and Shepherd, J. (2001) 'Bowling Along: Community Leaders in East London', *Voluntary Action*, 3, pp 27-45.

Low, N., Butt, S., Ellis Paine, A. and Davis Smith, J. (2007) *Helping Out: A National Survey of Volunteering and Charitable Giving*, London: National Centre for Social Research and the Institute for Volunteering Research for the Office of the Third Sector.

Lowe, P. and Speakman, L. (2006) (eds) *The Ageing Countryside: The Growing Older Population of Rural England*, London: Age Concern England.

LSE Public Policy Group (2008) *Maximising the Social, Policy and Economic Impacts of Research in Humanities and Social Sciences*, Report to the British Academy, London: LSE.

Lukka, P. and Ellis, A. (2001) 'An Exclusive Construct? Exploring Different Cultural Concepts of Volunteering', *Voluntary Action*, 3(3), www.ivr.org.uk/culturalconcepts.htm

Lund, B. (1999) '"Ask Now What Your Community Can Do for You": Obligations, New Labour and Welfare Reform', *Critical Social Policy*, 19(4), pp 447-62.

Lupton, R. (2003) *Poverty Street*, Bristol: The Policy Press.

Lyon, D. and Glucksmann, M. (2008) 'Comparative Configurations of Care Work across Europe', *Sociology* 42(1), pp 101-18.

Lyon, F., Teasdale, S. and Baldock, R. (2010) *Approaches to Measuring the Scale of the Social Enterprise Sector in the UK*, Working Paper 45, Birmingham: TSRC, www.tsrc.ac.uk/LinkClick.aspx?fileticket=Rc d7%2f7PK0CE%3d&tabid=500

McCabe, A. and Phillimore, J. with Mayblin, L. (2010) *Understanding Third Sector 'Below the Radar' Activities: A Review of the Literature*, Birmingham: TSRC, www.tsrc.ac.uk/LinkClick.aspx?fileticket=80 XsXl6tHkc%3d&tabid=500

McDonald, C. and Warburton, J. (2003) 'Stability and Change in Nonprofit Organizations: The Volunteer Contribution', *Voluntas*, 14(4), pp 381-400.

McDowell, L. (2004) 'Work, Workfare, Work/Life Balance and an Ethic of Care', *Progress in Human Geography*, 28(2), pp 145-63.

MacGillivray, A., Wadhams, A. and Conaty, P. (2001) *Low-Flying Heroes: Micro-Social Enterprise below the Radar Screen*, London: New Economics Foundation.

Machin, J. and Ellis Paine, A. (2008) *Management Matters: A National Survey of Volunteer Management Capacity*, London: Institute for Volunteering Research.

McKinlay, A. (2002) '"Dead Selves": The Birth of the Modern Career', *Organization*, 9, pp 595-614.

McLaughlin, J. (2006) 'Conceptualising Intensive Caring Activities: The Changing Lives of Families with Young Disabled Children 2006', *Sociological Research Online*, 11(1), www.socresonline.org.uk/11/1/mclaughlin.html

Macmillan, R. (2010) *The Third Sector Delivering Public Services: An Evidence Review*, Birmingham: TSRC, www.tsrc.ac.uk/LinkClick.aspx?fileticket=l9qruXn%2fBN8%3d&tabid=712

Marks, A. and Scholarios, D. (2007) 'Revisiting Technical Workers: Professional and Organisational Identities in the Software Industry', *New Technology Work and Employment*, 22(2), pp 98-117.

Marshall, F. (2004) *Young People in NDC Areas: Findings from Six Case Studies*, Research Report 20, Sheffield: Sheffield Hallam University.

Massey, D. (1994) *Space, Place and Gender*, Cambridge: Polity Press.

Martin, B.R. and Tang, P. (2007) *The Benefits of Publicly Funded Research*, SPRU Working Paper 161, Brighton: SPRU.

Merrell, J. (2000) '"You Don't Do it for Nothing": Women's Experiences of Volunteering in Two Community Well Woman Clinics', *Health and Social Care in the Community*, 8, pp 31-9.

Mesman, J. (2007) 'Disturbing Observations as a Basis for Collaborative Research', *Science as Culture*, 16(3), pp 281-95.

Milbourne, L. (2009) 'Remodelling the Third Sector: Advancing Collaboration or Competition in Community-Based Initiatives?', *Journal of Social Policy*, 38(2), pp 1-21.

Milligan, C. and Fyfe, N.R. (2004) 'Putting the Voluntary Sector in its Place: Geographical Perspectives on Voluntary Activity and Social Welfare in Glasgow', *Journal of Social Policy*, 33, pp 73-93.

Milligan, C. and Fyfe, N.R. (2005) 'Preserving Space for Volunteers: Exploring the Links between Voluntary Welfare Organisations, Volunteering and Citizenship', *Urban Studies*, 42(3), pp 417-33.

Mirvis, F. (1992) 'The Quality of Employment in the Nonprofit Sector: An Update on Employee Attitudes in Nonprofit Versus Business and Government', *Non-profit Management and Leadership*, 3(1), pp 23-42.

Mirvis, F. and Hackett, E. (1983) 'Work and Work Force Characteristics in the Nonprofit Sector', *Monthly Labour Review*, 106, pp 3-12.

Mitchell, M. (2010) AgeUK presentation and launch, Research for Later Life Inaugural Conference, AgeUK Nottingham, September.

Molas-Gallart, J. and Tang, P (2007) *Report of the ESRC Impact Evaluation Methods Workshop 20th March 2007*, Swindon: ESRC, www.esrc.ac.uk/ESRCInfoCentre/Images/ESRC%20Impact%20Evaluation%20Methods%20Workshop_tcm6-24818.pdf

Montgomery, K. and Oliver, A.L. (2007) 'A Fresh Look at How Professions Take Shape: Dual-Directed Networking Dynamics and Social Boundaries', *Organization Studies*, 28(5), pp 661-87.

Mooney, G. and Scott, G. (eds) (2005) *Exploring Social Policy in the 'New' Scotland*, Bristol: Policy Press.

Morgan Inquiry (2008) *An Independent Inquiry into Young Adult Volunteering in the UK*, London: Morgan Inquiry, www.morganinquiry.org.uk/

Moulaert, F. and Ailenei, O. (2005) 'Social Economy, Third Sector and Solidarity Relations: A Conceptual Synthesis from History to Present', *Urban Studies*, 42(11), pp 2037-53.

Moxham, C. and Boaden, R. (2007) 'The Impact of Performance Measurement in the Voluntary Sector: Identification of Contextual and Processual Factors', *International Journal of Operations and Production Management*, 27(8), pp 826-45.

Mumford, K. and Power, A. (2003) *East Enders: Family and Community in East London*, Bristol: The Policy Press.

Munoz, S. (2009) 'Social Enterprise and Public Sector Voices on Procurement', *Social Enterprise Journal*, 5(1), pp 69-82.

Murphy, R., Wedlock, E. and King, J. (2005) *Early Findings from the Home Office Citizenship Survey*, Home Office Online Report 49/05, London: Home Office, www.homeoffice.gov.uk/rds/pdfs05/rdsolr4905.pdf

Myers, P., Barnes, J. and Shemilt, I. (2004) *Using Existing Data in Sure Start Local Evaluations*, London: Birbeck, University of London, www.ness.bbk.ac.uk/support/GuidanceReports/documents/395.pdf

NAO (National Audit Office) (2005) *Working with the Third Sector*, London: NAO, www.nao.org.uk/publications/nao_reports/05-06/050675.pdf

Narushima, N. (2005) 'Payback Time: Community Volunteering among Older Adults as a Transformative Mechanism', *Ageing and Society*, 25(4), pp 567-84.

NCVO (National Council of Voluntary Organisations) (2009) *UK Civil Society Almanac 2009*, London: NCVO.

NCVO (2010) *Briefing on the 'Big Society'*, London: NCVO, www. ncvo-vol.org.uk/sites/default/files/Big_Society_Programme_ briefing_final.pdf

nef (new economics foundation) (2009) *Tools for You: Approaches to Proving and Improving for Charities, Voluntary Organisations and Social Enterprise*, London: nef, www.neweconomics.org/publications/ tools-you

nef (2010) *Cutting It*, London: nef, www.neweconomics.org/sites/ neweconomics.org/files/Cutting_it.pdf

NESS (National Evaluation of Sure Start) (2004) Sure Start Local Programmes and Improving the Employability of Parents, London: National Evaluation of Sure Start, http://www.ness.bbk.ac.uk/ implementation/documents/401.pdf

NHS Central Surrey Health (2010) www.centralsurreyhealth.nhs.uk/ Index.html

Nicholson, N. and West, M.A. (1989) 'Transitions, Work Histories and Careers', in M.B. Arthur, D.T. Hall and B.S. Lawrence (eds) *Handbook of Career Theory*, Cambridge: Cambridge University Press, pp 181-202.

Norman, J. (2010) *Big Society: Anatomy of the New Politics*, Buckingham: University of Buckingham Press.

Number10.gov.uk (2010) 'Prime Minister launches Big Society Awards', www.number10.gov.uk/news/latest-news/2010/11/big-society-awards-57376

Nutley, S., Walter, I. and Davis, H. (2007) *Using Evidence: How Research can Inform Public Services*, Bristol: The Policy Press.

Oakley, A. (1974) *The Sociology of Housework*, London: Martin Robertson.

Obama, B. (2007) *Dreams of My Father*, Edinburgh: Canongate.

ODPM (Office of the Deputy Prime Minister) (2003) *Community Involvement and Urban Policy: Searching for Solid Foundations*, London: HMSO and ODPM.

Omoto, A.M. and Snyder, M. (2002) 'Considerations of Community: The Context and Process of Volunteerism', *American Behavioral Scientist*, 45(5), pp 846-67.

ONS (Office for National Statistics) (2001) 'Neighbourhood Statistics', http://neighbourhood.statistics.gov.uk/dissemination/LeadHome. do;jessionid=ac1f930c30d58603e1beb3fa4404b73f8e8df1e8f066?m =0&s=1289919361695&enc=1&nsjs=true&nsck=true&nssvg=fals e&nswid=1162

ONS (2010a) 'Labour Force Survey', www.statistics.gov.uk/statbase/ Source.asp?vlnk=358

ONS (2010b) 'Standard Occupation Classification', www.ons.gov.uk/ about-statistics/classifications/current/soc2010/soc2010-volume-1-structure-and-descriptions-of-unit-groups/index.html#5

Onyx, J. and Leonard, R. (2000) 'Women, Volunteering and Social Capital', in J. Warburton and M. Oppenheimer (eds) *Volunteers and Volunteering*, Sydney: Federation Press, pp 113–24.

Onyx, J. and Maclean, M. (1996) 'Careers in the Third Sector', *Non-Profit Management and Leadership*, 6(4), pp 331–45.

Onyx, J. and Warburton, J. (2003) 'Volunteering and Health among Older People: A Review', *Australasian Journal of Ageing*, 22(2), pp 65–9.

O'Reilly, K. (2000) *The British on the Costa Del Sol*, London: Routledge.

Osborne, S. and McLaughlin, K. (2004) 'The Cross-Cutting Review of the Voluntary Sector: Where Next for Local Government–Voluntary Sector Relationships?', *Regional Studies*, 38, pp 571–80.

Osborne, S., Beattie, R. and Williamson, A. (2002) *Community Involvement in Rural Regeneration Partnerships in the UK: Evidence from England, Northern Ireland and Scotland*, Bristol: The Policy Press.

Osborne, S., Chew, C. and McLaughlin, K. (2008) 'The Once and Future Pioneers? The Innovative Capacity of Voluntary Organisations and the Provision of Public Services: A Longitudinal Approach', *Public Management Review*, 10(1), pp 51–70.

Pahl, R. (ed) (1988) *On Work: Historical, Comparative and Theoretical Perspectives*, Oxford: Blackwell.

Parkinson, C. and Howorth, C. (2008) 'The Language of Social Entrepreneurs', *Entrepreneurship and Regional Development*, 20(3), pp 285–309.

Parry, J., Pettinger, L. and Glucksmann, M. (2005) 'Confronting New Challenges of Work Today: New Horizons and Perspectives', in L. Pettinger, J. Parry, R. Taylor and M. Glucksmann (eds) *A New Sociology of Work?*, Oxford: Blackwell.

Parsons, E. and Broadbridge, A. (2004) 'Managing Change in Nonprofit Organizations: Insights from the UK Charity Retail Sector', *Voluntas*, 15(3), pp 227–42.

Pavey, B. (2006) 'Human Capital, Social Capital, Entrepreneurship and Disability: An Examination of Some Current Educational Trends in the UK', *Disability and Society*, 21(3), pp 217–29.

Paxton, W., Pearce, N., Unwin, J. and Molyneux, P. (2005) *The Voluntary Sector Delivering Public Services: Transfer or Transformation?*, York: Joseph Rowntree Foundation.

Pearce, J. (2003) *Social Enterprise in Anytown*, London: Calouste Gulbenkian Foundation.

Peattie, K. and Morley, A. (2008) *Social Enterprises: Diversity & Dynamics, Contexts and Contributions: A Research Monograph*, Swindon: ESRC.

Peredo, A.M. and McLean, M. (2006) 'Social Entrepreneurship: A Critical Review of the Concept', *Journal of World Business*, 41(1), pp 56–65.

Petchey, R., Williams, J. and Carter, Y. (2009) 'From Street-Level Bureaucrats to Street-Level Policy Entrepreneurs? Central Policy and Local Action in Lottery-Funded Community Cancer Care', *Social Policy and Administration*, 42(1), pp 59–76.

Peters, G.B. and Pierre, J. (2001) 'Developments in Intergovernmental Relations: Towards Multi-Level Governance', *Policy & Politics*, 29(2), pp 131–6.

Pettigrew, A. (2001) 'Management Research after Modernism', *British Journal of Management*, 12, pp 61–70.

Phillipson, C., Bernard, M., Phillips, J. and Ogg, J. (1999) 'Older People's Experiences of Community Life: Patterns of Neighbouring in Three Urban Areas', *Sociological Review*, 47(4), 715–43.

Plagno, A. and Huppert, F. (2010) 'Happy to Help? Exploring the Factors Associated with Variations in Rates of Volunteering Across Europe', *Social Indicators Research*, 97, pp 157–76.

Pollert, A. (1981) *Girls, Wives, Factory Lives*, Basingstoke: Palgrave Macmillan.

Poole, L. (2007) 'Working in the Non-Profit Sector: Contract Culture, Partnership, Compacts and the Shadow State', in G. Mooney and A. Law (eds) *New Labour/Hard Labour? Restructuring and Resistance inside the Welfare Industry*, Bristol: The Policy Press, pp 233–61.

Portes, A. (2000) 'The Two Meanings of Social Capital', *Sociological Forum*, 15(1), pp 1–12.

Power, M. (1999) *The Audit Society: Rituals of Verification*, Oxford: Oxford University Press.

Priestley, J.B. (1934, 2009) *English Journey: Rediscovering Priestley*, Ilkley: Great Northern Books.

Prochaska, F. (1988) *The Voluntary Impulse: Philanthropy in Modern Britain*, London: Faber and Faber.

Public Administration Select Committee (2008) *Public Services and the Third Sector: Rhetoric and Reality: Eleventh Report of Session 2007-08*, London: House of Commons.

Putnam, R. (2000) *Bowling Alone: The Collapse and Revival of American Community*, New York, NY: Simon & Schuster.

Raynes, N., Clark, H. and Beecham, J. (2006) *The Report of the Older People's Inquiry into 'That Bit of Help'*, York: Joseph Rowntree Foundation.

Richardson, L. and Mumford, K. (2002) 'Community, Neighbourhood and Social Infrastructure', in J. Hills and J. Le Grand (eds) *Understanding Social Exclusion*, Oxford: Oxford University Press, pp 202-25.

Ridley-Duff, R. (2007) 'Communitarian Perspectives on Social Enterprise', *Corporate Governance: An International Review*, 15(2), pp 382-92.

Ridley Duff, R. and Bull, M. (2011) *Understanding Social Enterprise: Theory and Practice*, London: Sage Publications.

Roberts, J. and Devine, F. (2004) 'Some Everyday Experiences of Voluntarism: Social Capital, Pleasure and the Contingency of Participation', *Social Politics*, 11, pp 280-96.

Robinson, J. and Tansey, J. (2006) 'Co-production, Emergent Properties and Strong Interactive Social Research: The Georgia Basin Futures Project, *Science and Public Policy* 33(2), pp 151–60.

Robson, P., Begum, N. and Lock, M. (2004) *Developing User Involvement: Working towards User-Centred Practice in Voluntary Organisations*, Bristol: The Policy Press.

Rochester, C. (2006) 'Making Sense of Volunteering: A Literature Review. The Commission on the Future of Volunteering, Volunteering England'. www.volcomm.org.uk/NR/rdonlyres/6EF238B5-0425-4F99-930E-E7665CAAEEC6/0/Making_sense_of_volunteering.pdf

Rochester, C. and Thomas, B. (2006) *Measuring the Impact of Employer Supported Volunteering: An Exploratory Study*, London: IVR.

Rochester, C., Ellis Paine, A., Howlett, S. and Zimmeck, M. (2010) *Volunteering and Society in the 21st Century*, Basingstoke: Palgrave Macmillan.

Rochester, C., Hutchinson, R., Harris, M. and Keely, L. (2002) *A Review of the Home Office Older Volunteers Initiative*, London: Home Office.

Ruddick, S. (1990) *Maternal Thinking: Towards a Politics of Peace*, London: Women's Press.

Russell, I. (2005) *A National Framework for Youth Action and Engagement*, London: HMSO, www.russellcommission.org/report/index.html

Russell, L. and Scott, D. (1997) *Very Active Citizens? The Impact of the Contract Culture on Volunteers*, Manchester: University of Manchester.

Ruston, D. (2003) *Volunteers, Helpers and Socialisers: Social Capital and Time Use*, London: Social Analysis and Reporting Division, ONS.

Sampson, R.J., McAdam, D., MacIndoe, H. and Weffer-Elizondo, S. (2005) 'Civil Society Reconsidered: The Durable Nature and Community Structure of Collective Civil Action', *American Journal of Sociology*, 111(3), pp 673-714.

Savage, M. (1988) 'The Missing Link? The Relationship between Spatial Mobility and Social Mobility', *British Journal of Sociology*, 39, pp 554-77.

Saxton, J. and Baker, J. (2009) *How Government Definitions Over-Estimate Levels of Volunteering: A Briefing by npfSynergy*, London: nfpSynergy.

SCEDU (Sheffield Community Enterprise Development Unit) (2008) *Get Ready for That Local Authority Contract*, London: Financehub.

Schervish, P.G. and Havens, J.J. (2002) 'The Boston Area Diary Study and the Moral Citizenship of Care', *Voluntas*, 13(1), pp 47-71.

Schoenberger, E. (1997) *The Cultural Crisis of the Firm*, Oxford: Blackwell.

Schumpeter, J. (1934) *The Theory of Economic Development*, Cambridge, MA: Harvard University Press.

Sciulli, D. (2005) 'Continental Sociology of Professions Today: Conceptual Contributions', *Current Sociology*, 53(6), pp 915-42.

Scott, M. (2011) 'Reflections on the Big Society', *Community Development Journal*, 46(1), pp 132-7.

Scourfield, P. (2005) 'Implementing the Community Care (Direct Payments) Act: Will the supply of personal assistants meet the demand and at what price?', *Journal of Social Policy*, 34(3), pp 469–88.

Scourfield, P. (2007) 'Social Care and the Modern Citizen: Client, Consumer, Service User, Manager and Entrepreneneur', *British Journal of Social Work*, 37(2), pp 107-22.

Seddon, N. (2007) *Who Cares? How State Funding and Political Activism Change Charity*, London: Civitas.

Sennett, R. (1998) *The Corrosion of Character*, New York, NY: Norton.

SEU (Social Exclusion Unit) (1998) *Bringing Britain Together: A National Strategy for Neighbourhood Renewal*, Cm 4045, London: HMSO.

Sevenhuijsen, S. (2003) 'The Place of Care: The Relevance of the Feminist Ethic of Care for Social Policy', *Feminist Theory*, 4(2), pp 179-97.

Shakespeare, T. (2000) 'The Social Relations of Care', in G. Lewis, S. Gewirtz and J. Clarke (eds) *Rethinking Social Policy*, London: Sage Publications, pp 52-65.

Shaw, E. and Carter, S. (2007) 'Social Entrepreneurship: Theoretical Antecedents and Empirical Analysis of Entrepreneurial Processes and Outcomes', *Journal of Small Business and Enterprise Development*, 14(3), pp 418-34.

Shaw, K. and Robinson, J.F.F. (2010) 'Centenary Paper: UK Urban Regeneration Policies in the Early Twenty-First Century, Continuity or Change?', *Town Planning Review*, 81(2), pp 123-49.

Shove, E. and Rip, A. (2000) 'Users and Unicorns: A Discussion of Mythical Beasts in Interactive Science', *Science and Public Policy*, 27(3), pp 175-82.

Showstack Sassoon, A. (1996) 'Complexity, Contradictions, Creativity, Transitions in the Voluntary Sector', *Soundings*, 4, pp 183–94.

Shucksmith, M. (2000) 'Endogenous Development, Social Capital and Social Inclusion: Perspectives from LEADER in the UK', *Sociologia Ruralis*, 40(2), pp 208-18.

Skill: National Bureau for Students with Disabilities (2010) *Welcome to Volunteer Voices* London: Skill, www.skill.org.uk/index.aspx

Small Business Service (2005) *GHK Review of the Social Enterprise Strategy: Summary of Findings*, London: Small Business Service.

Smith, M. (2010a) 'Public Services face Doing More with Less', *The Guardian*, 7 July, www.guardian.co.uk/public-services/how-to-do-more-with-less

Smith, M.J. (2010b) 'From Big Government to Big Society: Changing the State–Society Balance', *Parliamentary Affairs*, 63(4), pp 818-33.

Social Enterprise Coalition (2010a) *About Social Enterprise*, London: Social Enterprise Coalition, www.socialenterprise.org.uk/pages/about-social-enterprise.html

Social Enterprise Coalition (2010b) *Response to Third Sector Research Centre Survey on Social Enterprise*, London: Social Enterprise Coalition, www.tsrc.ac.uk/LinkClick.aspx?fileticket=fXeeXRJNIZk%3d&tabid=733

SOLACE (Society of Local Authority Chief Executives and Senior Managers) (2010) *Rebalancing the Public Finances: The end of the beginning*, London: SOLACE, www.solace.org.uk/library_documents/Rebalancing_the_public_finances_181010.pdf

South West Foundation (2008) *Influence: Older People's Forums Come of Age*, Taunton: South West Foundation.

Southern, A. (2011) 'Introduction: Enterprise and Deprivation', in A. Southern (ed) *Enterprise, Deprivation and Social Exclusion: The Role of Small Business in Addressing Social and Economic Inequalities*, London: Routledge, pp 1-15.

Sprigings, N. and Allen, C. (2005) 'The Communities we are Regaining but Need to Lose: A Critical Commentary on Community Building in Beyond-Place Societies', *Community, Work and Family*, 8(4), pp 389-411.

Stacey, M. (1969) 'The Myth of Community Studies', *British Journal of Sociology*, 20(2), pp 134-47.

Stebbins, R.A. (1996) 'Volunteering: A Serious Leisure Perspective', *Nonprofit and Voluntary Sector Quarterly*, 25(2), pp 211-24.

Stephenson, H.H. and Gumpert, D.E. (1985) 'The Heart of Entrepreneurship', *Harvard Business Review*, 63(2), pp 85-94.

Stevenson, H.H. and Jarillo, J.C. (1990) 'A Paradigm of Entrepreneurship: Entrepreneurial Management', *Strategic Management Journal*, 11, pp 17–27.

Sullivan, W. (1995) *Work and Integrity: The Crisis and Promise of Professionalism in America*, New York, NY: HarperCollins.

Sundin, E. and Tillmar, M. (2008) 'A Nurse and a Civil Servant Changing Institutions: Entrepreneurial Processes in Different Public Sector Organizations', *Scandinavian Journal of Management*, 24, pp 113–24.

Tajfel, H. and Turner, J.C. (1979) 'An Integrative Theory of Intergroup Conflict', in W.G. Austin and S. Worchel (eds) *The Social Psychology of Intergroup Relations*, Monterey, CA: Brooks–Cole, pp 33-47.

Tam, J. (2007) *Measuring Economic Impacts of Investment in the Research Base and Innovation: A New Framework for Measurement*, London: DTI.

Taniguchi, H. (2006) 'Men's and Women's Volunteering: Gender Differences in the Effects of Employment and Family Characteristic', *Nonprofit and Voluntary Sector Quarterly*, 35(1), pp 83–101.

Taylor, M. (2002) *Public Policy in the Community*, Basingstoke: Palgrave.

Taylor, R. (2004) 'Extending Conceptual Boundaries: Work, Voluntary Work and Employment', *Work, Employment and Society*, 18, pp 29-49.

Taylor, R. (2005) 'Rethinking Voluntary Work', in L. Pettinger, J. Parry, R. Taylor and M. Glucksmann (eds) *A New Sociology of Work?*, Oxford: Blackwell, pp 119-35.

Teasdale, S. (2010) *What's in a Name? The Construction of Social Enterprise*, Birmingham: TSRC, www.tsrc.ac.uk/LinkClick.aspx?fileticket=Mq mKeY9Ciss%3d&tabid=500

Thaler, R.T. and Sunstein, C.R. (2009) *Nudge: Improving Decisions about Health, Wealth and Happiness*, London: Penguin.

Thatcher, M. (1987) Interview with *Woman's Own* magazine, 31 October.

The Guardian (2010) 'Consumer Focus Watchdog to be Axed in 'Bonfire of the Quangos'', www.guardian.co.uk/money/2010/oct/10/consumer-focus-watchdog-to-be-axed

The Independent (2011) 'Liverpool pulls out of Big Society drive', 3 February. www.independent.co.uk/news/uk/politics/liverpool-pulls-out-of-big-society-drive-2203407.html

Third Sector (2010) 'Stockport Community and Voluntary Services Closes after Council Withdraws Funding', www.thirdsector.co.uk/news/Article/1032554/Stockport-Community-Voluntary-Services-closes-council-withdraws-funding/

Tolich, M.B. (1993) 'Alienating and Liberating Emotions at Work', *Journal of Contemporary Ethnography*, 22(3), pp 361-81.

Tonkiss, F. and Passey, A. (1999) 'Trust, Confidence and Voluntary Organisations: Better Values and Institutions', *Sociology*, 33(2), pp 257-74.

Townsend, P. (1957) *The Family Life of Old People*, London: Routledge and Kegan Paul.

Wann, M. (1995) *Building Social Capital: Self Help in a 21st Century Welfare State*, London: Institute for Public Policy Research.

Warburton, J. and McLaughlin, D. (2005) 'Lots of Little Kindnesses: Valuing the Role of Older Australians as Informal Volunteers in the Community', *Ageing and Society*, 25, 715-30.

Wardell, F., Lishman, J. and Whalley, L. (2000) 'Who Volunteers?', *British Journal of Social Work*, 30, pp 227-48.

Waring, M. (1988) *If Women Counted: A New Feminist Economics*, London: Macmillan.

Warry, P. (2006) *Increasing the Economic Impact of Research Councils: Advice to the Director General of Science and Innovation, DTI from the Research Council Economic Impact Group*, RCUK Report 06/1678, London: DTI.

Watson, J. (2009) 'Entrepreneurial Action, Identity Work and the Use of Multiple Discursive Resources: The Case of a Rapidly Changing Family Business', *International Small Business Journal*, 27(3), pp 251-73.

WBCSD (World Business Council for Sustainable Development) (2000) *Corporate Social Responsibility: Making Good Business Sense*, Geneva: WBCSD, www.wbcsd.org/web/publications/business-case.pdf

Webber, M. (1963) 'Order in Diversity: Community without Propinquity', in L. Wingo (ed) *Cities and Space*, Baltimore, MD: John Hopkins Press.

Webber, M.W. (1964) *Explorations into Urban Structure*, University of Pennsylvania, Pennsylvania.

Weiss, C.H. (1980) 'Knowledge Creep and Decision Accretion', *Knowledge: Creation, Diffusion, Utilization*, 1(3), pp 381-404.

Wenger, C. (1995) 'Myths and Realities of Ageing in Rural Britain', *Ageing and Society*, 21(1), pp 117-30.

Wenger, C. (2001) 'Introduction: Intergenerational Relationships in Rural Areas', *Ageing and Society*, 21(5), pp 537-45.

Wenger, E., McDermott, R. and Snyder, M. (2002) *Cultivating Communities of Practice*, Boston, MA: Harvard Business School Press.

Westall, A. (2009) *Value and the Third Sector: Working Paper on Ideas for Future Research*, Birmingham: TSRC, www.tsrc.ac.uk/LinkClick.aspx?fileticket=9T8hoUzuf/c%3d&tabid=500

Whittam, G. and Birch, K. (2011) 'Can the Market Deliver the Goods? A Critical Review of the Social Enterprise Agenda', in A. Southern (ed) *Enterprise, Deprivation and Social Exclusion: The Role of Small Business in Addressing Social and Economic Inequalities*, London: Routledge, pp 239-53.

Wilding, K. (2010) 'Voluntary Organisations and the Recession', *Voluntary Sector Review*, 1(1), pp 97-101.

Wilding, K., Clark, J., Griffith, M., Jochum, V. and Wainwright, S. (2006) *The UK Voluntary Sector Almanac: The State of the Sector*, London: NVCO.

Williams, C.C. (2003) 'Developing Community Participation in Deprived Neighbourhoods: A Critical Evaluation of the Third-Sector Approach', *Space and Polity*, 7(1), pp 65-73.

Williams, C.C. (2005) 'Fostering Community Engagement and Tackling Undeclared Work: The Case for an Evidence-Based "Joined Up" Public Policy Approach', *Regional Studies*, 39(8), pp 1145-55.

Williams, C.C. (2008) 'A Critical Evaluation of Competing Representations of the Relationship between Formal and Informal Work', *Community, Work and Family*, 11(1), pp 105-24.

Williams, C.C. (2011) 'Social-Spatial Variations in Community Self-Help: A Total Social Organisation of Labour Perspective', *Social Policy and Society*, 10, 3, pp 365-78.

Williams, C.C. and Windebank, J. (2006) 'Harnessing the hidden enterprise culture of advanced economies', *International Journal of Manpower*, 27(6), pp 535-51.

Williams, F. (2001) 'In and Beyond New Labour: Towards a Political Ethics of Care', *Critical Social Policy*, 21(4), pp 467-93.

Williams, F. (2002) 'The Presence of Feminism in the Future of Welfare', *Economy and Society*, 31(4), pp 502-19.

Williams, F. (2005) 'A Good Enough Life: Developing a Political Ethic of Care', *Surroundings*, 30, pp 17-32.

Williams, W.M. (1969) *The Sociology of an English Village: Gosforth*, London: Routledge and Kegan Paul.

Willmott, P. (1985) 'The Institute of Community Studies' in M. Bulmer (ed) *Essays on the History of British Sociological Research,* Cambridge: Cambridge University Press, pp 137-50.

Willmott, P. (1986) *Social Networks, Informal Care and Public Policy*, London: Policy Studies Institute.

Willmott, P. (1987) 'Introduction', in P. Willmott (ed) *Policing and the Community*, London: Policy Studies Institute, pp 1-15.

Willmott, P. (1989) *Community Initiatives, Patterns and Prospects,* London: Policy Studies Institute.

Willmott, P. and Young, M. (1960) *Family and Class in a London Suburb*, London: Routledge and Kegan Paul.

Wilson, J. (2000) 'Volunteering', *Annual Review of Sociology*, 26, pp 215-40.

Wolch, J.R. (1990) *The Shadow State: Government and the Voluntary Sector in Transition*, New York, NY: The Foundation Center.

Woodin, T., Crook, D. and Carpentier, V. (2010) *Community and Mutual Ownership: A Historical Review*, York: Joseph Rowntree Foundation.

Woolgar, S. (2000) 'The Social Basis of Interactive Social Science', *Science and Public Policy*, 27(3), pp 165-9.

Yeung, A.B. (2004) 'The Octagon Model of Volunteer Motivation: Results of a Phenomenological Analysis', *Voluntas*, 15, pp 21-46.

Young, M. and Schuller, T. (1991) *Life after Work: The Rise of an Ageless Society*, London: HarperCollins.

Young, M. and Willmott, P. (1957) *Family and Kinship in East London*, London: Routledge and Kegan Paul.

Zahra, S.A., Gedajlovic, E., Neubaum, D.O. and Shulman, J.M. (2009) 'A Typology of Social Entrepreneurs', *Journal of Business Venturing*, 24(5), pp 519-32.

Zappala, G. (2000) *How Many People Volunteer in Australia and Why Do They Do It?*, Camperdown, NSW: The Smith Family.

Zappala, G. and Burrell, T. (2002) 'Understanding the Factors Associated with Volunteer Commitment: A Case Study of Volunteers in Community Service', *Third Sector Review*, 8, pp 5-30.

Zerbinati, S. and Souitaris, V. (2005) 'Entrepreneurship in the Public Sector: A Framework of Analysis in European Local Governments', *Entrepreneurship and Regional Development*, 1, pp 43-64.

Zimmeck, M. (2001) *The Right Stuff: New Ways of Thinking about Managing Volunteers*, London: IVR.

Useful websites

ACEVO (Association of Chief Executives of Voluntary Organisations): www.acevo.org.uk/Page.aspx?pid=211 and www.acevo.org.uk/about+ACEVO

Association of Volunteer Managers: www.volunteermanagers.org.uk/about-us

Charity Commission: www.charitycommission.gov.uk/Showcharity/RegisterOfCharities/CharityWithPartB.aspx?RegisteredCharityNumber=234887&SubsidiaryNumber=0

Skill: National Bureau for Students with Disabilities: www.skill.org.uk/index.aspx

Turning Point: www.turning-point.co.uk/Pages/home.aspx

Bibliography

Index

V

'V' initiative 26, 35
VCS (voluntary and community sector) 2, 8–10
  careers in 52–63, 67–9
  paid workforce 59–62
  workforce 33–4
  see also volunteer managers (VMs); volunteers
VCSOs 9–10, 11–12, 83–4, 149–50
  'below the radar' groups 14, 86, 149, 150
  bureaucratic form 55–6
  chief executives 68–9, 73–4
  collectivist-democratic model 56
  diversity of 84–9
  and entrepreneurship 30, 94–5
  funding 90–1, 98–101, 103, 157, 158, 159
  innovation 92, 98
  organisational change 59, 95–6, 102–4
    cooperatives as care providers 105–9
    maintaining services and managing money 98–101
    public service delivery 96–8
    volunteers' responses to change 101–4
  provision of care 89–91
  as service providers 91–3
  stakeholder ambiguity 40, 62, 63, 91–2
  state-sponsored 89–91
  workforce
    paid 59–62, 67–9
    unpaid 33
  workplace model 55–6
  see also charities; cooperatives; social enterprises
Voluntary Action in the 21st Century (Conservative Party) 152
voluntary and community sector *see* VCS (voluntary and community sector)
voluntary help organisations (VHOs) 77–8
volunteer brokerage scheme 36, 80
volunteer management 10, 55–9, 63, 138
Volunteer Management programme 58
volunteer managers (VMs) 12, 57, 58–9, 62, 81–2
  job advertisements 56
  narratives 69–70
  peer support 78, 79
  professional identity 77–81
  role of 63
Volunteer Voices 26
volunteering 4–5, 21–2
  antecedents of 12, 44–8
  consequences of 12, 51–3

family, impact on 11, 50–1, 53
gender issues 7, 25, 47, 68, 142, 164–5
historical accounts 5–7
motives for 37–41, 44–8, 135, 139
pathways, case study 34, 41–4, 52–4
  consequences 51–2
  personal histories 44–8
  volunteers' work 48–51
and public policy 35–7
see also Brightville, case study; volunteers
Volunteering, self-help and citizenship in later life study 18
volunteering development manager 71–3
Volunteering England 78, 80
volunteers 33–4
  change, response to 93, 96, 101–4
  older people as 38, 47–8, 101–2, 104, 135, 142–3
  see also voluntary and community sector (VCS); volunteering
Volunteers' Forum 72
Volunteers' Newsletter 72

W

Warry Report 161
Watling, community study 114
Webber, M.W. 132, 145
welfare spending cuts 157
welfare-to-work policies 7, 35, 37
Westall, A. 94
Whittam, G. 30, 148, 164
Wicks, M. 158
Williams, C.C. 13, 117, 149
Williams, W.M. 113
Willmott, P. 112–13, 132–3
women
  career trajectory 64
  unpaid work 7, 164–5
Woolgar, S. 160
work 7, 13, 14, 25–9
  unpaid 7, 13, 14, 24, 25, 26–7
work communities 133
worker cooperatives 88
Workers Co-operative 106–7, 149
Working with the Voluntary Sector (House of Commons Committee of Public Accounts) 90

Y

Young, M. 112, 113, 135
young people 26, 35, 36–7